The Puritan Pulpit:
The Irish Puritans

James Ussher, D.D.
Bishop of Armagh
(1580–1655)

Edited by Dr. Don Kistler

Soli Deo Gloria Publications
. . . for instruction in righteousness . . .

Soli Deo Gloria Publications
A division of Ligonier Ministries, Inc.
P. O. Box 547500, Orlando, FL 32854
(407) 333-4244/FAX 333-4233
www.ligonier.org

*

*

1-56769-074-2

*

Library of Congress Cataloging-in-Publication Data

Ussher, James, 1581-1656.
 The Puritan pulpit : the Irish puritans / James Ussher ;
edited by Don Kistler.
    p. cm.
 ISBN 1-56769-074-2 (alk. paper)
1. Puritans–Sermons. 2. Puritans–Doctrines. 3. Sermons,
English–17th century. 4. Puritans–Ireland. I. Kistler, Don.
II. Title.

BX9323.U87 2006
252'.03–dc22

2006012976

Contents

Preface

These sermons are such as, several years since, were taken from the mouth of that man of God, the reverend Archbishop of Armagh. When, by reason of that bloody rebellion in Ireland, this star of the greatest magnitude was forced to quit his proper orb, it pleased the Lord to fix him as a shining, burning light for some time in Oxford. While there he constantly spent himself, and was spent, in preaching Christ and Him crucified. This he did with such soundness, diligence, evidence, faithfulness, and zeal that he seemed not only willing to impart the gospel, but his own soul unto us. A film of superstition and profaneness then grew over one of the eyes of someone in our island. Our pulpits turned, as it were, into stages, and sadly prostituted to froth and jerks at godliness. As for truly learned, soul-searching, soul-saving preaching, it was that which most of us either did not know or scorned. The mode of our sermons then was more to please the fancy than to pierce the heart; to tickle the ear rather than wound the conscience, or save the precious, immortal soul.

At that time the Lord was pleased to cause this star to arise and shine in our horizon, and by his light and influence to guide us to Bethlehem. A time of love it was, an accepted time, a time never to be forgotten, especially by those who, through grace, can from thence date the era of their sound conversion. The persuasion of Armagh's incomparable learning, the observation of his awful gravity, the evidence of his eminent and exemplary piety, all improved to the height by his indefatigable industry, drew students to flock to him as doves to the windows. It joys us to recollect how multitudes of scholars, especially the heads of our tribes, thronged to hear the sound of his silver bells; how much they were taken with the voice of this wise charmer; how their ears seemed, as it were, fastened to his lips. Here you might have seen a sturdy Saul changed into a submissive Paul, a persecutor transformed into a preacher. There a tender-hearted Josiah lamenting after the Lord, and with Ephraim smiting on his thigh, saying, "What have I done!" Others, with the penitent Jews, were so stabbed at the heart that they were forced to cry out in the bitterness of their souls, "Men, brethren, fathers, O what shall we do?" These were some of the blessings from on high which attended these sermons when preached to the ear. Oh, that a like or a greater might follow them now that they are printed!

These notes, it is true, were taken by such who all had the pens of ready writers, and after that completed by a strict comparing of several distinct papers. This is the body, the bulk of these heavenly sermons. The gloss, the spirit, the energy of them was and must be wholly from above. We trust the publishing of these notes will not be interpreted by any in the least to reflect on the unparalled worth of the preacher, to whose very dust we owe a sacred reverence. If anything seems not to speak him, let it be charged not on him, but the publishers, who have only this to add, namely, their fervent prayers that these sermons may find the like influence on the hearts of others in the reading that they had on their own in the hearing; then will both have abundant cause to bless the Lord.

Let those notes taken after him be testimonies how much he condescended, and let them serve for patterns to such as think it below them, especially in such audiences, to preach, as he did, a crucified Christ in a crucified style. The general subject of these sermons is of conversion, and mightily did the Lord bless them, not only to the edification and consolation of very many, but also to the conversion of some.

Joseph Crabb, William Ball,
Thomas Lye, Stanley Gower

1

Speedy Conversion the Only Means to Prevent Imminent Destruction, Part 1

"Again, he limiteth a certain day, saying in David, Today, after so long a time; as it is said, Today if ye will hear his voice, harden not your hearts." Hebrews 4:7

The chief matter of these words is the doctrine of the conversion of a sinner. Forasmuch as God's judgments are abroad upon the earth and hang over our heads, the only means to prevent and remove both temporal and eternal judgments is our speedy conversion and return unto God. Else He will whet His sword, bend His bow, and make it ready for our destruction (Psalm 7:12). God bore a deadly hatred against sin in the time of the psalmist, and so He does still; for His nature cannot be changed. If we do not return, we are but dead men. The eternal weight of God's wrath will be our portion, both here and in the world to come, if we do not repent.

In these words there are three observable points:

1. Continuance in sin brings certain death.

2. Since God's judgments for sin are on particular nations and persons, then if particular nations or persons turn away from their evil courses, no harm shall come near them. God takes no delight in the death of a sinner, nor that He should despair of His mercy; but would have us turn out of the broad way which leads to destruction.

3. Therefore, it behooves everyone to speedily set about the work of conversion.

Do not esteem this as a vain word. I bring you those

things whereon your life depends. Obey it and you are safe forever; neglect it and you are undone forever. Unless you embrace this message, God will bend His bow and make ready His arrows against you.

1. Continuance in sin brings certain death. There will be no way of escaping but by repentance, by coming in speedily unto God. The words of this text are taken from Psalm 95:8: "Harden not your hearts as in the provocation, and as in the day of temptation in the wilderness." If when God calls us either to doing this or leaving that undone, yet we are not moved, but continue in our evil ways, what is the reason for it? It is because we harden our hearts against Him. The Word of God is the power of God to salvation, and a two-edged sword to sever between the joints and the marrow. If the strength of the Almighty encounters our hard hearts and yet they remain like the stony and rocky ground, whereon though the Word is plentifully sown; if it fastens no root there, and though for a season it springs, yet suddenly it fades, and comes to nothing, we may have a little motion by the Word, yet there is a rock in our souls, a stone in our hearts. And though we may sometimes seem to receive it with some affection, and be made, as it were, sermon-sick, yet it holds but a while but makes us no better. Why? Because it is not received as an engrafted Word. Therefore, says James, "Receive with meekness the engrafted word" (James 1:21). Let the Word be engrafted in you; one sprig of it is able to make you grow up to everlasting life. Do not be content with hearing it, but pray to God that it may be firmly rooted in your hearts; this will cause a softening.

"Today, if ye will hear His voice, harden not your hearts" against Almighty God. If you do, expect Him also to come against you in indignation. Hearken to what He says by His prophet: "I will search Jerusalem with candles, and punish the men that are settled on their lees, that say in their heart, 'The Lord will not do good, neither will He do evil' " (Zephaniah 1:12). Mark it, "I will search Jerusalem, and punish those that are settled on their lees." When a man is thus settled and resolved to go on in his sins, to put the matter to hazard come what will, there is a kind of atheism in the soul. For when God tells him by His minister that He is preparing the instruments of death against him, what does he do but in a manner reply, "Do you think us such fools as to believe it?" What does this do but provoke God to swear that we shall never enter into His rest. What is the reason for this? It is because men have no change, they are settled on their lees. "Moab hath been at ease from his youth, and he hath settled on his lees, and hath not been emptied from vessel to vessel, neither hath he gone into captivity" (Jeremiah 48:11). Let us consider whether our security does not come from the same cause.

Why do we see so few conversions? There are two things that hinder it: the hardening of a man's heart against the Word, and our settling ourselves on our lees. When we have no change in grace, we are secure; we never see an evil day. And this is that which slays the foolish person. Woe to them who are at ease! It would be better for you to be emptied from vessel to vessel, to go into captivity. For as long as a man continues thus in an unregenerate condition, he can look for nothing but troubles. Certain judgments must necessarily follow, and as sure as God is in heaven, so sure may they expect misery on earth, and they shall receive the eternal weight of God's wrath treasured up against the day of wrath. Therefore see the necessity for our conversion if we will keep off either temporal or eternal wrath.

Our Savior makes the case of all impenitent sinners to be liable to wrath. One judgment befell the Galileans, another those on whom the tower of Siloam fell. But what did our Savior say, "Suppose ye that these were greater sinners above all men that dwelt at Jerusalem? I tell you nay, but except ye repent, ye shall all likewise perish" (Luke 13:3). All, everyone here present, if you do not turn from your sinful courses, God will surely meet with you one time or another, if you harden your hearts against Him. Whoever hardened his heart against God and prospered? As long as a man is in this condition, his state is woeful. As many as are in the state of unregeneracy are under the power of Satan (2 Timothy 2:25–26). Mark the apostle's words: "In meekness instruct those that oppose themselves, if God peradventure will give them repentance to the acknowledging of the truth. And that they may recover themselves out of the snare of the devil, who are taken captive by him at his will."

The state, then, of those who are hardened and settled on their lees is as a bird in a cage, taken alive at the will of the fowler. So is it here: as long as we continue obstinate and hardened, we are taken alive at Satan's will; we are at his disposal. While we are at liberty, we are waylaid by his nets and traps, and are taken at his pleasure. As long as we are hardened in heart, we are in the devil's cage. True repentance is that alone whereby we purchase our freedom, whereby we recover ourselves. Therefore, in Romans 2:5, hardness of heart and impenitence signify the same thing: "After thy hardness and impenitent heart, treasurest up unto thyself wrath against the day of wrath." What is a hard heart? It is an impenitent heart. Do you harden your heart? Then know that for the present you are a dead man. If, notwithstanding all God's threats out of His Word, you are not one jot moved, you are dead while alive, as the woman who lived in pleasure. And if you continue so, you treasure up wrath against the day of wrath, and the just revelation of God's judgments.

God's Word is the special means to recover you. So examine yourself: does the working of the Word gall you? It is a sign there is life in you. But if it makes no impression, if it does not move you, it is a sign of a dead heart. Consider, then, the danger of a man resolving to go on in his evil courses, never purposing to alter matters. It exceedingly hastens God's judgments.

2. The second point directs us how to work our escape. Though God threatens us, if God causes us to consider that we have to deal with a merciful Father, and makes us meet Him by humiliation, then, though our sins were as scarlet, yet if we submit ourselves to our Judge and live as obedient subjects, the storm shall pass from us. Notwithstanding God's threatening us, if He gives us grace to repent, then, let our sins be never so great, we may be sure of mercy.

Oh, that we could see with what a gracious God we have to deal! If you will but humble yourself, all these things shall speak peace unto you. As an impenitent sinner is under the power of Satan and liable to all misery, so whoever returns and seeks the Lord is sure to be under His wings and free from all evil. Do you think that God makes use of threatenings for your hurt? No, He does not deal with us as an angry Judge, but as a compassionate Father. Men will always put an enemy at a disadvantage when they may do him the most hurt. God's terrors overtake us. He threatens us that He will do this and that so that we may prevent it. He knows that unless His terrors awaken us, we will rest securely. Before He smites us He tells us that "He will whet His sword. He hath bent His bow and made it ready. He hath prepared His instruments of death" (Psalm 7:12–13). He could shoot you presently and instantly run you through, but He threatens you so that the Lord may not strike you.

See what the prophet Amos denounces from chapter 4: "I have given you cleanness of teeth . . . I have withholden rain" (verses 6–7). "I have smitten you with blasting and mildew" (verse 9). "I have sent amongst you the pestilence . . . yet have you not returned unto Me" (verse 10). "Therefore thus will I do unto thee, O Israel, and because

I will do thus unto thee, prepare to meet thy God, O Israel" (verse 12).

What judgments have befallen us, have befallen us for our own use, if we will be warned by them! The reason why God says He will overthrow us is not because He means to do it, but that we may prevent Him by repentance. Look into Jeremiah 3 and see what wonderful passages are to this purpose: "As a wife treacherously departeth from her husband, so have you dealt treacherously with me, O house of Israel." And yet see God's unspeakable mercy: "Return again unto Me," and, "Return, ye backsliding children, and I will heal your backslidings. Turn to Me, and I will not cause Mine anger to fall upon you" (verse 22). "Only acknowledge thine iniquity that thou hast transgressed against the Lord thy God" (verse 13). See how God speaks to the worst and most vile of all, and yet He entreats them to return. See then the conclusion of the second point; how, if God gives us grace to repent, let our former evils be what they will, the danger is past.

3. But I leave this and come to the third point, for which I chiefly chose this text. You have seen how dangerous a thing hardness of heart is, how it brings certain death, and that if we have the heart to repent we are safe. It is not falling into water, but lying under it that drowns a man. Are you fallen into sin? Only lift up your head, the promise of salvation belongs to you. The main thing, then, is this: it behooves us to set about the work of repentance speedily.

God is angry with us, and we do not know whether God will execute His judgments on us this day or not; therefore go about it speedily. God will put away all our sins if we will come to Him within a day. Now what madness is it to neglect it! After a certain time, says the apostle, according to what was said by the Psalmist, God has limited a certain day (Psalm 95:7). You have provoked the

Holy Ghost, and now He limits you to a day. Hebrews 3:7, "Wherefore," says the Holy Ghost, "today if ye will hear His voice." Now is it safe, do you think, to let this day pass? A hard heart is a provoking heart and, as long as it continues hard, it continues to provoke God and to despise the Holy Ghost. Today, therefore, hear His voice, that is, this present day. But which is that day? It is this very time, wherein you stand before God and in which you hear me. If you embrace the opportunity, you are happy; if not, you shall give as dear an account as for anything you ever heard in your life.

There is no dallying with God; take His offer, take Him at His Word in the matter of salvation. He calls to you today; perhaps He will speak no more. Therefore, in Hebrews 3:13, we find it is a limited day: "Exhort one another today, whilst it is called today, lest any of you be hardened through the deceitfulness of sin." When he says "while it is called today," he means, do not stay till tomorrow, but embrace the present opportunity. This day God holds out the golden scepter and, if you accept it, you will be saved. If you do not take it today, your heart will be more hardened tomorrow; and so it may be you will never touch it. God is angry with us, says Psalm 7:11. Why? He is our adversary because we bear arms against Him, and will contest for the mastery with Him. We oppose Him in hostile manner as long as we continue sinful against Him. What is the best counsel in this case? "Agree with thine adversary quickly while thou art in the way with him." It is wisdom to do that soon that must of necessity be done. If it is not, we perish forever. "Kiss the Son, lest He be angry, and thou perish from the right way" (Psalm 2:12).

OBJECTION. But what need is there for such haste? I may do it hereafter, when I come to my journey's end.

ANSWER. There needs to be haste for the day is limited. "I have heard thee in an accepted time, and in the day of salvation have I succored thee. Behold, now is the accepted time, now is the day of salvation" (2 Corinthians 6:2). It is a day of salvation, and would we not be glad to know this time? Behold, this is the accepted time. "Seek the Lord while He may be found; call on Him while He is near." This is the accepted time; this is the day of salvation. Embrace this time, for now He may be found; this instant is the time; the present is now. God at this time stirs the waters; if now you will step in and close with God, casting down your weapons, then this will be the day of your salvation. As this is called "God's day," so it is our day. O Jerusalem, Jerusalem, "if thou hadst known in this thy day the things that belong unto thy peace, but now they are hid from thine eyes" (Luke 19:42). Mark, "if thou hadst known in this thy day"; so that if we pass by in this acceptable time those things which belong to our peace, they will be hidden from our eyes.

Give me leave to press this upon you, for nothing more brings destruction than putting off from us the offers of God's grace. Unless we return to the Almighty, humbling ourselves, there will be bitterness in the end. Here is the matter, whether God must wait on us or we on Him? This is the day of salvation, says God, and must we take time to think whether it is seasonable or not?

• By this means we show the highest presumption; and this is no light thing to be inconsiderately passed over. Shall God make you such an offer, and will you be so presumptuous as to think another one more seasonable? It is high presumption for you to make yourself wiser than God, to neglect what He prescribes, and that with a promise too, as if you had God at your command. If you resolve to take it tomorrow, it is requisite that you have space to repent, and grace to do it. Now neither of these are in your own hands; if they were, you would have ground for a further delay. If you had the power to say, "I will live so long," or could by your own might prolong your life, it would be something—but it is otherwise. In refusing God's offer, you refuse Him who has your life in His hand. What high presumption is this! See it in Jezebel: "I gave her space to repent, but she repented not" (Revelation 2:21). It is as if God had said, "I gave her time to live when I might have cut her off in the midst of her sins."

Observe here the reason why God gives us this space: it is to repent. What presumption must that be when we will go quite contrary to God? And because we have space, therefore we will not repent. Why does God not smite you from heaven when you thus audaciously set yourself against Him? Why does He not strike you with a thunder-bolt? Surely He does not give you this space to spend it idly, but for another end; not to follow your lusts, neglecting God's call, but that you may remember yourself, and return with all your heart. Remember those words: "My times are in Thy hands" (Psalm 31:15). He did not say, "My times are in my own hands," for he knew that would be grand presumption. Why, then, should anyone challenge that to himself which belongs to God, as if he were the lord of his own life, supposing God's call to be unseasonable, and that he may think on it better hereafter?

May not a young man die soon? Even now an old man cannot live long. Many strong and lusty men are brought to the grave as well as the weak and feeble. And why should we suffer Satan to abuse us thus? Your space, then, is preserved in God's hands, and therefore you may not be lord and master of it.

But even if we were to admit that God grants you space, yet you may not have the grace to repent. That was Jezebel's case: though God gave her space, yet she did not repent (Revelation 2:21). What! Can you tell what may then become of you? Perhaps you may live long, yet you may never find so much as your thoughts on repentance, much less the grace to perform it; you may not have a desire that way, much less be able to do it. Repentance is not a thing at our own command. "In meekness," said the apostle, "instruct them that oppose themselves, if God, peradventure, will give them repentance to the acknowledging of the truth" (2 Timothy 2:25). *If* God will give it to them. It is a thing then that would seem to be in God's hand; it is His proper gift. Repentance is a grace out of our reach; it is not in a man's own power. Be meek, therefore, in instructing. The opening of the eyes of the blind is in God's hands; thank Him for what you see, and know that it is His gift.

The apostle, speaking of our Savior Christ, says, "Him hath God exalted with His right hand to be a Prince and a Savior, for to give repentance to Israel and forgiveness of sins" (Acts 5:31). The grace of repentance, then, is no herb growing in our own garden; it is a gift of God's bestowing. To this purpose is Acts 11:18: "When they heard these things, they held their peace and glorified God, saying, 'Then hath God also to the Gentiles granted repentance unto life.' " As God grants life, so He also grants repentance unto life. "I have heard Ephraim bemoaning himself thus," said the Lord, "Thou hast chastised me, and I was chastised, as a bullock unaccustomed to the yoke; turn Thou me, and I shall be turned" (Jeremiah 31:18). And to the same purpose is Lamentations 5:21: "Turn Thou us unto Thee, O Lord, and we shall be turned." It is as if Zion had said, "We are no more able to turn ourselves than a dead man." "After that," said Ephraim, "I was turned, I repented; and after I was instructed, I smote upon my thigh. I was ashamed, yea, even confounded." See then what high presumption it is for a man to presume he has this grace of God at his command.

• But as it is high presumption, so it is the highest contempt and despising of the grace of God. "Despisest thou the riches of His goodness and forbearance, and long-suffering?" (Romans 2:4). Thus is it here: God gives you space; you have it, but you do not employ it in what God gave it to you for. You defer the main business; and the apostle accounts it no better than despising the offers of God's grace and goodness. Do you think God will take this kindly from your hands? Will you despise Him, and think that He will not despise you? With the froward He will show Himself froward. God will come suddenly, if you do not make use of your opportunity, and take all away from you. The threatening is plainly laid down in Revelation 3:3: "If thou shalt not watch, I will come on thee as a thief, and thou shalt not know what hour I will come upon thee." It is spoken to us all, and therefore it concerns us all. Whoever has an ear to hear, let him hear. These are God's words I have spoken to you this day, and you shall be accountable for them. Do not let the devil steal this from you; hold it fast; this is your day: "If thou shalt not watch, I will come on thee suddenly as a thief." It is the heaviest judgment that can come on unconverted persons, on unregenerate souls, not to awake till God comes on them, never to stir themselves till hell rouses them up. Thus will it be with us unless we awake by repentance.

To pray against sudden death and not to fit yourself for it is to add contempt to your presumption and rebellion. The wise man tells us that "man knoweth not his time; as the fishes that are taken in an evil net, and as the birds that are caught in the snare, so are the sons of men snared in an evil time when it falleth suddenly upon them" (Ecclesiastes 9:12). Mark, when it falls suddenly, unaware. Here is your wisdom, then, to provide that you may not be taken suddenly. If the good man of the house knew at what time the thief would come, he would have watched, and not have suffered his house to have been broken up. And therefore Christ counsels us to watch, since we do not know the day or hour when the Son of man comes.

Here is the difference, then, between wisdom and folly. Hereby may we know whether we are wise men or fools: if we foresee this day and provide for it, it is an argument of wisdom, if we watch so that, when it falls, it may not fall suddenly on us. If we are negligent of this day, and allow our hearts to become like Nabal's—who had ten days for repentance, yet his heart was dead like a stone—then we shall despise the day of salvation, God's day and our own day. Then we will be a Nabal, no more moved than a pillar in the church, as I have found by experience.

But you may reply, "I suppose God will not put me at such a disadvantage. I trust I shall have life and space, and not be in Nabal's condition. I hope I shall have my senses about me to be able to cry, "Lord, have mercy upon me!"

But suppose God gives you a tender heart, and you are sensible of your danger so that you call and cry earnestly to God for mercy; yet even this is a miserable condition. You shalt find it will not be enough to cry, "Lord, be merciful to me!" If you neglect Him here, He will neglect you on your deathbed.

I am not speaking this as if it came from me. No, look what Wisdom says in Proverbs 1:24–26: "Because I have called and ye refused, I have stretched out My hand and no man regarded; but ye have set at naught all My counsel, and would none of My reproof, I also will laugh at your calamity. I will mock when your fear cometh." It is as if He had said, "You refused Me on My day. I called and cried unto you, but you set at naught My words, rejected My counsel, and were wiser than I. Therefore I will laugh at your destruction; when you are in misery, I will mock and deride instead of succoring."

It will be a terrible thing when, instead of hearing our cries to answer them, He shall deride us and laugh at our folly and madness. Verse 28: "Then shall they call upon Me, but I will not answer; they shall seek Me early, but they shall not find Me." See what folly then it is to let this time slip. This is the acceptable day. "Seek the Lord while He may be found; call on Him while He is near" (Isaiah 55:6). When a man refuses God's day, God will not hear his prayer; all his sighs and sobs, his groans and cries, shall not prevail. "I will choose their delusions, and will bring their fears upon them; because when I called, none did answer; when I spake, they did not hear" (Isaiah 66:4). When men will be choosers of what God would not have, God will have His choice too; and it shall be that which will be displeasing to them. "I will choose their delusions, and will bring their fears upon them."

2

*Speedy Conversion the Only Means to
Prevent Imminent Destruction, Part 2*

"Again, he limiteth a certain day, saying in David, Today,
after so long a time; as it is said, Today if ye will hear his
voice, harden not your hearts." Hebrews 4:7

The last day we opened this place and showed how the
Lord had proposed a limited time for our conversion unto
Him, in which we should hear and obey His voice. We
showed further how it was Satan's policy to make men
seem wiser than God so that when God proposes a certain
time and limits us to a day wherein He will be found, we
will not have His time frame but our own. It is folly in the
highest degree to trust the future when we have neither
space nor grace in our own hands for such a business.
God is the Lord and owner of them both, and will not part
with His prerogative. "Go to, ye that say, 'Today or tomorrow we will return unto the Lord.' " You add to presumption both folly and rebellion.

Seeing then these are not in your power, do not
harden your hearts as in the provocation, nor offer spite
to the Holy Ghost, by whom you are sealed to the day of
redemption. If we do not embrace God's day, we despise
the riches of His goodness, long-suffering, and patience.
"Despisest thou the riches of God's grace, not knowing
that the longsuffering of God leadeth thee to repentance?" (Romans 2:4). There can be no higher presumption than to bid defiance to the Spirit of God; nor can
there be greater contempt of mercy than to set light of

the time of our repentance and returning to God, making that the greatest argument of our delay which God uses to draw us to Him. God gives us space that we may repent, and we do not repent because He gives us space! He gives us life so that, with fear and trembling, we may set about the business of salvation, and we, through strong delusions, put from us the offers of His grace, as if they were unseasonably offered! What madness is it to frustrate the Almighty of His ends and purposes! The Lord is not slack touching His promise.

It is a great stop and hindrance to our progress in goodness and the work of repentance when we distrust God and do not take Him at His Word. He sends abroad His ambassadors, who proclaim, "This is the accepted time; this is the day of salvation. Today, if ye will hear His voice, harden not your hearts." Yet we put this day from us, and say that hereafter is a more acceptable time: "I have this delight, this pleasure to take first in the world. I am not so weaned from it as I would be." It is as if God should take it well from our hands that we should then return to Him when there is no remedy, and say, "I will first use all the pleasure the world affords me, and then saying, 'Lord, have mercy on me' will serve the turn." This is the very stifling of the beginnings and proceedings of Christianity. Let this be well and speedily weighed as we tender our good and comfort.

OBJECTION. But some may say, "Why must we be in haste? May we not use leisure? Soft and fair goes far."

ANSWER. True, soft and fair goes far, if a man goes fairly in the way. In this case, though you go but softly, you may come to your journey's end. But the doubt remains still; there is a question whether you are in the way or not. We are happy if we are in the way, although we can but halt and limp on in this way—although this should be no ground for us to content ourselves therewith. We must not trifle in the ways of holiness. It is what concerns our life, and must be seriously thought on, and that speedily too. "Agree with thine adversary quickly while thou art in the way with him." God is your Adversary; unless you agree with Him speedily, His patience will break forth into fury. "Kiss the Son lest He be angry, and thou perish from the right way." You have no assurance of your life; you may be snapped off while you think you have time enough to repent and return. As long as we are out of the way of repentance, we are on the way to hell; and the farther a man goes in a wrong way, the nearer is he to hell, and the greater ado it is to return back. In this regard, soft and fair may go far; but it is far out of the way, far on the way to perdition and destruction. As long as we are out of the right way to heaven and happiness, we are on the path that leads directly to the chambers of death.

But let me in this particular unrip the heart of a natural man. What is the reason that, when God gives men a day, and cries out, "This is the day of salvation, this is the accepted time," they put salvation far from them and hope to defer it and desire more time? Consider whether the thoughts that poise down our hearts are not groundless; see whether they will hold water in the end, and whether in making such excuses to great presumption we do not add the height of folly. Can it be expected that we should have our good in this world, and in the world to come too? This is well, if it might be so. But let us try the matter.

You are loath to part with your profits and pleasures, but consider what a grand iniquity this is. Can you offer God a greater wrong and indignity? Do you think this is the way to make your peace with God? What a high dishonor it is to Him that you should give Him your feeble and doting old age, and give the devil your lively and vigorous youth, your strength and spirits! Do you think He will accept you in the next world when you thus scorn Him in this one? "If you offer the blind for sacrifice, is it not an evil? If you offer the lame and sick, is it not evil? Offer it now unto thy governor; will he be pleased with thee, or accept thy person? saith the Lord of hosts" (Malachi 1:8). But mark how he goes on: "Cursed be the deceiver, which hath in his flock a male, and voweth and sacrifieth unto the Lord a corrupt thing" (verse 14). God accounts such service a corrupt thing.

Never look for a blessing from God in heaven when you sacrifice corrupt things to Him. We are to offer and present ourselves "a living sacrifice, holy and acceptable unto God" (Romans 12:1). Now judge whether they offer God the living who say, "When my doting days come, my lame days when I cannot go, my blind days when I cannot see, then I will offer myself as a sacrifice to God." Will this be acceptable to Him? "Is not this evil," says the Lord, "to offer Me such a corrupt thing?"

Nay, more, he is accursed who offers such an offering, such a polluted sacrifice. Do you thus requite the Lord? Do you think He will accept it at your hands? Go offer such a gift to your ruler, to your prince; will he accept it or be pleased with it? No, a landlord will have the best and the choice; and it must provoke God when we give Him the refuse. Let no man then thus delude himself with vain hopes, but let him consider how dishonorable a thing it will be to God, and how unprofitable to you, whoever you are.

It is the ready way to destruction. Heaven, happiness, and eternal life are laid up for those who embrace the acceptable time; death, horror, and eternal misery for those who refuse it—and will you hazard soul and body on this? Moses, on this ground, chose rather to suffer affliction in this world with the people of God than to enjoy the pleasures of sin for a moment. When these things are past, what profit will you have of those things whereof then you will be ashamed? When a man comes to see truly and thoroughly into himself, he will find no profit of such things as these. Death, both temporal and eternal will certainly follow us if we do not repent the more speedily; that is all the profit we shall find.

But suppose you prevent everlasting death by repentance, yet "what profit is there of those things whereof thou art now for the present ashamed?" The best that can come is shame.

You are loath to part with the pleasures of sin for a season, and hereafter you think you can amend all. But consider the particulars, and then you shall see how you are fooled in your hearts and souls. Believe it as an undoubted truth, there is nothing in the world by which Satan more deludes a man than by persuading him to neglect his day and repent well enough hereafter. That you may expel this suggestion out of your soul, pray to God that He would go along with His Word, and cause you to lay this to heart, that by His Spirit your understanding may be enlightened to see the truth. Though I make as clear as the sun that it is a false supposition and mere folly on which we build in deferring our return to God, yet God from heaven must teach you or you will be never the wiser. Know therefore that this very day God reaches out the golden scepter to you. And what folly would it be to neglect it since you do not know whether He will ever offer it to you again. Assure yourself that he is a liar who tells you that you can as easily repent hereafter as now; and this will appear whether we consider the order of outward things in the world or the nature of sin.

As for external things, every age after a man comes into the world (if he does not embrace the present opportunity for repentance) is worse than the other, and are each of them as so many clogs which come one after another to hinder it. Consider that the wisest of men gave you this counsel: "Remember thy Creator in the day of thy youth, before the evil days come, wherein thou shall say thou hast not pleasure in them." Here we find that it is a youthful thing, and should be a young man's practice. The more sin you commit, the less apt you are to repent. Custom in sinning makes you like Lot: the older you grow, the more loath you are to go out of Sodom.

Besides, consider what sin is in its nature. It is a weight: "Let us lay aside every weight, and the sin which doth so easily beset us" (Hebrews 12:1). Sin is then a weight, and so a heavy thing; but add sin to sin, a weight to a weight, and it becomes heavier and heavier. A man who is in a state of impenitence has this weight laid on him, and is subject to the devil; he is in a state of rebellion against God. One said well that if we consider sin rightly, it is like the rising of water, over which a man tries to pass; and finding it higher than it was wont to be, he stays awhile, and then tries again, and finds it higher than before. He stays yet longer, till it becomes impassable, so that he may not adventure without great disadvantage. Thus it is with sin: now, perhaps, the waters of iniquity are passable; if you will, you may go over; but if you delay the adventure, the streams of sin will run together into one channel and be more difficultly passed.

Add hereto the argument in the text: "Today if ye will hear His voice, harden not your heart," but repent while it is called today, showing that if we pass this day, we shall be harder and harder. Wherefore, says the apostle, "Exhort one another daily while it is called today, lest any of you be hardened through the deceitfulness of sin" (Hebrews 3:13). It is as if he had said, "If your heart is hard today, it will be harder tomorrow." Custom in sin hardens the heart and takes away the sense of it. Wherefore, says the apostle, "I speak after the manner of men because of the infirmity of your flesh. For as ye have yielded your members servants to uncleanness, and to iniquity unto iniquity, even so now yield your members servants to righteousness unto holiness" (Romans 6:19).

So we see that if a man once gives himself up unto sin,

he will not be satisfied therewith, but will give himself up to "iniquity unto iniquity." What is the meaning of that? It is as if he had said, "If we give ourselves up to iniquity we shall not rest there, but we shall add iniquity unto iniquity, sin unto sin. We shall be brought to such a custom in evil that it will be easier for an Ethiopian to change his skin and a leopard his spots than for those who have been accustomed to doing evil to learn to do well (Jeremiah 13:23). It will be to as much purpose to wash the color off of a black man as to try to put off that ill custom and shake off that second nature.

Sin is a hammer, and sin is a nail too. Every sin strikes the former sin home to the head so that, whereas before it might easily have been drawn out, it roots it in so fast that it can hardly be plucked out. Mark how the apostle described this cursed nature of sin: "Having eyes full of adultery, and that cannot cease from sin, beguiling unstable souls, a heart they have exercised with covetous practices" (2 Peter 2:14). What makes a man prompt in anything but exercise? When a man is exercised in sin, see the result of it: it brings him to that vicious habit so that at length he cannot cease from sin. If a man deals with a young twig, it will bend and break at his pleasure; but when it comes to full growth, it is beyond his strength. So it fares with sin: if you deal with it while you are young, before it has taken root, you may easily wield it, at least with more facility than otherwise you could. But if you let it run on to confirmed habits, it becomes immovable. Wherefore, said the apostle, "Let us lay aside the sin which doth so easily beset us" (Hebrews 12:1). The reason is evident, because else we shall be so hardened that we shall not be able. A man who has a green wound, if he will seek his cure right away, it may be quickly and easily remedied. But if he delays, the wound begins to fester and must be lanced, not without great pain and anguish to the patient.

Sin is such a wound: if it is let alone it corrupts. And

the more proud flesh grows up, the longer the cure is delayed. This therefore should be a chief thing we should take heed of, how we put from us God's time and the offers of mercy till another day.

But there is another sort who are as greatly fooled as these, yea, more, if more is possible. These are they who put it off till the hour of their death, till the last gasp, as if they desired to give God as little of their service as possibly they might. These think that if they can but cry, "I have sinned," and, "Lord, have mercy on me," when their breath departs their bodies, they show a good disposition and perform such acceptable service that God cannot fail to grant them a pardon. But do not think that all will be well, or that you shall shake hands with God at your journey's end, when you have not walked with Him all the way.

OBJECTION. But did not the thief repent at the very last on the cross? And why may not I do so on my deathbed?

ANSWER. This is no good warrant for your delay, for Christ might work this miraculously for the glory of His compassion. Do not trust therefore in this, nor content yourself with good intentions; but set about the business in good earnest and immediately. Our deathbeds will bring so many disadvantages as will make that time very unseasonable.

Consider the external hindrances, such as are pangs and pains in your body, which must be undergone: and you shall find it will be as much as you well can do to support yourself under them. Every noise will then offend you; yea, you will not be able to endure the speech of your best friends. Through the anguish of our spirits we shall be unfit to meddle with anything else, especially when the pains of death are upon us, the dread whereof is terrible. How it will make us tremble when death shall come to cut off our souls from our bodies, and put them into possession of hell unless we repent the sooner.

But suppose these outward hindrances are removed, so that neither pain of body nor fear of death seize you, neither care of wife or children, houses or lands distract you, but that you might then set about repentance with all your might. Though you seemed to be in the most penitent condition possible, yet where is the change or new nature that should follow your contrition? Unless we see this in truth, we can have but little comfort. Were I to see a sinner run on in his ill courses till the day of his death, and then set about this work, I could not conclude therefore the safety of his soul, because it is the change of the affections, not of the actions, that God looks for. The fear of death may extort this repentance where the nature is not changed.

For example, take a covetous man who dotes on his wealth more than anything else in the world; suppose him to be on a ship with all his riches about him, and a tempest comes and puts him in danger of losing both his life and his goods. In this difficulty, he casts out all his wealth so that he may preserve his life; shall we therefore say he is no longer covetous? No, we will account him nevertheless covetous for all this—not that he loved his goods less, but his life more.

It is so in this case when an impenitent person is brought upon his deathbed: he is apt to cry out in the bitterness of his soul, "If God will but grant me life and spare me now, I will never be a drunkard, swearer, or covetous person again." Where does this come from? Not from any change of his nature, or from a loathing of what he formerly loved, but because he cannot keep these and life together. Fear alters his disposition when the terrors of the Almighty lie upon him.

I myself have seen many at such a time as this, who have been so exceedingly full of sorrow and penitent expressions that the bystanders have even wished their souls to have been in the other soul's eases; and yet when God has restored them, they have fallen into their former courses again. Why is this? Because when repentance comes this way, it alters only the outward actions for the present, not the sinful dispositions; things that are extracted from a man alter the outward appearance, not the nature. How penitent were they when God's hand was on them! But let it be removed, and hear how God complains of them: "O Ephraim, what shall I do unto thee? O Judah, what shall I do unto thee? For thy goodness is as a morning cloud, and as the early dew it goeth away." Mark, "thy goodness is as a morning cloud," such a goodness as is extorted, that is as temporary as early dew.

But I draw to a conclusion. God has set us a certain day and, if we let the time pass, woe to us! For though He is full of mercy and patience, yet patience hurt oftentimes harms, and provokes the Almighty to fury. To this purpose is that parable: "A certain man had a fig tree planted in his vineyard, and he came and sought fruit thereon and found none. Then said he unto the dresser of his vineyard, 'Behold these three years I come seeking fruit on this fig tree, and find none; cut it down. Why cumbereth it the ground?' " (Luke 13:6–7). There is an appointed time, then, foreordained by God, wherein He offers us grace. It may be seven years or ten; it may be but two hours for all you know. No man knows the time and its continuance but He who has appointed it to this purpose.

You hear much talk of God's eternal and everlasting election, and we are too apt to rest on this, that if we are elected to salvation we shall be saved, and if not, we shall be damned, troubling ourselves with God's work of pre-destination, whereas this works no change in the party elected until He come unto Him in his own person. What is God's election to me? It is nothing to my comfort unless I myself am effectually called. We are to look to this effec-tual calling. The other is but God's love to sever me. But what is my effectual calling? It is when God touches my heart and translates me from the death of sin, to the life of grace.

Now there are certain times that God appoints for this effectual calling, wherein He uses the means to work on us, and of which He can say, "What could I do more than I have done?" And may you not fear an actual rejection since you have lived so long under the means of grace; that God has waited these many years, the dew of heaven continually falling on you, and yet you have remained unfruitful? Do you not fear that dismal sentence, "Cut it down, why cumbereth it the ground?" God's grace is not to be dallied with, as children do with their meals. If we thus slight Him, He may justly deprive us of all. A terrible place to this purpose is Hebrews 6:7–8: "The earth which drinketh in the rain that cometh oft upon it, and bringeth forth herbs meet for them by whom it is dressed, receiveth blessing from God; but that which beareth thorns and briers is rejected, and is nigh unto cursing, whose end is to be burned."

God calls us where the droppings of His grace are. Do we bring forth that fruit which is fitting, answerable to those continual distillings and droppings on us? If our consciences witness for us, happy are we. But when there have been these showers of grace out of God's Word flowing down upon us, and yet we have received so much grace in vain, oh, what can we then expect but a curse in this life, and eternal death in the world to come? What can we look for but the same curse which the barren fig tree received? The tree was not cut down, but withered. We are near the same curse, if we do not answer God's grace.

When we have had so long a time for the ministry of the Word, and yet suffer it to be lost through our barrenness, our condition is sad and woeful; we can look for nothing but withering. But, beloved, I must hope better things of you, and such as accompany salvation. Labor therefore to prevent, and arm yourselves against this suggestion and fallacy of Satan; resolve to hear God in this acceptable time, to set yourselves now to the work that, if we do, all will be well. God will be gracious to us. If it is otherwise, we are undone forever. Till you have learned this lesson, you can go no further. Wherefore do not let Satan possess you with that madness, to cause you to pass and let slip this golden opportunity through a false conceit, that you may have a more seasonable day of your own for repentance hereafter.

3

All Men Are Dead in Sin

"And you hath he quickened, who were dead in trespasses and sins; wherein in time past ye walked according to the course of the world, according to the prince of the power of the air, the spirit that now worketh in the children of disobedience." Ephesians 2:1–2

In the last discourse I declared unto you the duty that is required of us if we look to be saved, that we must not only take the matter speedily into consideration and not be deluded by our own hearts and the wiles of Satan, and that we must not do it superficially or carelessly, but must bring ourselves to the true touchstone and not look upon ourselves with false glasses because there is naturally in everyone self-love; and in these last and worst times men are apt to think better of themselves than they deserve. If there is any beginning of goodness in them, they think all is well, when there is no likelihood of their being any more than half-Christians. Such a person thinks that if he has escaped the outward pollutions of the world through lust, and is not as bad as formerly he has been, and not as bad as many men in the world are, therefore he is well enough; whereas his end proves worse than his beginning.

This superficial repentance is but like washing a hog: the outside is only washed, the swinish nature is not taken away. There may be in this man some outward abstaining from the common gross sins of the world, or those which he himself was subject unto; but his disposition to sin is the same. His nature is not changed; there is no renovation,

26

no casting in a new mold, which must be in us. For it is not a little reforming that will serve the turn, no, nor all the morality in the world, nor all the common graces of God's Spirit, nor the outward change of the life. They will not do unless we are quickened and have a new life wrought in us; unless there is a supernatural working of God's Spirit, we can never enter into heaven.

Therefore, in this case, it behooves every man to prove his own work (Galatians 6:4). Men are rarely drawn to be exact examiners of themselves. Even a heathen could say, "To know a man's self is a heavenly thing." And it is a heavenly thing indeed if we have a heavenly Master to teach us. The devil taught Socrates a lesson that brought him from the study of natural to moral philosophy, whereby he knew himself; yet the devil knew morality could never teach him the lesson indeed. All the morality in the world cannot teach a man to escape hell; we must have a better instructor herein than the devil or ourselves. The Lord of heaven must do it if ever we will be brought to know ourselves aright.

Paul was brought up at the feet of Gamaliel, one of the most learned doctors of the Pharisees, and yet he could not teach him this. When he studied the law he thought himself unblamable; but coming to a higher and better Master, he knew that in him, that is, in his flesh, dwelt no good thing (Romans 7:18). By self-examination a man may find many faults in himself; but to find that which the apostle afterwards found in himself, to see the flesh as rottenness, the sink of iniquity that is within him, and to find himself as bad as indeed he is—unless it pleases the Lord to open his eyes and to teach him, he can never attain to it.

Now we come to this passage wherein we see the true glass of ourselves. The Spirit knows what we are better than we do, and the Spirit shows us that every one of us either was or is such as we are here set down to be. We are natural before we can be spiritual; there is not a man but has been or is yet a natural man, and therefore we see the large description of a natural man before he is quickened, before God, who is rich in mercy, enlivens him who was dead in sins, and saves him by grace in Christ. Thus is it with us all, and thus must it be; and we shall never be fit for grace till we know ourselves thus far, till we know ourselves as far out of frame as the Spirit of truth declares us to be.

In this place of Scripture we will consider:

1. Who this carnal man is; what they are whom the apostle speaks of as being "dead in sins," and who "walk after the course of the world," led by the devil, and who "have their conversation after the flesh," being "children of wrath." These are big words and heavy things. So we will consider, first, the subject of whom this is spoken.

2. Then follows what that ill news is which he delivers to them.

1. Who they are of whom this is spoken, and that is you: "*You* hath He quickened who were dead." And then it is "ye" in the words following, "that in times past *ye* walked after the course of the world." In the third verse it is "we": "Among whom also *we* all had our conversation in times past." He speaks now in the first person, as before in the second, so that the subject is "we" and "ye all." There is not a man in this congregation but is or was as bad as the Holy Ghost here makes him out to be. But to come to that which is delivered of him: he is one who is "not quickened" and who is "dead in sins." He is no better than nature made him; he has that corrupt nature which he received from Adam till he is thus spiritually enlivened.

Now he is described first by the quality of his person and second by his company: "even as others." You may think yourself better than another man, but you are no better. You are "even as others," you are not so alone, but as bad as the worst. There is not a man more evil in his nature than you are. When you go to hell, perhaps there will be some difference in your various punishments, according to your various acts of rebellion; but yet you shall all come short of the glory of God. But for the matter of quickening, you are all alike.

First, then, concerning their quality: and this is declared,

• By their general disposition: they are "dead in trespasses and sins." They are dead, and therefore are unable and indisposed to the works of a spiritual living man. And they are not only indisposed and unable thereto, but dead in trespasses and sins. This person lies rotting in his own filth, like a rotten carcass and stinking carrion in the nostrils of the Almighty, so loathsome is he, all which is drawn from original sin. He is not only disenabled to any good, but prone to all sin and iniquity.

• By his particular conversation, and that appears in the verse following: "Wherein in time past ye walked." How? Not according to the Word and will of God, not according to His rule, but you walked after three other wicked rules. A dead man, then, has his walk, you see! This is a strange thing in the dead, but who directs him in his course? These three: the world, the flesh, and the devil, the worst guides that may be. Yet, if we look to the conversation of a natural man, we see that these are his pilots which are here set down.

The world. "Wherein in time past ye walked according to the course of the world." He swims along with the stream of this world. Nor will he be singular, nor so precise as some are, but he will do as the world does, run wherever that carries him. See the state of a natural man. He is apt to be brought into the slavery of the world.

The devil. The devil leads him as well as the world: "According to the prince of the power of the air, the spirit that now worketh in the children of disobedience." Instead of having the Spirit of God to be led by, he is posted by the spirit of Satan, and the works of his father the devil he will do. He does not have a heart to resist the most vile lusts the devil shall persuade him to. When Satan fills his heart, he has no heart to anything else other than to follow him.

The flesh. "Amongst whom also we all had our conversation in times past in the lusts of the flesh, fulfilling the desires of the flesh, and of the mind" (verse 3). So you see the three guides of a natural man; and he is as bad as these three can make him. And until the stronger Man comes and pulls him out, in this condition he remains, and in this natural estate he is a son of disobedience. We see, then, the state of disobedience described to be wretchedness.

This further appears by that which must follow, which is cursedness. Rebellion and wretchedness going before, cursedness will follow. For God will not be abused, nor suffer a rebel to go unpunished. "Therefore," says the apostle, "we are by nature the children of wrath." Being the natural sons of disobedience, we may well conclude that we are the children of wrath. If we can well learn these two things of ourselves—how deep we are in sin and how the wrath of God is due to us for our sins—then we may see what we are by nature. Thus much concerning the quality of a natural man.

The second thing we see is his company: "even as others." By nature we are "the children of wrath, even as others." That is to say, we go in that broad, wide way that leads to damnation, that way we all naturally rush into. Though we may think it otherwise, and think ourselves better, yet we are deceived. For it is with us even as with others. Naturally we are in the same state that the worst men in the world are; so that we see the glass of a natural man, or of a man who has made some beginnings, till Christ comes and quickens him.

QUESTION. We see then who it is spoken of to be

dead men, those who are rotten and putrid, as bad as the
world, the flesh, and the devil can make them. Who would
these be?

ANSWER. It is you: "*You* hath He quickened."

But you might say, "This refers to the Ephesians, who
were in times past heathens: I hope it does not refer to us!
They were Gentiles and pagans who did not know Christ.
Verse 12: 'Aliens from the commonwealth of Israel, and
strangers from the covenants of promise, having no hope,
without God in the world.' Atheists, as the text renders it,
and therefore they might well be so. But I hope it is not
referring to me! I was never a pagan or heathen. I was
born of Christian parents, and am of the church."

But put away these conceits. Look at the third verse:
"Among whom *also we* had our conversation," and "*wherein
ye yourselves.*" It is not only spoken of the Gentiles, but veri-
fied of us also. It is as if he had said here, as in Galatians
2:15, "We who are Jews by nature, and not sinners of the
Gentiles." He paints out not only "you" the Gentiles in
such ugly colors, but "we" Jews also, we of the commonwealth of Israel. "We," before we were quickened, were in
the same state that "you" are described to be in.

OBJECTION. "Oh, but the apostle may do this out of
fellowship, and to avoid envy, as it were, making himself a
party with them, as Ezra did in Ezra 9, including himself in
the number of the offenders, though he had no hand in
the offense: 'O our God, what shall we say? Our evil deeds
. . . .'" And "how shall we stand before Thee because of
this?' making a particular confession, whereas he was not
at fault, but was merely trying to sweeten it to them."

ANSWER. But here the apostle does not so; he was not
thus minded. But it is "we all." He puts a universality into
it. So it is clear that before conversion and quickening by
grace from Christ, we all, all of us, are in as foul and filthy
a condition as what is here described and set down. This is
the point: it is not spoken of some desperate sinners, but is

the common state and condition of all the sons of Adam.

DOCTRINE. All men, every man and woman in this place, either is or has been in the state that here the apostle describes him or her to be.

Therefore we all have need to examine ourselves, whether we yet remain in that condition or not. The apostle brings this description to testify the truth of the point: "The Scripture hath concluded all under sin" (Galatians 3:22). The whole current and course of the Scripture shows the universality of it, that it is true of all. The apostle speaks of himself and the rest, saying, "We ourselves also," not only you of the Gentiles, but "we ourselves also were foolish, disobedient," and so on, "but after the kindness of God towards man appeared" (Titus 3:3–4), that is, before the "day-star of grace did arise in our hearts," there is not the best of us all but have been thus and so.

The apostle insists on the point expressly in Romans 3:19, "that every mouth might be stopped," to show the state of all men naturally. Having laid down a large bedroll of the iniquities of the heathen, he comes afterward to convince the Jews: "What are we better than they? No, we have proved that all are under sin; there is none good, no not one."

OBJECTION. "But though you bring many places to prove that all are sinners, yet I hope the Virgin Mary was not."

ANSWER. All are sinners. "There is none righteous, no not one." The drift of the apostle in this is to show that these things are not spoken of some heinous sinners only, but no one is to be exempted. And therefore, in his conclusion he says, "That every mouth may be stopped, and all the world become guilty before God; and that by the deeds of the law no flesh can be justified from sin" (verses 19–20).

So that now having proved this so clearly to you, consider with yourselves how needful it is to apply this to our own souls. Many men, when they read such things as these in the Scripture, read them but as stories from strange countries: "What! Are we dead in sins and unable to stir one foot in God's ways? We are bad, indeed, but dead, rotten, and stinking in sins and trespasses? What, as bad as the world, the devil, and flesh can make us? What, children of wrath? Firebrands of hell?" Few can persuade themselves that it is so bad with them. Therefore take this home to yourselves; think no better of yourselves than you are, for thus you are naturally. Therefore consider, if you were now going out of the world, what state are you are in? Are you a child of wrath, a child of Belial, or the like? Set about the work speedily; go to God, pray, and cry earnestly. Give yourself no rest till you know this to be your condition. Do not let your corrupt nature deceive you and make you think better of yourself than God says you are.

Now, that we may better know to whom these things belong, know that it is you and I. We all have been, or are, in this state until we have supernatural grace; and therefore we are declared to be children of wrath and children of disobedience until we are regenerated. Why? Because that is our nature, it belongs to all. We know the common nature always appertains to the same kind; there is nothing that is natural but is common with the kind. If then by nature we are children, then certainly it belongs to every mother's son of us, for we are all sons of Adam. "In Adam we all die" (Romans 5). That is the fountain whence all misery flows to us. As you received your nature, so you received the corruption of your nature from him; for "he begat a son in his own likeness." This, therefore, is the condition of everyone.

The apostle, in 1 Corinthians 15, speaks of two men: "the first was from the earth, earthy; the second was the Lord from heaven." What, were there not many millions and generations more? True, but there were not more men like these, men of men, two headmen, two fathers of all other men. There were but two by whom all must stand or fall. By the fall of the first man we all fell; and if we do not rise by the second Man, we are yet in our sins. If He did not rise, we cannot be risen. We must rise or fall by Him. He is the Mediator of the second covenant. If He rises and we are in Him, we shall rise with Him; but if not, we are dead still.

So it is with the first Adam: we all depend on him; he is the root of all mankind. It is said in Isaiah 53 that our Savior would rejoice to see His seed. That is to say, He is the common Father of all mankind, I mean of all those who shall proceed from Him by spiritual generation. He shall present them to His Father, as when one is presented to the university. "Behold here am I, and the children that Thou hast given Me." So in Adam, he being the head of the covenant of nature, that is the law, if he had stood, none of us would have fallen; if he falls, none of us all can stand. He is the peg on which all the keys hang: if that stands, they hang fast; but if that falls, they fall with it.

We see this in matters of bondage and servitude. If the father forfeits his liberty and becomes a bondman, all his children are bondmen to a hundred generations. And this is our case spiritually. We were all once free, but our father has forfeited his liberty; and if he becomes a slave, he cannot beget a freeman. The Jews declared themselves to be freemen: "We were never bondmen," though it was false. Even Cicero himself could tell a Jew that he was a slave, although they had a good opinion of themselves. But our Savior said, "You are bondmen unto sin and Satan." For till the Son makes you free, you are all bondmen; but when He makes you free, then you are free indeed.

2. This is our condition, and this is the bad news the apostle delivered: we are dead in trespasses and sins, that is, there is an indisposition in us to all good works. A dead man cannot walk, speak, or do any act that a living man

can; so these cannot do the actions of men who are quickened and enlivened. They cannot pray with the Spirit, they cannot love God, they cannot do those things that shall be done hereafter in heaven. There is not one good duty that this natural man can do. If it should be said unto him, "Think just one good thought, and for it you shall go to heaven," he could not think it. Till God raises him from the sink of sin, as He did Lazarus from the grave, he cannot do any thing that is pleasing unto God. He may do the works of a moral man, but to do the works of a quickened and enlightened man is beyond his power. For if he could do so, he must then have some reward from God; for however we deny the merit of good works, yet we cannot deny the reward of good works to a man that is in Christ. There is no proportionable merit in a cup of cold water and the kingdom of heaven, yet "he that giveth a cup of cold water to a disciple in the name of a disciple shall not lose his reward."

Here then is the point: the best thing that a natural man does cannot so please God that He should take delight in it or reward it; whereas the least good thing that comes from another root, from a quickened spirit, is acceptable and well-pleasing to Him. Consider for this end that verse set down in Proverbs 15:8. Take the best works of a natural man, his prayers or sacrifice, and see there what is said: "The sacrifice of the wicked is an abomination to the Lord." It is said again in Proverbs 21:27, where there are additions: "The prayers of the wicked are an abomination to the Lord; how much more when he brings it with a wicked mind?" Suppose there should come upon this man a fit of devotion, where he has or should have some good motions; is it then accepted? No, it is so far from being accepted that it is an abomination to God; how much more then if he brings it with a wicked mind? That is, even if he does not bring it with a wicked mind, it is an abomination; how much more with it? See the case set down in Haggai

2:12–14: "If one bear holy flesh . . . shall he be unclean? And the priest answered, 'No.' Then said Haggai, 'If an unclean person touch any of these, shall it be unclean?' And he said, 'It shall be unclean.' Then answered Haggai, 'So is this people, so is this nation before me,' saith the Lord, and so is every work of their hands, it is unclean."

A man may not say prayer is a sin, because it is so in them; no, it is a good duty, but spoiled in the carriage. He mars it in the carriage; and therefore, instead of doing a good work, he spoils it, and so, instead of a reward, he must look for punishment. "The end of the commandment is love out of a pure heart, a good conscience, and faith unfeigned" (1 Timothy 1:5). Let the things you do be according to the commandment; see that what you do is according to the middle, end, and beginning of the commandment. If you are wrong in all these, then though the work is never so materially good, being faulty in the original, middle, or end, it is so far from being a good work that God will not accept it, and you may rather expect a plague for spoiling it than a cure.

See then the beginning of a good work: it must be from a pure heart. A man not engrafted into Christ is a defiled, polluted person; his very mind and conscience are defiled. The conscience is the purest thing a man has; it holds out last, and takes part with God. As Job's messenger said, "I only am escaped to tell thee," so conscience only remains to declare a man's faults to God, and to witness against the man. And yet this very light, the eye of the soul, is defiled. Therefore, if you have a corrupt fountain, if the heart is naught, the fountain muddy, whatever stream comes from it cannot be pure.

Again, the end of it is love. Consider when you do any duty, what moves you to do it? Is it love that constrains you? If love does not constrain you, it is manifest that you do not seek God but yourself, and are to every good work a reprobate; that is, you are not able to do anything that

God will accept. The best thing you do will not stand with God. It is a hard estate indeed that when a man shall come to appear before God, he shall not have one good thing that he has done in all his life which God will own. Some there are who take a great deal of pains in coming to the Word, in public and private prayer, in charity and giving to the poor. Alas, when you shall come to an account, none of these things shall defend you, not one of them shall speak for you; but all will be lost—how heavy will your case be! "Look to yourselves, that we lose not the things that we have wrought" (2 John 8). By being indisposed to do the works of a living man, we lose all; that is to say, God will never own or accept them. We shall never have reward for them.

So here is your case: you being dead, unable to perform the works of a living man, can have no reward from heaven at all until you are quickened and have life from Christ. "Without Me," said our Savior, "ye can do nothing." Augustine on this passage, observed that Christ did not say, "Without Me you can do nothing great," no, but "unless you are cut off from your own stock, taken from our own root, are engrafted into Me, have life from Me, and are quickened by Me, you can do nothing at all." Nothing, either great or small; all that you do is lost. So if there were nothing but this being dead, you could do no good action.

"I know that in me, that is, in my flesh," said Paul, "there dwelleth no good thing": that is, nothing spiritually good; nothing for which I may look for a reward in heaven. The Lord will say of such a man, "You have lived ten, twenty, forty, or, it may be, fifty years under the ministry, and yet have not done a good work or thought a good thought that I can own. Cut down this fruitless tree; why does it encumber the ground?" And this is the case of every one of us while we continue in our natural condition; till we are engrafted into Christ and live by His life,

God will own nothing we do.

But we are not only dead and indisposed to the works of a living man—though this is a very woeful case, and we need no more misery; for this will bring us to be cut down and cast into the fire, if we continue so—but a natural man is not only indisposed to good works, he is very active and fruitful in the works of darkness. The others were sins of omission; here he is wholly set upon the commission of sins and trespasses. He not only does not bring forth fitting fruit or good fruit, or even no fruit, but he brings forth thorns and briers, and is therefore rejected, and "nigh unto cursing, whose end is to be burned" (Hebrews 6:8).

You are not only found to be a barren tree, and so deserve to be cut down, but you bring forth thorns and briers and deserve to be burned! There is not only no good fruit, but noxious, bad, and poisoned fruit—and this mightily aggravates the matter. Now for us who have lived so long under the ministry, and the Lord has watered, dressed, and hedged us, do we think the Lord expects from us no good fruit? Had we lived among heathens, or where the Word is not taught, then so much would not be expected; but we have heard the Word often and been powerfully taught. And therefore it is expected that we should not only bring forth fruit, but meet fruit, answerable to the means. Where God affords the greatest means, there He expects the most fruit. If a man lives thirty or forty years under powerful means, the Lord expects answerable fruit which, if he brings it forth, he shall have a blessing from the Lord. But when a man has lived long under the means and brings forth no fruit pleasing to God, but all God's cost is lost; when notwithstanding the dew and the rain which falls oft upon him, he brings forth nothing but thorns and briers, is rejected and nigh unto cursing, whose end is to be burned, he is nigh unto the curse.

Now if we consider the particulars and search into

God's testimonies, we shall see how bad this man is.

QUESTION. But who is this man?

ANSWER. We have God's own Word for it. It is men, all men.

See it in the thoughts. "God saw the wickedness of man was great in the earth, and that every imagination of the thoughts of his heart was only evil continually" (Genesis 6:5). Every word is, as it were, a thunderbolt: and was it not time, when it was thus with them, for God to bring a flood? The thoughts are the original ones, from which the words and actions usually proceed. All their thoughts were evil. What! Was there no kind of goodness in their thoughts? No, they were only evil continually; and that was the reason the flood came.

"Well, but though it was so before the flood, yet I hope they were better after the flood." No, God said again after the flood, "The imagination of the thoughts of man's heart is evil" (Genesis 8). Men are all of one kind till they receive grace from Christ. We are all of one nature, and naturally all the thoughts and imaginations of our hearts are only evil continually.

See it in the understanding, "The natural man perceiveth not the things of the Spirit of God, neither can he know them, for they are foolishness unto him" (1 Corinthians 2:14).

See it in his will. "It is not subject to the will of God, neither indeed can it be" (Romans 8:7). Our Savior anatomizes the heart of such a man. "Those things which proceed out of the mouth come from the heart, and they defile the man; for out of the heart proceed evil thoughts, murders, adulteries" (Matthew 15:18). These are the things that defile a man because they come from his heart, from within. If a man goes by a house and sees great flakes of fire coming out of the chimney, though he does not see the fire within, yet he cannot but know there is fire within because he sees the flakes without. I am not able to see the heart of any man and to declare to you what I have seen with mine eyes, but if I see such flakes coming forth as murders, thefts, blasphemies, lying, and the like, I may say there is hellfire in the heart; your heart is a little hell within you. These manifestations from without make it appear to be so. The words of this man are rotten words and filthy words, and his heart is much more.

So this is the point: we are utterly indisposed, aliens to all good, and bent to all evil. "I am carnal," said the apostle. We are sold under sin, slaves to it; sin is our lord and we are its slaves. We have generally forfeited our happy estate, and are servants to Satan, whom we obey. Therefore this is a thing not easily to be passed over: this is our condition, of which if we were ever truly persuaded, we would never give ourselves any rest till we were got out of it.

If the person who goes to the physician could but know his disease, and cause the physician to know it and the causes of it, whether it came from a hot cause or a cold, it would be easily cured. The chief reason why so many miscarry is because their disease is not perfectly known. That is the reason we are not better, because our disease is not perfectly known; that is the reason we are no better, because we do not know how bad we are. If we once know our disease, and know ourselves to be heart sick, and not like the Laodiceans, who thought themselves rich and wanted nothing, when they were poor, blind, and naked, then we could seek out and be on the way to being cured.

4

The Sinner's Disease and Remedy

"For if a man think himself to be something, when he is nothing, he deceiveth himself. But let every man prove his own work, and then shall he have rejoicing in himself alone, and not in another." Galatians 6:3–4

When Satan cannot prevail with a sinner to say to his soul, or to think with himself, "I will embrace the offers of God's grace later," or "I will embrace them at the day of my death," when he cannot prevail with him to defer it and leave it quite undone for the present, then he will give way to his doing a little towards it, but it shall be so superficial and on such false grounds that he may as well leave it undone,

Regarding conversion, there are two things to be thought on. The first thing is what state the sinner is in for the present; and then when he has made search and found it to be amiss, the next thing is that he must turn to God and resolve to amend.

Since it is uncertain how soon God may enter into judgment with you, it is wise to be always ready. "Let us search and try our ways, and turn again unto the Lord" (Lamentations 3:40). Let us first see how the matter stands with us at the present; let us examine ourselves and our ways and see if all is well, and then we may go on with comfort in the way wherein we are.

But when we have searched and found things not to go as well as they ought, or that we are not in a right way, then after our searching we must turn unto the Lord.

Thus the prophet did: "I thought on my ways, and turned my feet unto Thy testimonies" (Psalm 119:59). First, he made haste and thought on his ways, and then he turned.

I took this text to show that the neglect of one of these is as dangerous as the other, and how apt men are to deceive themselves in their search and examination. It is as dangerous not to prove your ways as it is to put off and defer turning to God. This is a dangerous disease when men come to examine and try their spiritual estates, and they have false weights and unequal balances to prove themselves by. They are very willing to save themselves the labor, though they are deceived. A man is loath to be deceived by another, but his folly is that he is willing enough to deceive and betray himself.

In the words of my text we see the disease and the remedy.

The disease is in the third verse: "If a man think himself to be something when he is nothing." This is a common and dangerous disease, and a disease that, as it is both common and dangerous, is the more to be feared, and the more careful must the physician be. This is the more common disease, for there is not a man but finds some of it in his own heart. And it is the most dangerous; for who is in more danger than he who is blind, and will be blind, who is willing to be cheated by Satan and himself? This is the patient. Now what his disease is, and the danger of it, the apostle tells us. He thinks himself to be something and is nothing. This is the patient to be cured, and that is his disease; and no disease is more common than this one. Even the worst of men will say, "I thank God I am something, and I am not half as bad as the preacher would make me. I have some good thing in me."

Now this person's disease stands in two things. First, that he is nothing; and, second, that he thinks himself to be something.

He is nothing. For a man to be brought before God's

judgment seat and have nothing to answer, how will it fare with him then? But this man cannot help thinking that he is something. Well, then, something he is, but nothing to the purpose; nothing that can plead for a man when he holds up his hand at God's bar.

He thinks himself to be something though he is nothing. He thinks he shall come to heaven though he is not on the way to heaven. He is like the foolish virgins, who thought they should be let in, and did not fear the contrary till they came there. So these men walk in their way all their life, and yet expect entrance into heaven till they receive sentence to the contrary. If these men knew themselves to be nothing, they would seek something for themselves; but now they are nothing, though they think themselves to be something. This is their disease.

The remedy is in the next verse: "Let him prove his own work." That is, let him look at himself in a true glass. And that is the point we shall insist on. If Satan cannot delude us in deferring and putting off our repentance, do not let him deceive us with a false conceit of our ways and estate so that we do not make ourselves something when we are nothing.

Therefore let us see what false glasses they are that men get to themselves. If Satan brings us to have a good opinion of ourselves and our condition, and persuades us that it is not with us as these precise preachers tell us; that it is no such matter to go to heaven, but that it may be done with less pains and more ease; when Satan lulls a man to sleep with such plausible things as these—he has him exactly where he would have him. It is no marvel, then, if this man likes his ways when he looks upon them with false glasses.

The first false glass is self-love; and the property of love is to make the good things in the party it loves very great, and the vices very little. Self-love represents nothing in its true shape. The apostle, speaking of the latter days, said,

"There shall be perilous times" (2 Timothy 3:1). And wherein does the peril lie? "Men shall be lovers of their own selves." It is as if he had said, "It is one of the worst perils for a man to have a great conceit of himself." If one is sick because of this disease, it will so blind him that he shall never see a thing in its right place.

We may see it by the contrary in the want of love. Suppose a neighbor, for example, is full of malice and envy towards his neighbor. Consider what a false glass this is, the man who lacks love can see how the good and bad deeds of his neighbor show themselves to him! When he looks on the good actions of his neighbor they appear but very small; he is always abridging and contracting his virtues and good things, making them seem less than they are. On the other side, all things he sees amiss in him, this want of love makes them far greater than they are.

But love produces the contrary. When a man loves himself, his good things seem very great, and his evil things very small; those he abridges and contracts. When such a man looks upon his own sins, they appear small to him; but when he looks on the infirmities of others, they seem very great. With one eye he looks on himself, with another his neighbor. This man, perchance, is a drunkard as well as his neighbor, covetous as well as him; yet he concludes them great evils in his neighbor, but extenuates them within himself. Self-love is what causes this difference. As long as we love things because they are our own, we shall never be able to guess at our own condition.

Self-love is a deceitful glass, and looking therein a man will be favorable to himself, and so deceive himself; for it renders things in a bigger shape than they are. But the second false glass is when a man says or thinks, "I thank God that my neighbors, and all others who know me, speak well of me. I have not only a good conceit of myself, but every man about me can speak well of me. I have a good report of all men." If this were enough and sufficient to assure you of the goodness of your estate, it would be well—but it is not enough. True, a good report from men for fair and honest dealing is not to be despised; yet it will do no good unless you have it from God. To have a good report from men, and also from the truth, is a happy thing: but having it not from the truth, "Woe to us when all men speak well of us." What folly is it to rest upon a good report from men when I do not have it from the truth? It is as much madness for a man to trust in the absolution of his fellow prisoner when the law of the land condemns him. Shall a sick man be so mad as to say he is well because others say so? No, "Let every man prove his own work, and then shall he have rejoicing in himself, and not in another" (Galatians 6:4). "He is a Jew which is one inwardly, whose praise is not of men but of God" (Romans 2:29). Not as if this did turn out the praise of men; but it is comparatively spoken; and it is meant of those whose praise is not so much of men as of God.

So this is the second false glass, when a man concludes himself to be in a good estate because men praise him; when he thinks it well with him because others think so and say so. He has a good opinion of himself, but that is not all, other men give him a good report too. A man needs never fear flattery from others who does not flatter himself.

Perhaps you will say, "But these are not my only grounds for having so good an opinion of myself, and that others speak so well of me; but when I compare myself with myself, I find wherein I may rejoice."

That brings us to the third false glass, which is when a man compares himself with others and himself.

When he compares himself with others. "I thank God," he says, "that I am better than twenty of my neighbors. I know this man follows such courses, and another lives in such a foul sin. Surely I am not such a sinner as these; therefore I am happy, and I have no doubts of having a room in heaven." This is the reason that the Pharisee went home unjustified, because, looking on other men, he justified himself: "God, I thank thee I am not as other men, no extortioner," and so on. This fellow is so far from begging anything of God that he fills up his time with thanksgiving; he thinks he lacks nothing, and that is his error. He looks on other men, and compares himself with them, and thence concludes that he is well enough because he is not as bad as this or that man.

This is the common deceit, when men take it for a rule that because they are not as bad as the off-scouring of the world, but are better than the ordinary sort of men, therefore they suppose they are very well, or as well as they need to be! As if a sick man should say, "I am not so sick as such a man who is at the point of death; therefore I am very well." I would desire such men who look on those who are under them to cast their eyes on those who are above them. You look on the publican, this and that man, and bless yourselves because you are not as bad as these who, perchance, are before you in points of morality. If you stand on comparisons, look on those who are above you, who go beyond you in grace and zeal, and do not look so much on the sins of others as your own. Another man's sins may condemn him, but they cannot save you. When a thief and a murderer are both arraigned at the bar for their lives, will the thief say to the murderer, "Your sin is greater, your fault is of a higher nature, therefore I shall be saved because mine is not so heinous," when they both are punishable with death? The fault of another will not make your case any better. It is no point of justification thus to deceive yourself, and to conclude that, because another is worse than you, therefore your estate is blessed.

So we see the degrees of false glasses. Self-love or self-conceit, then a good opinion from men, and then comparing a man's self with some others. He is better than they; therefore his estate is good. This is an absurd conclusion; the devil will mightily insult over such as he can so easily deceive.

But this man goes further: "I not only compare myself with others, but myself too, and find good ground to conclude the safeness of my condition. I remember a time when I was vain and idle, when I ran in a way contrary to God. But, whereas before I was loose and dissolute, now I am careful to do my duty, to serve God. I am not so profane as I was formerly; my state must be good." This is a very dangerous thing to say, that because I am not so bad as I was, I am therefore good. And shall this serve to excuse you, by comparing yourself with others who are worse, and with yourself, that because you have mended yourself in some particulars, therefore you are on the way to heaven? It is a false and foolish conclusion.

Now we come to the main thing, another false glass, which we call partial obedience. When a man goes farther, looking upon the letter of the commandment only, and says, "Thank God, I forbear many sins and do many duties. I am not a thief, nor a murderer, swearer, drunkard, or covetous person. I do not take God's name in vain. I have not broken the Sabbath, though I doubt whether that law is moral or not. I have served God by coming to His house, giving obedience to my parents, and so on." And looking on this, he concludes, doubtless, that all is well with him. But when I have a thousand thorns in my feet, and have three or four taken out, will this help me? Because I do not have the stone or the gout, shall I conclude I am well, as if I could be sick without this or that disease? Because I do something that God requires, shall I think I do as much as I need to do? No, we must take heed of that kind of thinking. God will not be contented with partial obedience. He will have the whole heart or none.

OBJECTION. "But mine is not partial obedience. I endeavor, as far as I am able, to do what God requires. I thank God that I do what I can, and I see no reason why more should be required. I conform myself as I am able and as I see it needful to the greatest duties of Christianity. I lead such a blameless life that no man can tax me in any particular that God has enabled me to do; and according to moral philosophy, I do not know how more can be required. Surely this is not partial obedience!"

ANSWER. I am not speaking against morality, but let me tell you that if you have no more than morality, it will not bring you to heaven. A moral man is an excellent stock whereon to graft grace and virtue; it is a good help to heaven, yet it comes far short of bringing him there. Natural reason was once a full and fair glass till it was broken by the fall; but now it is insufficient. This glass which then was so perfect is now broken, and is not as perfect as it was, though there is something yet remaining in it. We may see something of its ancient luster in the Gentiles, "for these having not a law, are a law unto themselves." There are practical principles yet remaining in the tables of our hearts, so that they who do not care for the law shall be judged by the natural light that is in them. We have a conscience to show the difference between good and evil. This is the truth. It is a part of the image of God implanted in us that we are not to despise, lest we be judged with those who hold the truth in unrighteousness.

The truth is the principle of difference between good and bad. The soul was to have a seat as a queen to rule all our actions; but now this queen has been taken captive and all is lost. Morality and inward principles are to be much esteemed as things that God at first planted, yet they come short of bringing a man to heaven. The young man in the gospel had a good esteem of himself, was doubtless esteemed of others, and did many things; yet our Savior told him how hard a thing it was to come to heaven. Our Savior told him of the commandments: "All these," he said, "have I kept from my youth." That must be a good moral man indeed who had done so much; but this was not enough. "One thing is lacking: go and sell all that thou hast." Yet because there was so much in him, we read, "Jesus loved him" (Mark 10:21). Christ showed him that his cause was heavy, and that going so far would not attain his end; but this was not to be despised, for Jesus loved him. So 1 Kings 14:13: "He only of Jeroboam shall come to the grave, because in him are found some good thing." If there are but some good things in a man, they remain of God's work, and God loves His own work.

Here is the point then: morality is good, and natural reason is good; it remains in us since the state of our first creation. This was a pure and a full glass, made by God Himself, but since the fall it is much darkened. If we consult with natural reason and moral philosophy, it will reveal many things; yet these come short. There is an abundance of things that it cannot discover, manifold defects. The apostle said, "I had not known sin but by the law; for I had not known lust" to have been a sin had "not the law said, 'Thou shalt not lust.' "

We have many sins we cannot know but by the law, yea, such secret sins as must be repented of. Our Savior overthrew the tables of the money-changers, and would not suffer them to carry burdens through the temple, though for the use of those who sacrificed, it was a thing which had some show of religion in it. He whipped both out, not only those who had residence there, but those who passed through. He would suffer none but those who could justify what they did by the law.

Now, as God would not have sin lodge and make its abode in the soul, so He would not have it made a thoroughfare for sin. He would not have vain thoughts come up and down in the heart. Now, "by the law comes the knowledge of these secret things." Reason is a glass much to be esteemed for what it can show, but it is not a perfect glass. Sometimes it shows a sin, but many times diminishes it, so that we cannot see it in full proportion. The apostle makes this use of the law, that by it sin became exceedingly sinful. You may see sin to be sin by natural reason, but to see it as exceedingly sinful, this morality comes short of; you must have this from the law of God.

There is another false glass, which is when the devil transforms himself into an angel of light, when he preaches another gospel to a man. Beware of the doctrine when the deceiver preaches. This may be his doctrine: "He that believeth and is baptized shall be saved." From this, by Satan's cunning delusion, the natural man thus concludes: "A mere heathen shall be shut out of heaven's gates, but I believe in the Father, the Son, and the Holy Ghost; therefore I am in a good condition. Why then should I trouble myself any further? No man can accuse me, and my own good works will testify unto me that I do enough. Strictness in religion is troublesome, and it is an unreasonable thing to do more." But this is but a mere delusion of Satan, for there is nothing more quiet and satisfies a man than religion; there is nothing in the world more reasonable than the service of God.

First, then, know your disease, and then apply those sweet balms. It is no easy matter for a man to believe; it must be done by the mighty power of God. It is as great a work of God as the creation of the world to make a man believe; it is the mighty power of God to salvation. Such a one must not only receive Christ as a Savior, but as a Lord too. He must renounce all to have Him and must take Him on His own terms. He must deny the world and all, looking beforehand what it will cost him.

Now for a man to take Christ as His Lord, denying himself, the world, and all, to resolve to pluck out his right eye and cut off his right hand rather than to part with him, and account nothing so dear to him as Christ, is no small matter. You cannot be Christ's spouse unless you forsake all for Him. Thou must account all things as dung and dross in comparison of Him. And is not this a difficult thing? Is this an easy task? Easily spoken indeed, but not as easily done.

It must be here as in the case of marriage: a man must forsake all others, yea, the whole world, else Christ will not own him. Observe the speech of the apostle: "What is the exceeding greatness of His power to usward that believe" (Ephesians 1:19). Mark, is to believe so easy a matter, do you think? Why, unless the mighty power of God is engaged in it with that strength which was engaged in raising Christ from the dead, it cannot be. When you are to believe and be united unto Christ, the agreement is not that you shall take Him as your wife, and that you shall be His husband. No, He must be your husband, and you must obey Him.

Now for a man to be brought out of his natural condition and to take Christ on any terms, so that he may be saved by Him in the end, is not so easy. Can you think there is nothing more required than the outward baptism, or that there is nothing more in baptism but the outward washing of the flesh? No, "He is not a Jew that is one outwardly, neither is that circumcision which is outward in the flesh; but he is a Jew that is so inwardly, and circumcision is that of the heart."

You, then, enter into God's livery. Mark this, for by it I strive only to bring you back to yourself. You enter into covenant with Him; you bind yourself to forsake the world, the flesh, and the devil. And we should make this use of baptism now to put it in practice.

When we promised, there were two things in the indenture: one was that God would give Christ to us; the other was that we must forsake all the sinful lusts of the flesh. This is what makes baptism to be baptism indeed to us.

The other thing required is that we forsake all. It is not confined to the very act, but it has a perpetual effect all the days of your life. I add, it never has its full effect till the day of our death, till the abolition of the whole body of sin. The death of sin is not till the death of the body, and therefore it is said, "We must be buried with Him by baptism into His death." Now, after death we receive final grace; till then, this washing and the virtue thereof does not have its consummation.

Let no man, therefore, deceive you with vain words; take heed of looking on yourselves in these false glasses. Do not think it an easy thing to get to heaven; the way is straight, and the passage narrow. There must be a striving to enter; there must be an ascending into heaven, a motion contrary to nature. And therefore it is folly to think we shall drop into heaven; there must be a going upward if ever we would come there.

5

The Purpose of the Law

"But the Scripture hath concluded all under sin, that the promise by faith of Jesus Christ might be given to them that believe." Galatians 3:22

You see in this excellent portion of Scripture the two covenants of Almighty God: to wit, the covenant of nature and the covenant of grace. The covenant of nature, which was written by God on man's heart, is the holy law of God, by virtue whereof a man was to continue in that integrity, holiness, and uprightness in which God had first created him, and to serve God according to that strength He first enabled him with, so that he might live thereby.

But when man broke this covenant and entered into a state of rebellion against God, he was shut up in misery, but not in misery forever as the angels that fell were, being reserved in chains till the judgment of the great day. No, the Lord shut him up in prison only for a while so that He may better make a way for his escape and deliverance, and for his entrance into the second covenant of grace. This was to make him see his own misery, wherein by nature he is, and cutting him off from his own stock, he may be engrafted into Christ, draw sap and sweetness from Him, and bring forth fruits to everlasting life. This is the method the Scripture uses. It concludes "all under sin, that the promise by faith of Jesus Christ might be given to them that believe." It is no new doctrine devised by us, but it is the course and method of the Scriptures; for it begins in this great work with imprisoning and shutting up.

The law is like a justice of the peace who, by his warrant, commands us to prison. It is a sergeant who arrests a man and carries him to the jail. But why does the Scripture do this? It is not to destroy you with famine; the law does not send you there to starve you, or to kill you with the stench of the prison, but thereby to save and preserve you alive, and that you may hunger and thirst after deliverance. So we find the reason added in the text: "The scripture concludes all under sin." Why? It is that "the promise by faith of Jesus Christ might be given to them that believe." You are shut up as prisoners and rebels so that, having felt the smart of it, seen your misery, and learned what it is to be at enmity with God, and the folly of trying to make yourselves wiser and stronger than God, you may submit yourselves, cast down your plumes, and desire Christ with a hungry and thirsty appetite, not only as a Priest to sacrifice Himself for you, and as a Prophet to teach and instruct you, but as a King to be ruled by Him. Your soul will then earnestly crave to be His subject, and to be admitted into the privilege of His subjects in the commonwealth of Israel; you will esteem it your greatest shame that you have been aliens so long, so long excluded. The Scripture, then, concludes you under sin and shut up by it, not to bring you to despair, but to bring you to salvation; as a physician who gives his patient bitter medicine, not to make him sick, but that he may restore him to health; or as a surgeon who cuts the flesh, not with an intent to hurt, but to cure the wound.

This is the Scripture method: it concludes all under sin; it has shut up all. The text does not say "all men" in the masculine gender, but "all things" in the neuter. And it is as if the apostle had said, "The Scripture arrests not only your person, but your actions." The Scripture lays hold not only of the man, but of everything in him. This word "all" is a forcible word, and empties us clean of everything so that we may truly confess with the apostle, "In me, that is, in my flesh, dwelleth no good thing" (Romans 7:18). It is impossible that a man should by nature think thus of himself, that there is no good in him; or that he should, by asking others, find himself half so bad as the law makes him to be. But the Scripture does so by shutting up a man under sin, and all things in a man, yea, all good, whatever good you may think is in you.

And this it does that you may come to Christ, as is enlarged in the two verses following. "Before faith came," says the apostle, "we were kept under the law, shut up unto the faith, which should afterwards be revealed; wherefore the law was our schoolmaster to bring us unto Christ, that we might be justified by faith." Until you have faith, then (which is the day salvation comes to your house), you are kept under the law. You are not assured of salvation, nor can you expect till then that God should show you mercy. We may have a conceit that though we are never transplanted nor cut off from our own stock, yet God will show us mercy; but we shall beguile ourselves to hell therein for we are kept under the law till faith comes so that we may know ourselves.

"We are kept." That word "kept" is a metaphor drawn from military affairs, as when men are kept in a garrison and kept in order. The law is God's garrison, which keeps men in good awe and order. The law does this not to terrify you too much, or to break your minds with despair, but to fit you for the faith. It is a shutting up to that faith which should afterwards be revealed. He is a miserable preacher who ends with preaching the law; the law is for another end, to fit us for faith. It is our schoolmaster to bring us to Christ. We do not thunder the law to make men run away from God, but to bring them home to Him.

The schoolmaster, by the smart of his rod, makes the child weary of his bondage and desire earnestly to be past this stage of his life; and this is the schoolmaster's end, not that he delights to hear him cry. Thus are we beaten by the law, not that God delights or loves to hear us sigh or sob, but that we may grow weary of our misery and cruel bondage and may desire to be justified by faith. The law, then, is a schoolmaster so that, by making us smart, it may bring us home. We see then the course and method of the Scripture: "it has concluded all under sin that the promise by faith of Jesus Christ may be made to them that believe."

Now because men do not like this kind of doctrine, to begin with preaching of the law, and think there may be a shorter and nearer way to preach Christ first, I will therefore make known unto you this method of the Scripture, and I will justify it to you.

There must be this preparative, or else the gospel will come unseasonably. If Christ is preached before we are soured by the leaven of the law, He will be unsavory and unpleasant to us. Did God, at the first preaching of the gospel, begin with Adam by preaching Christ, before he saw his sin and wickedness? No, He did not say to him as soon as he had sinned, "Well, Adam, you have sinned and broken My covenant. Yet there is another covenant: you shall be saved by one who comes out of your loins." Rather, God first summoned him to appear. He brought him out of his shelters and hiding places, told him of his sin, and said, "Have you eaten of the tree which I forbade you to eat of?"

Then the man shifted it off to the woman, and the woman shifted it off to the serpent: "The serpent beguiled me, and I did eat." Yet all this did not excuse them. God's judgments were declared, man's sin was made apparent, and he saw it. Then, being thus humbled, the promise of the gospel came: "The seed of the woman shall break the serpent's head." Be open, then, you everlasting doors, and the King of glory shall come in.

John the Baptist, who was the harbinger to prepare the way for Christ, preaching to the scribes and Pharisees, warned them, "O generation of vipers." He came to "throw down every high hill, and to beat down every mountain." He called them "serpents." His office was to lay the axe at the root of the tree.

Christ Himself came into the world and preached to Nicodemus: "Unless a man be born again, he cannot enter into the kingdom of God" (John 3:3). A man in his natural condition can never enter into heaven, for he is wholly carnal. "That which is born of flesh is flesh, and that which is born of the Spirit is spirit." It is carnal, and must be born again. A little patching will not serve the turn. You must be new born, newly molded; a little mending is not sufficient. A man must be a new creature, newly made.

So this is the substance of this doctrine of Christ, that if you are not better than moral virtue or civil education can make you, if you have anything less than regeneration, believe me, you can never see heaven. There is no hope of heaven, then, till you are born again. Until then, our Savior excludes all false fancies.

The apostles began to gather the first church after Christ's resurrection. They do not begin to preach Christ first, His virtue and efficacy; but first they told the people of their great sin in crucifying the Lord of life: "Whom with wicked hands you have taken and crucified" (Acts 2:23). But what was the end of their doing this? It is set down in verse 37: They were "pricked to the heart," and then they cried out, "Men and brethren, what shall we do to be saved?" This was the end of all, their being humbled so that, by declaring what they had done, they might be pricked at the heart; so that now they saw that if it was no better with them than for the present, it is likely to go ill with them. This made them cry out, "What shall we do?"

And it was then that Peter said unto them, "Repent and be baptized, and ye shall receive the gift of the Holy Ghost." After he had told them their lost condition and had brought them to a search, which is their first work, then came the promise of Christ.

Observe the apostle's method in the epistle to the Romans, which is a perfect catechism for the Church; it contains these three parts of divinity: humiliation, justification, and sanctification. See how the apostle orders his method. From the first chapter to part of the third he treats all of the law, and convinces both Jew and Gentile of sin. Then mark his conclusion: "that every mouth may be stopped" (Romans 3:19). When he had stopped every mouth, cast down every stronghold which lifted itself up against God, when he had laid all at God's feet and left them bleeding, as it were, under the knife of God, then he comes to Christ: "The righteousness of God without the law is manifested" (Romans 3:21). He had done his first business in humbling them, in showing them their sins by the law; and as soon as that was done, when every mouth was stopped, then came "the promise by faith in Jesus Christ to all them that believe."

You see, then, that the method of Scripture is first to conclude all under sin, and so to fit men for the promise of Jesus Christ. Know, therefore, that the law is the highway to the gospel, the path that leads to it, that way which must be trodden in. We are still out of our way till we have begun our walk in this path. And if you are not terrified by the law, and terrified at the sight of your sins, if you are not at your wits' end, as it were, weary of your condition and bondage, you are not on the way yet. Our sowing must be in tears. And it is said that, in the church triumphant, "all tears shall be wiped away from our eyes." That is a promise; but is it possible that tears should be wiped from our eyes before we shed them? Shall we look to go to heaven in a way that was never yet found out? Shall it be accounted a point of preciseness to walk in this way, or a soul-torturing doctrine to preach it? This is the way in which our forefathers have both preached and gone. This is that time of sowing spoken of in Psalm 126:5–6: "They that sow in tears shall reap in joy." It brings us joy in the end to begin our sowing in tears. It waters that precious seed, and makes it bring forth joy unto us in abundance, yea, such as no man can take from us.

So, then, having laid this point for a foundation, we now come to the next point. Until we come to Christ, the law lays hold of us. Till Christ comes, we are shut up under the law, kept under it. And if there were nothing else in the world to make a man weary of his condition, this would be enough. Until a man has given himself over to Christ and renounced his own righteousness, he is subject to the law, kept under it, not under grace. This only brings a man to the place where grace is. Put this therefore close to your consciences, and do not jumble these two together. First, nature comes, and while you are under that, you are under the law. Never think you are under the covenant of grace till you believe (of this belief we shall speak more hereafter). While you are under the law you are held under it. "Whoever is under the law is under the curse."

Now that I may unfold it, and show what a fearful thing it is to be under the law, to be held under it (although many think it is no great matter), hearken to what the apostle says of it: "Cursed is every one that continueth not in all things that are written in the book of the law to do them" (Galatians 3:10). Are you under the law? Then never think of being under grace at the same time (not but that we may hope to be under grace afterwards). By this law we must be judged, and the judgment of the law is very severe; it requires not only that you do this or that good thing, but if you do not continue in everything that is written therein, it condemns you.

Men have strange conceits nowadays, and strange divinity is brought forth into the world! For example, if a man does as much as lies in him, and what he is of himself able to do; nay, further, though he is a heathen who does not know Christ, yet if he does the best he can; if he lives honestly towards men, according to the conduct of his reason, and has a good mind towards God—it is enough, he needs not question his eternal welfare! It is a cursed and desperate doctrine they conclude hence: "Why may not this man be saved as well as the best?" But if it is so, I ask such, What is the benefit and advantage of the Jew more than the Gentile? What is the benefit of Christ? Of the church? Of faith? Of baptism? Of the sacrament of the Lord's Supper? This thread of Pelaganianism is abhorrent, when we shall undertake to bring a man to salvation without Christ; whereas, if he is not under grace, under Christ, he is accursed. If you will be saved by the law, is it not your endeavor of doing what lies in you that will serve the turn? Every jot and tittle that the law requires must be fulfilled.

What would be your state if you should be examined according to the strict rigor of the law? You must give account for the least word or thought that is contrary to it. If you stand upon your own foundation, or look to be saved by your own deeds, there is not one vain word which you speak but you shall be questioned for, cast down for, and condemned for.

Consider, then, the great difference of being under Christ and grace, and of being under the law. When we are under Christ we are not liable to answer for those evil things which we have committed. There is a comfortable passage in Ezekiel: "All his iniquities that he hath done shall not be mentioned unto him." When a man comes to forsake his old ways, his evils are cast out of mind, which should be a marvelous comfort to a Christian. Whereas if a man is not in Christ, he must be accountable for every idle word; if he in Christ, he shall never hear of the greatest sin he ever committed. All they who stand on God's right hand hear only of the good things they have done: "You have fed, clothed, and visited Me." But they on the left hand hear not a word mentioned concerning the good they have done; only their evil deeds are reckoned up.

Now that I may declare to you the difference between the law and the gospel, I will show the differences in three particulars:

1. The law rejects any kind of obedience besides that which is thorough, sound, full, and perfect, without any touch of the flesh. It rejects all cracked payment; it will take no clipped coin. That obedience which has any imperfection joined with it will not be accepted. But here I must not speak apart from Scripture. "We know that the law is spiritual, but I am carnal" (Romans 7:14), and then concludes, "O wretched man that I am."

"The law is spiritual." What is that? We may know the meaning of it by the particle "but," "but I am carnal." The law is spiritual, that is, it requires that all our works be spiritual, without any carnality or touch of the flesh. If in any point of our obedience there is a smell of the cask, it is rejected. Though the beer is ever so good, yet if it has an evil taste, it will not relish us. Let our services have this savor of the flesh, and they will not stand with God. And thus "the law is spiritual, but we are carnal."

Now it is otherwise here in the state of the gospel. Alas! We are carnal, it is true. The apostle himself complains that there is a law in his members rebelling against the law of his mind, and leading him captive. Yet, notwithstanding, the gospel accepts our obedience, though the law will not. What is the reason for this? Why, it is plain. When the law comes, it looks for justice; it puts a strict rule to us; it requires that we be perfect. But the gospel does not; it requires not a justification of our own, but looks that, being justified by God's free grace, we should show forth our thankfulness, and express that we are so in heart by our obedience to our utmost power. Here is all the strictness of the gospel. "If there be a willing mind, it is accepted according to that a man hath, and not according to that a man hath not" (2 Corinthians 8:12). God takes well the de-

sires of our mind. This is then our blessed condition under
the gospel: it does not require perfect obedience, but
thankfulness for mercies received, and a willing mind.
Suppose we cannot do what we would; that is no matter.
God looks to our affections and the willingness of our
minds; if it is according to the strength that you have, it is
received with acceptance.

2. The law does not consider what you now have, but
what you once had. If you say, "I have done my best; and
would you have a man do more than he can do?" The law
does not heed that; it does not consider what you do, but
what you ought to do. It requires that you perform obedience according to your first strength, that perfection God
once gave you, that all you do should have love as its
ground; that you should "love the Lord thy God with all
thy soul, mind, heart, and strength."

Here the law is like those taskmasters in Egypt, who laid
burdens on the Israelites too heavy for them to bear. They
had materials at first, and then they delivered in the full
tale of bricks; but when the straw was taken from them,
they complained of the heaviness of their burden. What
was the answer? "Ye are idle, ye are idle, ye shall deliver the
same tale of bricks as before." So stands the case here. It is
not enough to plead, "Alas, if I had the strength I would
do it; but I have not strength, I cannot do it!" But the law
is peremptory; you must do it; you are compelled by force;
you *shall* do it. The impossibility of our fulfilling it does not
exempt us, as appears by comparing Romans 8:3 with Romans 7:6. Although it is impossible, as the case stands, for
the law to be fulfilled by us, yet we are held under it, as appears plainly in this example. Suppose I give a man a stock
of money whereby he may gain his own living and be ad-
vantageous to me. But he spends it; and when I require my
money back with interest, he tells me, "It is true, sir, I received such a sum of money of you for this purpose; but I
have spent it, and am unable to pay." Will this serve the

turn? Will it satisfy the creditor or discharge the debt? No, no, the law will have its own way with him. If you do not pay your due, you must be shut up under the law. But it is otherwise under the gospel. The gospel accepts a man according to what he does not have.

3. Under the gospel, although I am fallen, yet, if I repent, the greatest sin I have ever committed cannot condemn me. By repentance I am safe. Let our sins be ever so great, yet if we return by repentance, God accepts us. Faith and repentance remove all.

The law knows no such thing. Look into the laws of the realm. If a man is indicted and convicted of treason, murder, or felony, though this man pleads, "True, I have committed such an offense, but I beseech you, sir, pardon it, for I am heartily sorry for it. I never did the like before, nor ever will again." Though he thus repents, shall he escape? No, the rigor of the law will execute justice on him. There is no benefit had by repentance; the law will seize him; he should have thought of that before.

If you commit murder or burglary, it is not enough to put one good deed for another, to say, "I have done this and that for the king. I won such a town for him." This will not serve your turn; this will not save your neck. The law takes no knowledge of any good thing done, or of any repentance. This is your estate.

Consider, then, what a case they are in who are shut up under the law. Until a man has faith, it is no excuse that things are required that are far above your power to perform. No repentance is accepted; and therefore we may well make this conclusion: "As many as are under the law are under the curse; as it is written, 'Cursed is everyone that continueth not in all things which are written in the book of the law to do them.' "

But now, where are we thus shut up? It is under sin, as the apostle tells us: "For the law discovers sin to be sin indeed, that sin by the commandment may become exceeding sinful" (Romans 7:13). The law makes us see more of it than we did, or possibly could come to have seen. "By the law cometh the knowledge of sin. I had not known sin but by the law" (Romans 3:20; 7:7). Yes, perhaps I might have known murder, adultery, and the like, to have been sins; but to have known them to have been exceedingly sinful, I could not have known but by the law. To know what a kind of plague sin is in itself so as not to make a game of it, or a small matter, as many usually make it; to see the ugliness of it, I cannot do without the law.

But that we may know what sin is, and that we may see it to be exceedingly sinful, I will here bring you a few considerations which I would have you ponder on and enlarge them to yourselves.

• Consider the baseness of him who offends, and the excellency of Him who is offended. You shall never know what sin is without this twofold consideration; lay them together and it will make sin to be sinful beyond measure. See it in David: "The drunkards made songs and ballads of him." He aggravated the indignity offered him in that he was their king, yet those wretched and filthy beasts, the drunkards, made songs of him. See it likewise in Job 29, when he had declared unto them in what glory he once was, that he was a king and prince in the country. Then see 30:1: "They that are younger than I have me in derision, whose fathers I would have disdained to have set with the dogs of my flock." He aggravated the offense, first, from the dignity of the person wronged, a king and a prince; then from the baseness and vileness of those who derided him: they were such as were younger than he, such as whose fathers he would have disdained to have set with the dogs of his flocks. A great indignity was mightily aggravated by these circumstances, that a king should be abased by such vile persons.

Now there might be some proportion between David and the drunkards, or between Job and these men, but between you and God what proportion can there be? Who are you, therefore, who dares to set yourself in opposition and rebellion against God? What! A base worm that crawls on the earth, dust and ashes, and yet you dare your Master! "Do you," says God, "lift yourself up against Him before whom all the powers of heaven tremble? Whom the angels adore? Do you exalt yourself against Him who inhabits eternity? What! Does a base creature oppose almighty God, his Creator!" Consider this, and let the baseness of the delinquent, and the majesty and glory of that God against whom he offends, be the first aggravation of sin, and you shall find sin to be sinful beyond measure.

• Consider the smallness of the motives, and the littleness of the inducements which persuade you, so vile a creature, to set yourself against so glorious a God. If it were great matters that set you to work, such as saving your life, it would be something; but see how small and little a thing usually draws you to sin. It may be a little profit or a little pleasure; it may be neither of these. When you breathe out oaths and belch out fearful blasphemies against God; when you rend and tear His dreadful and terrible name—what makes such a base and vile villain as you to thus fly in God's face? Is there any profit or delight in breathing forth blasphemies? You can take no profit; and if you take pleasure in it, then the devil is in you—yea, then you are worse than the devil himself. This is the second consideration which may make us to see the vileness of sin and abhor ourselves for it: the slenderness of the temptations and the smallness of the motives to it.

• Add what strong helps and means God has given you to keep you from sin. As you should consider the baseness of the delinquent, the glory of the Offended, the mean motives which cause so base a creature to do so vile an act, so also consider the great means God has given you to keep you from sin.

He has given you His Word, and it will greatly ag-

gravate your sins to sin against it. When God convinced
Adam, He proceeded thus with him: "Hast thou eaten of
the tree whereof I commanded thee that thou shouldst
not eat?" (Genesis 3:11). What! Have you purposely
crossed God? God has given you an express command to
the contrary, and yet have you done this! Have you so often heard the law, and prayed, "Lord have mercy on me,
and incline my heart to keep this law," and yet will you lie,
swear, commit adultery, and deal falsely, and that contrary
to the command of God? Will you obstinately disobey
Him!

Now God has not only given this great means of His
Word and commandment, but great grace, too. Understand that there is not only final grace, but degrees of
grace; else the apostle would not have said, "Receive not
the grace of God in vain" (2 Corinthians 6:1). Consider
then how much grace you have received in vain. How
many motions to good you have rejected! Perhaps your
heart is touched by this sermon, though my tongue, nor
the tongue of the most elegant in the world, can touch the
heart, but the Spirit that comes along with His Word. Now
when you find with the Word a Spirit to go with it, it is a
grace. If your conscience is enlightened, and your duty is
revealed to you, so that it tells you what you are, what you
ought to do and not do, it is a grace. Now if for all this you
blindly run through and are never the better, but obstinately set yourself against God and do many things which
others who have not received the same grace would not
have done, know then that you receive this grace in vain,
and your case is lamentable.

• Consider God's great goodness towards you. First,
there is His goodness in Himself. There is nothing but
goodness, infinite goodness in Him; and can you find in
your heart to sin against so good a God? To offend and
wrong a well-disposed person, one of a sweet nature and
affection, aggravates the fault; it is pitiful to wrong or hurt

such a one who injures nobody. Now such a one is God, a good God, infinite in goodness, rich in mercy, very goodness itself; and therefore it must aggravate the foulness of sin to sin against Him.

But He is not only good in Himself, but He is good to you. "Despisest thou the riches of His goodness and forbearance?" (Romans 2:4). What do you have that you have not received from His bountiful hand? Consider this, and let this be a means to draw you off from your sinfulness. When David had greatly sinned against God, and when God brought his murder home to him, He pleaded thus with him: "When thou wert nothing in thine own eyes, I brought thee to the kingdom. I took thee from the sheepfold and exalted thee, and brought thee to a plentiful house." And may not God say the same to us? And will you thus requite the Lord, O you foolish people and unwise, so that the more His mercy and goodness is to you, the higher your sins should be against Him?

• Consider more than this, we have the examples of good men before our eyes. God does not command us to do what we cannot do. If God had not set some before our eyes who walk in His ways and do His will, then we might say that these are precepts which none can perform. But we have patterns, of whom we may say, "Such a man I never knew to lie, such a one never to swear," and this should be a means to preserve us from sinning. Noah was a good man and, being moved with fear, did not set at naught the threatening of God, but built the ark, and thereby condemned the world (Hebrews 11:7). His example condemned the world in that they did not follow it, although it was so good, but continued on in their great sins. So, are you a wicked, debauched person? There is no good man but shall condemn you by his example. It is a great crime in the land of uprightness to do wickedly, to be profane, when the righteous, by their blameless lives, may teach you otherwise.

• Consider the multitude and weight of your sins. Had
you sinned but once or twice, or in this or that, it would
be somewhat tolerable. But your sins are great and many;
they are heavy, and you continually increase their weight
and add to their number. "A lion out of the forest shall
slay them, and a wolf of the evenings shall spoil them; a
leopard shall watch over their cities, and every one that
goeth out thence shall be torn in pieces." Why? "Because
their transgressions are many, and their backslidings are
increased" (Jeremiah 5:6). If you had committed but two,
three, or four sins, you might have hope of pardon. But
when you shall never have done with your God, but will
still increase and multiply your sins, how can you be pardoned? Thus David sets out his own sins in their weight
and number: "Mine iniquities are gone over my head as a
heavy burden; they are too heavy for me" (Psalm 38:4).
Continually multiplying them adds to their heap, in both
number and weight.

Thus I have shown you what the law does in respect of
sin, the benefit of being under the law, that it makes sin
appear in its own colors, and sets it forth to be, as indeed
it is, exceedingly sinful. But the law does not yet leave sin,
nor let it escape thus. But as the law discovers our sinfulness and accursedness by sin, its wretchedness, and man's
misery by it, till his blessedness comes from the hands of his
Jesus, so it lays down the miserable estate that befalls him
for it. If he will not spare God his sins, God will not spare
him His plagues. Let us consider this accursedness which
sin brings on us. God will not let us go so; but as long as we
are under the law, we are under the curse; and till we are
in Christ, we can expect nothing but that which should
come from the hand of a provoked God. Assure yourself,
you who pleasure yourself in your abominations, that God
will not take this at your hands, that by so base a creature
as you are, so vile a thing as sin is should be committed
against Him. But of the woeful effects of sin, more later.

6

The Consequences of Sin

"Woe unto us that we have sinned." Lamentations 5:16

Heretofore we considered the state of a natural man, a man who is not newly-fashioned, newly-molded, a man who is not cut off from his own stock, a man who is not engrafted into Christ. He is the son of sin; he is the son of death. First, I showed you his sinfulness; and now, second, I shall show you his accursedness, that which necessarily follows unrepented sin. I declared before what the nature of sin is; and now I come to show what the dreadful effects of sin are, the cause, the consequence that follows upon sin, and that is woe and misery. "Woe unto us that we have sinned." A woe is a short word, but there lies much in it.

DOCTRINE. Woe and anguish must follow him who continues to sin against God. When we hear this from the ministers of God, it is as if we heard that angel "flying through the midst of heaven, saying with a loud voice, 'Woe, woe, woe to the inhabitants of the earth' " (Revelation 8:13). The ministers of God are His angels; and the same that I now deliver to you, if an angel should now come from heaven, he would deliver no other thing. Therefore consider that it is a voice from heaven saying that this "woe, woe, woe" shall rest upon the heads, upon the bodies and souls of all those who will not yield to God, who will not stoop to Him, who will be their own masters and stand against Him. Woe, woe, woe unto them all. Woe unto us. It is the voice of the church in general, not of one man, saying, "Woe unto us that we have sinned."

69

That I may now declare unto you what these woes are, note that I do not speak to any particular man, but to every man in general. It is not for me to make particular application; you do that yourselves. We are all children of wrath by nature. In our natural condition we are all alike, we are all of one kind; and every kind produces its own kind. It is a hereditary condition, and till the Son makes us free, we are all subject to this woe. "By nature we are all children of wrath as well as others" (Ephesians 2:3). Now that I may not speak of these woes in general, I have shown how two woes are past, and a third woe is coming. God proceeds punctually with us. And are not our proceedings in judiciary courts after this manner? When the judge pronounces a sentence he particularizes the matter: "You shalt return to the place from whence you came; you shall have your bolts knocked off; you shall be drawn to the place of execution; you shall be hanged; you shall be cut down and quartered"; and so he goes on. And this is that which is the witness of justice. Thus is it here. The Spirit of God does not think it enough to merely say, "The state of a sinner is a woeful estate." But these woes are punctually numbered, and this shall be my practice.

1. The first thing that follows after sin is this: after the committing of sin, there comes such a condition into the soul that it is defiled, polluted, and becomes abominable. This is the first woe.

2. The soul being thus defiled and abominable, God loathes it; for God cannot endure to dwell in a filthy and putrid carrion soul. He startles, as it were, and seems afraid to come near it. He forsakes it and cannot endure it. And that is the second woe. First sin defiles it, then God departs from it; there must be a divorce.

3. When God has departed from the soul, then the devil enters in; he immediately comes in and takes up the room; there will be no emptiness or vacuum. And this is a fearful woe indeed; for as soon as God has departed from

a man, he is left to the guidance of the devil, his own flesh, and the world. There will be no emptiness in the heart. No sooner does God depart, but these step in and take God's place.

4. After all this is done, sin comes and cries for its wages, which is death; that terrible death which comprehends in it all that bedroll of curses which are written in the book of God; and not only those, but the curses also which are not written (Deuteronomy 28), which are so many that they cannot be written. Though the book of God is a complete book, and the law of God a perfect law, yet here they come short and are imperfect. For the curses not written shall light upon him, which are so many that pen and ink cannot set down, nay, the very pen of God cannot express them, so many are the calamities and sorrows that shall light upon the soul of every sinful man.

Now let us take these woes one after another:

1. The first woe is the polluting and defiling of the soul by sin. It may be that we think little of this, but once God opens our eyes and shows us what a black soul we have within us, and that every sin, every lustful thought, every covetous act, every sin sets a new spot and stain upon the soul and tumbles it into a new puddle of filth, then we shall see it, and not till then—for our eyes are carnal, and we cannot see this. If we could but see our hateful and abominable spots, that every sin tumbles us afresh into the mire; could we see what a black devil we have within us— we would hate and abhor ourselves as Job did. It would be so foul a sight that it would shake us out of our wits, as it were, to behold it. A man who is but natural cannot imagine what a black devil there is within him. But though he does not see it, yet He who has eyes like a flame of fire (Revelation 1:14) sees our stains and spots.

Our Savior shows the filthiness of the heart by that which proceeds out of the mouth: "Those things which proceed out of the mouth come from the heart" (Matthew 15:18). And, "Out of the heart proceed evil thoughts" (verse 19). Observe, of all evils, we account evil thoughts the least. We think what Christ says is strange. "What, thoughts defile a man? What, so light a matter as a thought? Can they make any impression?" Yes, and they defile a man too, leaving such a spot behind them which nothing but the blood of Christ can wash away. So many evil thoughts, so many blasphemies, so many filthy things come from the heart, every one being a new defilement and pollution, that a man is made so filthy by it that he cannot believe that it is as bad with him as indeed it is.

The Apostle Paul, having shown the Corinthians their former life and exhorted them against it in 2 Corinthians 6, goes on: "Let us cleanse ourselves from all filthiness of flesh and spirit" (2 Corinthians 7:1). Mark then, there is a double filthiness, a filthiness of the flesh and a filthiness of the spirit. The filthiness of the flesh everyone acknowledges to be filthy: carnality, fornication, adultery, and the like. These bestial lusts everyone knows to be unclean. But then there is a filth of the spirit too, and such are evil thoughts; they are the filth of the spirit. The corruption that cleaves to the best thing is worst. The soul is the best thing, the most noble thing; the filthiness which cleaves to it, therefore, must be the greatest. Fleshly filthiness, such as adultery, is filthy; but contemplative adultery, to dwell thereupon, is worse: however. Such a man may be pure from the filth of the flesh, yet if he delights himself in filthy thoughts, his spirit is abominable in the sight of God. There is a stain left behind by everyone of your impure thoughts. However, an actual sin is far greater than the sin of a thought, yet if that is but once committed, and these are frequently in you; if you always lie tumbling in the suds of your filthy thoughts—your continuing therein makes your sin more abominable than David's outward act which he only committed once. So we see that there is filthiness of the spirit as well as the flesh.

In James 1:21, we have a word that sets out the filthiness of it, which is "superfluity." James says, "Lay aside all filthiness and superfluity of naughtiness." It is expressed by the name of filthiness, showing there is nothing that so defiles a man as sin. Then it is called "superfluity of naughtiness." But does that mean that there is some naughtiness to be borne with, and whatever exceeds that is superfluous? No, that is not the meaning of the place. The word "superfluity" means the vilest filth, the absolute refuse. Though the comparison is homely, yet it shows the filthiness of sin. God would thereby show that those things that are most offensive to every man are not as filthy to man as sin is to God. So you see how the case stands with a sinful man: sin defiles and pollutes him.

2. In the next place, it makes God's soul to hate and abhor the sinner. It is true, there are some sins that every man imagines to be shameful and filthy; but all sins are so to God; they are filthiness of flesh and spirit. A man may hate carnality and fleshy filthiness; perhaps he may also hate covetousness—but pride and prodigality, that he may get (he thinks) credit by, he cannot maintain the reputation of a gentleman without them. It is a miserable thing that a man should account that a garnish of the soul which defiles and pollutes it. Well, when we thus defile ourselves by sin, God cannot endure us. He is forced to turn from us, and He abhors us.

When you have made yourself such a black soul, such a dunghill, such a sty, then God must be gone. He cannot endure to dwell there. It does not stand with His honor, and with the purity of His nature, to dwell in such a polluted heart; there must now be a divorce: "Holiness becomes His house forever. His delight is in the saints." He is King of the saints, and He will not be in a sty. When you have thus polluted and defiled your soul, God and you must immediately part. God puts you off, and you put God off too.

We read in Ephesians 2:12 that before they knew Christ, they were "without God in the world," atheists. And in chapter 4:18, "Having the understanding darkened, being alienated from the life of God through the ignorance that is in them." The presence of God is the life of our souls; and we, having through sin and ignorance banished God, become strangers until the time of our engrafting into Christ. We are aliens to the life of God, whereupon comes a mutual kind of abhorring one another. God abhors us, and we vile and filthy wretches, abhor God back. There is enmity between God and us, and between all that belongs to God and all that belongs to us. There is an enmity between God and us, and observe the expression of it: "If ye shall despise My statutes, or if your souls shall abhor My judgments, so that ye will not do all My commandments . . ." (Leviticus 26:15). See here how we begin to abhor God, and then see God's judgment on such persons: "My soul shall abhor you" (verse 30). We are not the responder with God in this abhorring: "My soul loathed them, and their soul abhorred me" (Zechariah 11:8). When we begin to abhor God, God's soul also abhors us. When a man has such a polluted soul, he becomes a hater of God, and he is hated by Him. When you have such a stinking soul, God must loathe it as a most loathsome thing; and so you are not behind God here either. Your filthiness makes God abhor you, and you abhor Him. This is your case: by hating God you are hated by God.

Nor is this all the enmity there is between you and God. There is enmity also between all that belongs to God and all that belongs to us. God's children and the wicked ever have an enmity between them, such an enmity as will never be reconciled. It is set down in Proverbs 29:27: "An unjust man is an abomination to the just, and he that is upright in his way is an abomination to the wicked." Just as it is between God and the seed of the serpent, so it is between both the seeds. A wicked man is an abomination to the just, and an upright man is an abomination to the wicked. There is a pale of abomination set between them. This is the second woe.

3. That which immediately follows is God's leaving us. When we have polluted ourselves with sin, and God by reasons thereof abhors us and turns from us, then there are others ready presently to take up the room. As soon as God departs, the devil steps in and becomes your god. He was your god by creation, and now by usurpation. God was your father, who would have given you every good thing; but now you are fatherless, or worse, you have the devil for your father, and would be better off without one. When the devil is your father, you must do his works. When "the Spirit of God departed from Saul, presently the evil spirit entered into him" (1 Samuel 16:14). If the good Spirit is gone, the evil spirit soon comes in; he comes and takes possession, and is therefore called "the god of this world." We are in that state where we walk after the course of him who works in the children of disobedience. We would account it a terrible thing for ourselves, or any of our children, to be possessed by a devil; but what it is to be possessed of this devil, you do not know. It is not half as bad to have a legion of devils possess your body as to have but one possess your soul. The devil becomes your god, and you must do his work; he will tyrannize you. What a fearful thing therefore it is that as soon as God departs from us and forsakes us, and we Him, the devil should presently come in His room and take up the heart? Mark Ephesians 2:2: "Wherein in time past ye walked according to the course of this world, according to the prince of the power of the air, the spirit that now worketh in the children of disobedience." As soon as God leaves a man, what a fearful company assails him! They all concur together, the world, the flesh, and the devil. These take God's place.

The world is like the tide; when a man has the tide with

him, he has great advantage over him who rows against the tide. But here is the devil too. The world is as a swift current, and besides this comes the devil, the prince of the power of the air, and fills the heart. While you were carried with the world, you went with the stream, and had the tide with you; but now that the devil has come, you have both wind and tide—and how can he fail to run whom the devil drives?

But this is not all; there must be something in your own disposition too, that it may be completely filled. Though there is wind and tide, yet if the ship is a slug, it will not make that haste which a light ship will. Therefore here is the flesh too, and the fulfilling the desires thereof, which is a quick and nimble vessel, and this makes up the matter. So if we consider the wind and tide, and the lightness of the ship, it will appear how the room is filled. And how woeful must the state of that man be! It is a fearful thing to be delivered up unto Satan, but not so fearful as to be delivered up to one's own lusts. But observe this for a ground: God never gives us up. God never forsakes us till we first forsake Him. He is still the Initiator in doing us good; but in point of harm, we ourselves are first. In the point of forsaking we are always initiating with God.

If it should be proposed to you whether you will forsake God or the devil, and you were to forsake God and choose the devil, you deserve that he should take possession of you. When a man obstinately renews his gross sins, does he not deserve to be given up? Observe the case in our first parents: God told the woman one thing and the devil persuaded her of another; she hearkened to the devil and believed him rather than God. And when we desire to serve the devil rather than God, the God who made us, and who made heaven for us, do we not deserve to be given up to him? For his servants we are whom we obey.

And thus we see how fearful a thing it is to be delivered up to ourselves and to the devil in Psalm 81:11–12. First, they forsake God. God comes and offers Himself unto them: "I will be thy God, thy Father; thou shall want nothing." Yet, notwithstanding, "Israel would not hear; they would have none of Me." And then, "If you will have none of Me, I will have none of you," says God. Then see what follows in verse 12. God commits the prisoner to himself: "I gave them up to their own hearts' lusts." And there is no case so desperate as this, when God shall say, "If you will be your own master, then be your own master." To thus be given up to a man's self is worse than to be given up unto Satan. To be given up unto Satan may be for your safety, but there is not a mountain of God's wrath greater than to give a man up unto himself. We would fain go over the hedges; but when God loves us, He hedges up our ways (Hosea 2:6). If God loves us, He will not leave us to ourselves, though we desire it. But when God says, "Go your way. If you will not be kept in, be your own master," this is a most fearful thing. So there you have the third woe. First the soul is polluted with sin; it forsakes God and God forsakes it. Then the world, the flesh, and the devil fill up the room. And then what follows when these three rule within but all kinds of sin, and so all kinds of punishment? And that is the next woe.

4. This woe brings in all the curses of Almighty God, a world of evils. Sin calls for its wages, death. That is the payment of all: "The wages of sin is death." Death in general must of necessity follow sin, that you who have forsaken the Fountain of Life are liable to everlasting death. For this see some passages of Scripture: "The wages of sin is death" (Romans 6:23). Consider then first what these wages are. Wages are something that must be paid. If you have a hireling, and your hireling does not receive his wages, you are sure to hear of it. And God will hear of it too: "He which keeps back the wages of the laborer, or of the hireling, their cry will come into the ears of the Lord of sabaoth" (James 5:4). As long as hirelings' wages are

unpaid, God's ears are filled with their cries, "Pay me my wages, pay me my wages." So sin cries, and it is a dead voice, "Pay me my wages, pay me my wages."

The wages of sin is death. And sin never stops crying, never lets God alone, never gives Him rest, till its wages are paid. When Cain had slain Abel, he thought he would never have heard any more of it. But sin has a voice: "The voice of thy brother's blood cries unto Me from the ground." So the Lord says concerning Sodom, "Because the cry of Sodom is great, and their sin very grievous, therefore I will go down and see whether they have done according to the cry that is come up into Mine ears" (Genesis 18:20). It is as if the Lord had said, "It is a loud cry. I can have no rest from it, therefore I will go down and see." If a man had his ears open, he would continually hear sin crying unto God, "Pay me my wages, pay me my wages, kill this sinful soul." And even though we do not hear it, it is so. The dead and doleful sound thereof fills heaven; it makes God say, "I will go down and see." Till sin receives its wages, God has no rest.

See Romans 7:11: "Sin, taking occasion by the commandment, deceived me, and by it slew me." We think that sin is not so great a matter as it is. We think about a matter of profit or pleasure, and thereupon are enticed to sin; but here is the mischief of sin, it deceives us. It is a weight; it presses down; it deceives men; it is more than they deem it to be. Committing sin is, as it were, running yourself upon the point of God's blade.

Sin at first may flatter you, but it will deceive you. It is like Joab's kiss to Amasa. Amasa was not aware of the spear that was behind till Joab smote it into his ribs and killed him. When sin entices you on by profits and pleasures, you are not aware that it will slay you; but you shall find it to be bitterness in the end.

A sinner who acts a tragedy in sin shall have a bloody catastrophe! "What fruit had ye then in those things whereof ye are now ashamed" (Romans 6:21)? Blood and death is the end of the tragedy. "The end of those things is death. The sting of death is sin" (1 Corinthians 15:56). What is sin? It is the sting of death; death would not be death unless sin were in it. Sin is more deadly than death itself. It is sin that enables death to sting, enables it to hurt and wound us.

We may look on sin as the barbarians looked on the viper on Paul's hand: they expected continually that he would swell and burst. Sin bites like a snake which is called a fiery serpent; not that the serpent is fiery, but because it puts a man into such a flaming heat by their poison. And such is the sting of sin, which carries poison in it, that had we but eyes to see our ugliness by it, and how it inflames us, we would continually, every day, look when we will burst with it. James 1:15 uses another metaphor: "Sin, when it is accomplished, brings forth death." The original Greek says, "Sin is pregnant with death." The word is proper to those in labor who are in torment till they are delivered. Now as if sin were thus represented, he uses it in the feminine gender. Sin is in pain, cries out, and has no rest till it has brought forth death.

Now consider, death is a fearful thing. When we talk of death, how it amazes us! The priests of Nob were brought before Saul for relieving David, and he said, "Thou shalt surely die, Ahimelech." This is your case: you shall surely die. Death is terrible even to a good man. Hezekiah, though he was a good man, yet with a sad heart entertained the message of death. The news of it frightened him; it went to his heart; it made him turn to the wall and weep. How does it come to pass that we are careless of death, that we are so full of infidelity, that when the Word of God says, "Thou shalt die, Ahimelech," we are not at all moved by it? What! Can we think these are fables? Do we think God is not in earnest with us? And by this means we fall into the temptation of Eve, questioning whether God's threats are true or not! That which was the deceit of our first parents is ours also.

Satan does not dispute whether sin is lawful or not: whether eating the forbidden fruit was unlawful, whether drunkenness or the like are unlawful. He will not deny that it is unlawful. But when God says, "If you eat of it you shall die," that he denies and says, "Ye shall not die." He would hide our eyes from the punishment of sin. Thus we lost ourselves at the first, and the floods of sin came on in this manner: we did not believe God when He said, "If you eat, you shall surely die."

And shall we renew that capital sin of our parents, and think if we sin we shall not die? If anything in the world will move God to show us no mercy, it is when we slight His judgments or do not believe them. This adds to the height of all our sins, that when God says, "If you live in sin, you shall die," and yet we will not believe Him; that when He comes and threatens us, as He does in Deuteronomy 29, when He curses us and yet we "bless ourselves in our hearts, and say, we shall have peace though we go on. The Lord will not spare that man, but the anger of the Lord and His jealousy shall smoke against him."

It is no small sin when we will not believe God. This is like being thirsty before, we now add drunkenness to our thirst; that is, when God pronounces curses on a man, he yet blesses himself and says, "I hope I shall do well enough for all that." See what follows in Deuteronomy 29: "The anger of the Lord and His jealousy shall smoke against that man."

We have now entered into the point; but it would make your hearts ache and throb within you if you should hear the particulars of it. All that I have done is to persuade you to make a right choice, to take heed of Satan's delusions. Why will you die? "Therefore cast away your sins, and make you a new heart and a new spirit, for why will ye die" (Ezekiel 18:31)? Where the golden candlestick

stands, there Christ walks; there He says, "I am with you."
Where the Word and sacraments are, there Christ is; and
when the Word shakes your heart, take that time to now
choose life. Why will you die? Consider the matter. Moses
put before the people life and death, blessing and cursing;
we put life and death before you in a better manner. He
was a minister of the letter; we are ministers of the Spirit.
Now choose life.

But if you will not hearken, but will try arguing with
God, therefore, because you will come to your own con-
clusions and will not hearken unto God, because you will
not obey Him when He calls, therefore He will turn His
deaf ear unto you; and when you call and cry, He will not
answer (Proverbs 1). I am pressing this point the more to
move you to make a right choice.

But now I turn to the other side. As there is nothing
but death as the wages of sin, and as I have shown you
where death is, so give me leave to direct you to the Fountain of Life. There is life in our blessed Savior. If we have
but a hand of faith to touch Him, we shall draw virtue
from Him to raise us up from the death of sin to the life of
righteousness. He who "hath the Son hath life; he that
hath not the Son hath not life" (1 John 5:12). You have
heard of the death that comes by the first Adam and sin;
and to that stock of original sin we had from him, we have
added a great heap of our own actual sins, and so have
treasured up unto ourselves wrath against the day of
wrath.

Now here is a great treasure of happiness on the other
side in Christ: have the Son and have life. The question is
now whether you will choose Christ and life, or sin and
death? Consider now that the minister stands in God's
stead, and beseeches you in His name. He does not speak
of himself, but from Christ. When he draws near to you
with Christ's broken body and His shed blood, and you
receive Christ then, as your life and strength are preserved

and increased by these elements, so you also have life by Christ. If a man is kept from nourishment awhile, we know what death he must die. If we do not receive Christ, we cannot have life. We know that there is life to be had from Christ, and he who shall, by a true and lively faith, receive Christ shall have life by Him. There is, as it were, a pair of indentures drawn up between God and a man's soul: there is blood shed, and by it pardon of sin and life conveyed unto you on Christ's part. Now if there is faith and repentance on your part, and you accept Christ as He is offered, then you may say, "I have the Son, and as certainly as I have the bread in my hand, I shall have life by Him." I speak this so that the sun might not set in a cloud, that I might not end only in death, but that I might show that there is a way to recover ourselves out of that death to which we have all naturally precipitated ourselves.

7

Death, the Wages of Sin

"The wages of sin is death." Romans 6:23

I declared the cursed effects and consequences of sin, and in general showed that it is the wrath of God; that where sin is, there wrath must follow. The apostle said in the epistle to the Galatians, "As many as are under the works of the law are under the curse." Now all that may be expected from a highly-offended God is comprehended in Scripture by this term, "death." Wherever sin enters, death must follow. "Death passed over all men, forasmuch as all had sinned" (Romans 5:12). If we are children of sin, we must be children of wrath. We are then "children of wrath, even as others" (Ephesians 2:3).

Concerning death in general, the state of an un-converted man is a dead and desperate estate: he is a slave. It would frighten him if he knew his own slavery, and what it is that hangs over his head; that there is but a span between him and death. He could never breathe any free air; he could never be at any rest; he could never be free from fear. Hebrews 2:15 says that Christ came to deliver those who, through fear of death, were all their lifetime subject to bondage. This bondage is a deadly bondage in that, when we have done all that we can do, the payment of the service is death. And the fear of this deadly bond-age, if we were once sensible, if God opened our eyes and showed us, as He did Belshazzar, our doom written, if we could see it, would make our joints loose and our knees knock against each other. Every day you live, you approach nearer to this death, to the accomplishment and consumption of it; death outside and death within; death in this world, and death in the world to come.

But you face death—not only death in general, but in particular also. And to unfold the particulars of death, and to show you the ingredients of this bitter cup, that we may be weary of our state, that we may be drawn out of this death, and be made to fly to the Son so that we may be free indeed, observe that death here is not to be understood only as a separation of the soul from the body, but a greater death than that, the death of the soul and body. We have made mention of a first resurrection: "Blessed and holy is he that hath his part in the first resurrection, for on such the second death hath no power" (Revelation 20:6). What is the first resurrection? It is a rising from sin. What is the second death? It is everlasting damnation. The first death is a death unto sin, and the first resurrection is a rising from sin.

So again, for all things, a man suffers all the judgments or troubles that pertain to this death before. It is not, as fools think, the last blow that fells the tree, but every blow helps forward. It is not the last blow that kills the man, but every blow that goes before makes way unto it. Every trouble of mind, every anguish, every sickness, all these are as so many strokes that shorten our life and hasten our end, and are, as it were, so many deaths. Therefore it is said by the apostle, "It is appointed for all men once to die." Yet we see the apostle referring to the great conflicts that he had in 2 Corinthians 11:23, saying that he was "in labors abundant, in stripes, above measure, in prisons frequent, in deaths oft." In death oft? What is that? That is, though he could die but once, yet these harbingers of death— these stripes, bonds, imprisonments, sicknesses, and the like—all of them were as so many deaths; all these were comprehended under this curse and are parts of death. Inasmuch as he underwent that which was a furtherance to death, he is said to die. So we read in Exodus 10:17 that Pharaoh could say, "Pray unto your God that He would forgive my sins this once, and entreat the Lord that he will take away from me but this death only." The locusts were not death, but are said to be so because they prepared and made way for a natural death. Therefore the great judgments of God are usually in Scripture comprised under this name, death. All things that may be expressions of the wrath of a highly-provoked God are comprehended under this name. All the judgments of God that come upon us in this life or the one to come, whether they be spiritual or temporal, are under the name of death.

Now to come to particulars, look particularly on death, and you shall see death begun in this world, and seconded by a death following: the separation of the body and soul from God in the world to come.

In this life he is always a dying man who is born of a woman. He is ever spending upon the stock; he is ever wasting like a candle, burning still, and spending itself as soon as lighted, till it come to its utter consumption. So he is born to be a dying man. Death seizes upon him as soon as it finds sin in him: "In the day that thou eatest thereof, thou shalt die," said God to Adam in Genesis 2:17, though he lived many years later. How then could this threatening hold true? It did in that immediately Adam fell into a languishing state, subject and inclined to miseries and calamities, the hasteners of death.

If a man is condemned to die, but the sentence is delayed and he is kept prisoner three or four years, we still account him as a dead man. Now, if this man's mind shall be taken up with worldly matters, earthly contentments, purchases, or the like, would we not account him a fool or a stupid man, seeing he lightly esteems his condemnation because he is not executed at the earlier hour? Such is our case: we are, while in our natural condition in this life, dead men, ever tending towards the grave, towards cor-

ruption. We are as the gourd of Jonah: as soon as it began
to sprout forth, there was a worm within that bit it and
caused it to wither.

The day that we are born there is within us the seed of
corruption, and that wastes us away with a secret and in-
curable consumption that certainly brings death in the
end. So at our very birth our progress to death begins. We
have a time, and we have a way, but it leads to death. Until
you come to be reconciled to Christ, every hour tends to
your death; there is not a day that you can truly say you
live in; you are ever posting on to death, death in this
world and eternal death in the world to come.

And as it is thus with us at our coming into the world,
so it is true of that little time we have above ground—our
days are full of sorrow. But when I speak of sorrows here,
you must not take them for such afflictions and sorrows as
befall God's children, for theirs are blessings to them.
Chastisements are tokens of God's love. "For as many as I
love I chasten." Affliction to them is like the dove with an
olive branch in her mouth, to show that all is well.

But take a man who is under the law, and then every
cross, whether it is loss of friends, loss of goods, or diseases
on his body, all things, everything to him is a token of
God's wrath, not a token of His love, as it is to God's children. It is as His impress money, as partial payment of a
greater sum, an earnest of the wrath of God, the first part
of the payment thereof.

It is the apostle's direction that, among the other armor, we should get our feet shod that we might be able to
go through the afflictions we shall meet with in this life:
"Let your feet be shod with the preparation of the gospel
of peace" (Ephesians 6:15). What, is the shoeing of the feet
a part of the armor? Yes, for in the Roman discipline there
were things they called "caltrops," which were cast in the
way before the army, before the horse and men. They had
three points, so that whichever way they were thrown, one

point was upwards. Now to meet with and prevent this mischief, the soldiers had brazen shoes so that they could tread upon these "caltrops" and not be hurt. We read that Goliath, among other armor, had boots of brass. It is to this the apostle seems to be referring in this metaphorical speech. The meaning is that as we should get the shield of faith and the sword of the Spirit, so we should have our feet shod so that we might be prepared against all those outward troubles that we might meet with in the world, which are all as so many stings and pricks.

All outward crosses are such. And what is it that makes all these hurt us? What is it that makes all these as so many deaths unto us but sin? If sin reigns in you and bears rule, that puts a sting into them. It is sin that arms death against us, and it is sin that arms all that goes before death against us. Have you been crossed in the loss of your wife, children, or good friends? Why, the sting of all is from sin; sin is what makes us feel sorrow. What shall we then do? Why, get your feet shod with the preparation of the gospel of peace. Prepare yourself; get God to be at peace with you. And if God is at peace with you, you are prepared; and then whatever affliction comes, however it may be a warning to someone else that God's wrath is coming, to you it is a messenger of peace.

Now these outward troubles are the least part of a wicked man's payment, though all these are a part of his death as long as he remains unreconciled. Whatever comes upon him, whereby he suffers either in himself or in any thing that belongs to him, they are all tokens of God's wrath, and are the beginnings of his death. In Leviticus 26 and Deuteronomy 28, the particulars of it are set down. The law of God is a perfect law, and nothing is to be added to it; yet the variety of the curses belonging unto an unreconciled man are so many that the ample book of God cannot contain them: "All the curses which are not written . . ." (Deuteronomy 28:61). See the diversities of plagues in verse 27. All these are made parts of the curse. They are part of the payment of God's wrath in hell: "I will send a sword amongst you, which shall avenge the quarrel of My covenant" (Leviticus 26:25). The sword which shall destroy you, that when you shall hear of war, of the coming of the sword (which the children of God need not fear, all is alike unto them), shall be to avenge the quarrel of God's covenant.

The book of God does not comprehend all the curses that are to light on the wicked. And therefore we find in Zechariah, a book, a great book, every side whereof was full of curses. "He said unto me, 'What seest thou?' And I said, 'I see a flying roll, the length whereof is twenty cubits, and the breadth thereof is ten cubits' " (Zechariah 5:2). Here is a large book indeed; but mark what is in it. Surely it is not for nothing that the Holy Ghost sets down the dimensions of it: "The length thereof is twenty cubits, and the breadth ten cubits," a huge volume. Nor is it a book, but a roll, so that the thickness goes into the compass, and this is written thick within and without, and is full of curses against sin. Now for the dimensions of it, compare this place with 1 Kings 6:3, and you shall find them the very dimensions of Solomon's porch, which was a great place where the people were wont to come to hear the Word; and not only in that time, but it was continued to the time of Christ and the apostles. We read how our Savior walked in Solomon's porch, and that, in Acts 5:12, the apostles were in Solomon's porch.

So large then was this roll that it agreed in length and breadth with Solomon's porch; and so many curses were written in it as were able to come in at the church door. It is as if we should see a huge book now coming in at the church door that should fill it up. Such a thing was presented unto him, and it was a roll of curses; and all these curses shall come on those who do not obey all the commandments; all shall come upon them and overtake them.

"Cursed shalt thou be in the city, and cursed shalt thou be in the field; cursed in thy basket and in thy store, cursed when thou comest in and when thou goest forth" (Deuteronomy 28:16–19). Till a man comes to receive the promises, till he comes to be a son of blessing, till he is in Christ, he is so beset with curses that if he lies down to sleep, there is a curse on his pillow; if he puts his money in his coffer, he lays up a curse with it which, like rust, eats it out and cankers it; if he begets a child, he is accursed. There is a curse against his person, his goods, and all that belongs unto him. There is still a curse over his head.

The creditor in this world, by the laws of the realm, may choose whether he will have his debtor's person seized, or his goods and chattels. But it is not so here; this writ is executed against his person, and his goods, and all that belongs unto him. So "it is a fearful thing to fall into the hands of the living God." If this is the condition of a wicked man, that his very blessings are curses, what a woeful case it is! There is nothing, till he is reconciled to Christ, that does not have a curse at the end of it.

Consider that passage in Malachi where the very blessings are accursed; not only when God sends diseases or the sword, but in blessings the man is accursed. " 'If you will not hear, and if you will not lay it to heart to give glory unto My name,' saith the Lord of hosts, 'I will even send a curse upon you' " (Malachi 2:2). But how? See how this curse is threatened: "I will curse your blessings; yea, I have cursed them already, because ye do not lay it to heart." Is it not a great blessing that God yet affords the Word, that we yet enjoy it; but if we come to hear it only formally, and do not lay it to heart, God curses even this blessing. Yea, "I have cursed it already," says the Lord.

When you pray in hypocrisy, your prayer is a curse to you. If you receive the sacrament unworthily, the cup of blessing is a cup of poison, a cup of cursing to you. Do not stay therefore one hour longer quietly in this cursed condition, but fly to Christ for life and blessing. Run to this city of refuge, for otherwise there is a curse at the end of every outward thing that you enjoy. "I have cursed these blessings already." It is as sure as if it was already passed on you. What a woeful thing then is it, do you think, to be liable to the curse of God!

But what has become of the soul now? Why, if you saw the cursed soul that you carry in your body, it would amaze you. These outward curses are but trifles to the blow that is given to the soul of an unregenerate man, that deadness of spirit which is within. If you saw the curse of God that rests upon the soul of this man, even while he is above ground, it would even astonish you.

There are two kinds of blows that God gives the soul of an unregenerate man. One is a terrible blow; the other, the worst of the two, is an insensible blow. The sensible blow is when God lets the conscience out and makes it fly in the face of a man, when the conscience comes and terribly accuses a man for what he has done. This blow is not so usual as the insensible blow; but the insensible blow is far more heavy.

In this world, sometimes before the glory in heaven, the saints of God have here a glimpse of heaven and certain communion with God and Christ, certain love tokens, "a white stone, a new name engraven, which no man knoweth but he that receiveth it." And this is the testimony of a good conscience, which is hidden joys. Private intercourse is between Christ and them. And as God's children meet with a heaven upon earth sometimes, and are, as Paul, "caught up into the third heaven," which to them is more than all the things in the world besides, so the wicked sometimes have flashes of hell in their consciences. If you had but seen men in the case that I have seen them in, you would say they had a hell within them; they would desire rather, as they have expressed it, to be torn in pieces by wild horses so that they might be freed from the horrors in their consciences. When the conscience recoils and beats back upon itself, as a musket overcharged, it turns a man over and over: and this is a terrible thing. Sometimes God gives men such a conscience in the world. And mark, where the Word is most powerfully preached, there is this froth most raised, which is why many men do not come where the Word is taught, because it galls their consciences. They desire the mass instead because they say the mass does not bite. They desire a dead minister who will not rub against their consciences; they would not be tormented before their time. They wish it so, but it is not their choice. God will make them feel here the fire of hell, which they must endure forever hereafter. This is the sensitive blow, when God lets loose the conscience of a wicked man; and he needs no other fire, no other worm to torment, nothing else to plague him. He has a weapon within him, his own conscience, which, if God lets loose, it will be hell enough.

But now, besides this blow that is not so frequent, there is another more common and more insensible blow. God says that the sinner is a dead man, a slave to sin and Satan. Yet the sinner thinks himself the freest man in the world. God curses and strikes, and the sinner does not feel it. This is an insensible blow, and like a dead palsy. You are dead, and yet walk about and are merry, though everyone who has his eyes open sees death in your face. Oh, this deadness, this senselessness of heart is the heaviest thing which can befall a sinner in this life. It is the reason the apostle speaks of in Romans why God delivers a man up to a reprobate mind. In Ephesians 4:19, Paul declares such a man to be past feeling: "Who, being past feeling, have given themselves over to lasciviousness, to work all uncleanness with greediness." Although every sin is, as it were, the running of a man's self on the point of God's sword, yet these men, being past feeling, run on and on and on to commit sin with greediness, till they come to the very pit of destruction. When this insensibleness comes upon them, not even God's goodness can work upon them. Who are you who "despisest the riches of God's goodness, not knowing that the goodness of God leadeth unto repentance?"

God's judgments will not move them; they leave no impression. "And the rest of the men which were not killed by these plagues, yet repented not of the works of their hands, that they should not worship devils, and idols of gold, and silver, and brass, and stone, and of wood, which neither can see, nor hear, nor walk" (Revelation 9:20). They did not repent, though they were spared, but worshipped gods which cannot see, hear, or speak; so brutish were they to be led away by stocks and stones. I think the papist gods cannot do it unless it be by deception; yet such is their senselessness that, though God's fury is revealed from heaven against papists, such as worship false gods, yet are they so brutish that they will worship things which can neither hear, see, nor walk. "They that made them are like unto them, and so are all they that worship them," as brutish as the stocks themselves. They have no heart to God, but will follow after their puppets and their idols, and such are they also that follow after their drunkenness, covetousness, and the like. "Who live in lasciviousness, lusts, excess of ruin" (1 Peter 4:3), who run into all kinds of excess, and marvel that you do not do so too. They marvel that you who fear God can live as you do, and yet they speak evil of all good men; they call you hypocrites, dissemblers, and I know not what other nicknames.

This is a most woeful condition; it is that dead blow when men are not sensible of mercies or of judgments, but run into all excess of sin with greediness. And this is a death begun in this life, even while they are above ground.

But then comes another death. God does not intend for sin to grow to an infinite height. His Spirit shall not always strive with man, but at length God comes and crops him off, and then comes the consummation of the death begun in this life: then comes an accursed death.

After you have lived an accursed life, then comes an accomplishment of curses. First, a cursed separation between body and soul, and then of both from God forever—and that is the last payment. This is that great death of which the apostle speaks: "Who hath delivered us from that great death." So terrible is that death that he calls it "great." This death is but the severing of the body from the soul; this is but the Lord's harbinger, the Lord's sergeant to lay His mace on you, to bring you out of this world into a place of everlasting misery, from whence you shall never come till all is satisfied, which will be never.

Consider the nature of this death, which, though every man knows, yet few lay to heart. What does this death do?

1. It takes from you all the things which you spent your whole life in getting. It robs you of all the things you ever had. You have taken pains to heap and treasure up goods for many years, but when this blow is given, all is gone. Death takes honor and preferment from you; it bars you from pleasure in idle company keeping. Mark, this is the first thing that death does: it not only takes away a part of what you have, but all that you have; it leaves you as naked as when you came into the world. You thought it was your happiness to get this and that. Death now begins to undeceive you. You were bewitched before, when you ran after all those worldly things; but now death undeceives you. It makes you see what a notorious fool you were.

You had many plans and projects, but when your breath is gone, then all your thoughts perish; all your plotting and projecting go away with your breath. Is it not a strange thing to see a man like Job, the richest man in the east, and yet in the evening we say that someone is "as poor as Job; he has nothing left him now." Though death does not take all things from you, yet it takes you from them all; all your goods, all your books, all your wealth, all your friends—you must now bid farewell, adieu forever, never to see them again.

2. Death does not rest there, however, but seizes upon your body. It has bereaved you of all that you possessed, of all your outward things; they are all taken away. But now it comes to touch your person. It touches you in that it rends your soul from your body; those two loving components that have so long dwelt together are now separated. The man who dies does not deliver up his spirit, as our Savior did: "Father, into Thy hands I commit My Spirit." Nor does he deliver his spirits, as Stephen did: but it is taken from him. Death pulls a man from himself.

QUESTION. But when a man is thus pulled asunder, what becomes of the parts separated?

ANSWER. The body, as soon as the soul is taken from it, hastens to corruption. Yea, it becomes so full of corruption that your dearest friend could not then endure to come near you. When the soul is taken from the body, of all carcasses man's is the most loathsome; none is so odious as that. Abraham loved Sarah well, but when he came to buy a monument for her, see his expression: "He communes with the men, and saith, 'If it be your mind to sell me the field, that I might bury my dead out of my sight' " (Genesis 23:8). Though he loved her very well before, yet now she must be buried out of his sight. It is sown in dishonor, and it is the basest thing that can be. Therefore, when our Savior was going near the place where Lazarus lay, his sister said, "Lord, come not near him, for he smells." Job said, "I have said to corruption, 'Thou art my father,' and to the worm, 'Thou art my mother and my sister' " (Job 17:14), as in the verse before, "The grave is my house. I have made my bed in the darkness." Here then he has a new kindred; and though before he had affinity with the greatest, yet here he gets new affinity: "He saith to corruption, 'Thou art my father,' and to the worm, 'Thou art my mother and my sister.' " The worm is our best kindred here; the worm then will be our best bed; yea, worms will be your best covering, as is said in Isaiah 14:11. Thus is it your father, your mother, and your bed; nay, it is your consumption and destroyer also (see Job 24:20). Thus it is with your body: it passes to corruption so that your best or dearest friend can neither behold it or endure it.

But what becomes of the soul then? The soul appears naked; there is no garment to defend it, no proctor appears to plead for it. It is brought singly to the bar, and there it must answer. "It is appointed for all men once to die." But what then? "And after that to come to judgment" (Hebrews 9:27). "The body returns unto the earth from whence it was taken, but the spirit to God that gave it" (Ecclesiastes 12:7). All men's spirits, as soon as their bodies and souls are parted, go to God to be disposed of by Him, where they shall keep their everlasting residence.

When you hear the bell ring out for a dead man, consider that if you had the wings of a dove to fly, and could fly after him and appear with him before God's tribunal to see the account that he must give unto God for all things done in the flesh; and when no account can be given— what a state of misery and horror would you see him in! And this is a silent kind of judging. The last day of judgment shall be with great pomp and solemnity. This is a matter closely carried between God and yourself; but then you must give an account of all that you have received. And if you cannot give a good account, then your talent will be taken from you. God will say, "I gave you learning; how did you use it? I gave you other gifts of mind; how did you employ them?"

God has given you wisdom, wealth, moral virtues, meekness, patience, and the like, all which are good things. But whatever good things you had in this world are now taken from you. If a man could but see the degrading of the soul, he would see that those moral virtues in which his hope of comfort lay (though they could never bring him to heaven), yet they shall be taken from him.

When a knight is degraded, first his sword is taken from him, then someone comes with a hatchet and chops off his golden spurs, and then he is told, "Go, sir knave." Such is the degrading of the soul before the judgment is received. The moral virtues are taken from him, and then you will see what an ugly soul he has. He had hope before, but now he is without hope; he had some patience in this world, but he made no good use of it, and now his patience is taken from him. And when you shall come to a place of torment, and your hope and patience are taken from you, what case will you be in then? Patience may hold a man up in trouble, and hope may comfort a man in torment, but both these are taken away. This is a thing we very seldom think of; but if we seriously considered this first act of the judgment before the sentence, we would not be idle in this world.

Last, the man who dies is put into an unchangeable estate. As soon as death lays God's mace on him, he is put into a state of unchangeableness. Such is the terribleness of it, that now, though he yells, groans, and pours out rivers of tears, there is no hope of change.

Consider what a woeful case this is. If a friend of this man's should now come to him, would he not tell his friend, "We have often been very merry together, but if you knew the misery that I am in, you would be troubled for me. Half those tears that I now pour forth would have put me into another place, had I taken the season; but now it is too late." Oh, therefore, make use of tears; a little may do it now, but hereafter it will be too late.

I now come to speak of the second death, but that which is everlasting deserves an hour's worth of speaking, and an age's worth of thinking on it. Therefore, of that everlasting torment, horror, and anguish that God has reserved for those who do not make peace with Him, I shall speak more in the next time.

8

The Place of Torment

"But the fearful, and unbelieving, and the abominable, and murderers, and whoremongers, and sorcerers, and idolaters, and all liars, shall have their part in the lake which burneth with fire and brimstone, which is the second death." Revelation 21:8

The last day I entered upon the miserable estate of an unreconciled sinner at the time of his dissolution, when his soul shall be taken from him and he is presented naked before Christ's tribunal, there to receive according to the works which he has done in the flesh. I showed that the woefulness of that estate consisted in two acts done upon him: the one before he comes to his place, before he is thrust away from God's presence into hellfire; the other is the woefulness of his estate once he comes to his final place. This act done to the sinner's soul before he is sent to hell is the deprivation of his light, the taking away of his talent. For while a man is in this world, he has many good things, too good to accompany him to hell. All these excellent gifts and natural endowments, which adorned a wicked man's soul before that soul is hurled into hell, must be taken away from him.

There is a kind of degradation of the soul; it is de-priested, as it were, and becomes like a degraded knight who has his honor taken from him. All the rich talents, and all the rich prizes that were put into the fool's hand, shall be taken from him. Is there any moral virtue? Are there any common graces and natural endowments in the miserable soul? It shall be stripped of all and packed off to hell. You who have abused the learning and gifts which God has given you, do you think they shall go with you to hell? No, you shall be very sots and dunces there. All your learning shall be taken from you, and you shall go to hell as arrant blockheads. He who had fortitude in this world shall not carry one drachm of it to hell; all his courage shall then be abased, and his cowardly heart shall faint for fear. Fortitude is a great advantage to a man in distress, but the damned soul need not expect the least advantage. The fortitude he had while he was in the way shall be taken from him.

It may be that he had patience in this world; but patience is a virtue unfit for hell; therefore, it shall be taken from him. If a man were in the most exquisite torments, yet, if he had patience, it would bear it up; but this shall add to his torments, that he shall not have any patience left to allay it. A man has perhaps hope in this world, and, as the proverb is, were it not for hope, the heart would burst; yet even this, too, shall be taken away from him. He shall have no hope left of ever seeing God's face again, or of ever having any more tastes of His favor. And so what has been said of some may be said of all his graces and endowments: he shall be clean stripped of all ere he is sent to hell.

I come now to speak of the place of torment itself, wherein the sinner is to be cast eternally, which is the second death. But have no thoughts that I am able to discover the thousandth part of it, no, nor any other man. God grant that no soul here present may ever come to find by experience what it is. What a woeful thing is it that many men should take more pains to come to this place of torments than it would cost them to go to heaven; that men should willfully run themselves upon the spikes, not considering how painful it is, nor how sharp those spikes are! I shall endeavor to my power to set this forth to you.

This text declares unto us two things: first, who they are for whom this place is provided; and, second, the place itself and the nature of it.

1. For whom the place is provided. The text contains a catalogue of the grand criminals, the ringleaders to destruction, the mother sins. We have, first, "the fearful." Hereby is not meant those who are of a timorous nature (for fear is not a sin), those who are simply fearful, but such as place their fear on a wrong object, not where it should be. This refers to those who do not fear God, but other things more than Him. If affliction and iniquity were put to their choice, they will choose iniquity rather than affliction; rather than have anything cross them, rather than incur the indignation of men, rather than part with their life and goods for God's cause, they will venture on anything, choosing iniquity rather than affliction. They are afraid of what they should not fear, never fearing the great and mighty God. These are "the fearful" meant here. See how it is expressed in Job 36:21: "This hast thou chosen . . . iniquity rather than affliction; to sin rather than to suffer."

Christ bids us not to fear poor, vain man, but the omnipotent God who is able to both kill and to cast into hell. The man who fears his landlord, who is able to turn him out of his house, and does not fear God, who is able to turn him into hell, this dastardly spirit is one of the captains of those who go to hell; that man is one of those timorous and cowardly persons who tremble at the wrath or frowns of men more than of God.

But why should men thus stand more in fear of men than of God? Why, it is because they are sensible of what men can do to their bodies, but they cannot by faith see what that is which is invisible. They are full of unbelief; for if they had faith it would banish all false fears. See what the Lord says: "Fear not, thou worm Jacob, I will help thee" (Isaiah 41:14). He does not say, "Fear not, you men," or, "you man," for then perhaps you might be thought to have some power to resist. But He says, "Fear not, thou worm." A worm, you know, is a poor, weak thing, apt to be crushed by every foot. Yet this is your case: even if you are a worm unable to resist the least opposition, yet "fear not, thou worm."

"Fear not?" Why not? "For I will help thee, saith the Lord." Could you but believe in God, this would make you bold; and if you had faith, you would not fear. When word was brought to the house of David that two kings were coming to invade the land (Isaiah 7:2), it is said, "His heart was moved, as the trees of the wood are moved with the wind." But what was the remedy for this fear? See Isaiah 8:12–13: "Fear not this fear, nor be afraid." That was a false and a base fear, but "sanctify the Lord in your hearts, and let Him be your fear, and let Him be your dread." In Isaiah 51:12, there is an object of our faith and comfort, and a remedy against fear proposed: "I, even I, am He that comforteth thee. Who art thou that shouldest be afraid of a man that shall die, and the son of man that is as grass?" What! Are you one who has God on your side? How unworthy you are of such high favor if you fear man! The greatest man who lives cannot shield himself from death, and from a covering of worms; and will you "be afraid of a man, and forget the Lord thy Maker?" The more you are taken up with the fear of man, the less you fear God; and the more you remember man, the more you forget your Maker.

You have seen the ringleaders, these fearful, faithless, dastardly, unbelieving men. Now see who the filthy rabble are who follow after: they are abominable, murderers, and the like. They are "abominable," that is, unnatural, such as pollute themselves with things not fit to be named, but to be abhorred, whether it be by themselves or with others. The abominable here meant are such as Sodom and Gomorrah, who were "set forth to such as an example, suffering the vengeance of eternal fire" (Jude 7). Let them carry it ever so secretly, yet are they here ranked among the rest, and shall have their portion in the burning lake.

After these come "sorcerers, idolaters, liars." Though these may be spoken fairly of by men, yet that cannot shelter them from the wrath of God; they shall likewise have their part in this lake of fire when they come to a reckoning. If there is a generation of people who worship these, say what you will of them, when they come to receive their wages, they "shall receive their portion in that burning lake with hypocrites." Those who make so fair a show before men and yet nourish hypocrisy in their hearts, these men, though in regard of the outward man they so behave themselves that none can say of them that they have a black eye; though they cannot be charged with those notorious things before mentioned; yet, if there is nothing but hypocrisy in their hearts, let it be spun with ever so fair a web, ever so fine a thread, yet they shall have their part and portion in the lake of fire.

Then it seems that this "black guard" has a peculiar interest in this place. It is said of Judas that "he was gone to his proper place" (Acts 1:25). So long as a man who is an enemy of Christ and will not yield Him obedience is out of hell, so long is he out of his place. Hell is the place assigned to him and prepared for him; he has a share there, and his part and portion he must have; till he comes there he is but a wanderer. Christ tells us that the scribes and Pharisees went about to gain proselytes, and when they were all done, they made them "seven times more the children of hell than themselves." A father has no more right to his son than hell has to these. He is a vessel of wrath filled brim full of iniquity, and a child of the devil. We say that the gallows will claim its right, and just so, hell will claim its due.

But do not mistake me, all that I speak concerning hell is not to terrify and frighten men, but, by warning them, to keep them from going there. For after I have shown you the danger I shall show you a way to escape it, and how the Lord Jesus was given to us to deliver us from this danger. But if you will not hear, but will try arguing with God, then you must go to your proper place, to the lake that burns with fire and brimstone.

Hell is a lake, a river, a flaming river, as Tophet is described to be. It is a "lake burning with fire and brimstone," a metaphor taken from the judgment of God on Sodom and Gomorrah, as mentioned in Jude, and also in 2 Peter 2:6, where it is said, "God turned the cities of Sodom into ashes, making them an example to all them that should after live ungodly." Mark the judgment of God upon these abominable men: the place where they dwelt was destroyed with fire, and the situation was turned into a lake full of filthy, bituminous stuff. This was made an instance of the vengeance of God, and an emblem of eternal fires. Therefore God said, "You shall have your portion with Sodom."

An even stronger word comes from Christ. Though they were so abominable that the lake was denominated from them, yet it shall "be easier for Sodom and Gomorrah than for you," if you do not repent while you can, but go on to despise God's grace. Can there be a greater sin than the sin of Sodom? Yes, for make the worst of the sin of Sodom, it is but a sin against nature: but your impenitence is a sin against grace and the gospel, and therefore deserves a hotter hell, and a higher measure of judgment in this burning pit.

But what is the second death? Surely it has reference to some first death or other going before. A man would think, as commonly is, that this second death is opposed to that first death, which is the harbinger to the second, and separates the soul from the body—but it is far otherwise. That, alas, is but a petty thing, and does not deserve to be put in the number of deaths. The second death in the text has relation to the first resurrection: "Blessed and holy is he that has his portion in the first resurrection; on such the second death shall have no power" (Revelation 20:6). The first death is that from whence we are acquitted by the first resurrection, and that is the death; for that is a kind of death (as Paul, speaking of a wicked and voluptuous widow, says, "She is dead while she liveth"). And the "time shall come, and now is, when they that are dead shall hear the voice of the Son of man, and they that hear shall live." Again, "Let the dead bury their dead."

So the first resurrection is when a man, hearing the voice of the minister, is roused up from the sleep of sin and carnal security, and the first death is the opposite thereunto. So that the death of the body is no death at all; for if it were, then this would be the third death. For then there would be a death of sin, a death of the body, and a death of body and soul. This death of the body is but a trifle in comparison with the other two. The second death is the separation of the body and soul from God, and this death is the wages of sin; and God must not, will not, lie in arrear to sin, but will pay its wages to the full.

All the afflictions a wicked man meets with here are but as God's down payment, a partial payment of that greater sum. But when he dies, the whole sum comes then to be paid. Before he merely sipped the cup of God's wrath, but he must then drink the dregs of it down to the bottom—and this is the second death. It is called death. Now death is a destruction of the parts compounded; a man is compounded of body and soul, and both are by this death eternally destroyed. That death (like Samson, pulling down the pillars whereby it was sustained, pulled down the house) draws down the tabernacles of our bodies, pulls body and soul asunder. This thing would have little hurt in itself were it not for the sting of it, which makes it fearful. To die is esteemed far worse than to be dead in regard of the pangs that are in dying, to which death puts an end. This temporal death is in an instant, but this other eternal, whereby we are ever dying and never dead; for by it we are punished with an everlasting destruction, "and that from the presence of the Lord, by the glory of His power" (2 Thessalonians 1:9). I have no need to add more to this passage, forasmuch as can be said of men and angels is fully comprehended in it. The apostle terms this a "fearful thing indeed" in Hebrews 2:15, whereon if a man will but think (if he has his senses about him), he would for fear of it be all his life long subject to bondage. He would scarcely draw any free breath, but would be studying how to avoid it, and would be in bondage and drudgery till he were delivered. Thus I have declared the nature of the place, and of this second death.

That I may now go further, know that this lake and this place that the Lord has provided for His enemies, is the Lord's slaughter house; it is called "a place of torments" in Luke 16:28, a place wherein God will show the accomplishment of His wrath and revenge upon His enemies: "Those Mine enemies that would not have Me to reign over them, bring them forth and slay them before My face." Bring those vessels of wrath, those rebels; the King is enraged, and His wrath is as the roaring of a lion, which makes all the beasts of the forests to tremble. And where there is the wrath of such a King, the issue thereof must be death (Proverbs 19:12). "The wrath of a king is as messengers of death" (Proverbs 16:14); how much more fearful is the wrath of the King of kings!

God has sharp arrows, and He sets a wicked man as His target to shoot at, to show His strength and the fierceness of His wrath. See the expression in Job 6:4 regarding this: "The arrows of the Almighty stick fast in me, and the venom thereof hath drunk up my spirit." In so few words there could not be a higher expression of the wrath of God. First, God will make you a target; then, you will be shot at, and that by God's arrows. And they are not shot by a child, but (as the man is, so is his strength) by the Almighty, by His bow wherein He draws the arrow to the head. Then, these arrows are poisoned arrows, and such poison as shall drink up all your soul and spirit. Oh, what a fearful thing it is to fall into the hands of such a God!

It was a saying of Moses, "Who knoweth the power of Thine anger?" (Psalm 90:11) The power of God's anger is unknown. And so Moses in his song sets it out in some measure: "A fire is kindled in Mine anger, which shall burn unto the lowest hell" (Deuteronomy 32:22). So that the King, being thus provoked, is provoked to curse you. In Matthew 25:41, it is put into the form of a sentence; this cursing shall be your lot in hell; it shall be your very sentence: "Go, ye cursed, into everlasting fire." There is nothing but cursing. As Job cursed himself and the day of his birth, so then shall cursing be all your song. You will curse yourself that you did not hearken to the preacher, that you would not accept Christ, and the means of mercy and grace when they were offered you. You will curse the time that you were acquainted with this man and that man, and others will curse you for drawing them to sin. God will curse you and man will curse you; and God does not curse in vain when He curses. Others will curse you, and you will curse yourself and others—and think then how cursed will be your condition! All the curses that can be thought on, and all the curses that cannot be thought on, shall rest on the head of an impenitent sinner, to show God's terrible and just indignation against Him. O beloved, to deliver us from this curse, Christ, the Son of God, was made a curse for us. The curse is so great that nothing else can free us from it.

But now, that I may rank these punishments of the damned, and bring them for memory's sake into some order (although there be no order there, for it is a place of confusion), you may consider that the penalties of God's enemies are penalties partly of loss and partly of sense.

1. They are penalties partly of loss, and those consist in the deprivation of everything that might administer the least comfort to him; for this reason hell is termed "utter darkness." Darkness is a deprivation of all light, so hell is a deprivation of all comfort, to show that there is not the least thing there that may give you contentment, nor is there the poorest thing you can desire to be had. Darkness was one of the plagues of Egypt, though there was no kind of sense in it; yet we may think what a plague and vexation it was to them to sit so long in darkness. The darkness of hell is darker than darkness itself. "They shall not see light," says the Scripture; they shall not have so much as a glimpse of it. To be cast into this utter darkness, where there shall be nothing to administer the least comfort, what an infinite misery will that be! Were it only the loss of the things we now possess and enjoy, of all which death robs us—such as pomp, honor, riches, and preferment—this would be grievous to a wicked man. These things death dispossesses a man of cannot follow him; nothing but your works accompany you. Your friends may follow you to the grave, but they shall leave you there. To have been happy and now to be miserable is the greatest woe; to have lived in good fashion and to be wretched is the greatest grief. How will this add to the sinner's misery, when he shall say to himself, "I once had all good things about me, but have now for my portion nothing but woe. I once had a bed of down, but it is now exchanged for a bed of fire. I was once honorable, but now I am full of shame and contempt." This will greatly add to his misery.

But all this is nothing; these are but the beginnings of his sorrow in regard of loss. For a man to be rich and wealthy today, and tomorrow to be stripped of all, and left nothing worth a coin, to have all swept away—this is a woeful case.

But if this is so grievous, what is it to lose heaven? Certainly to lose the highest and greatest good is the greatest evil and punishment that can be inflicted upon a creature; and this makes many divines think that the penalties of loss are far greater than those of sense, though they do not seem to make that impression. It is another thing to judge things by sense than by losses. For example, a man who is greatly troubled with a toothache thinks his case more miserable than any, and thinks no man ever endured so much misery as himself; he judges his misery by senses. Another man who has tuberculosis may have little or no pain at all; yet if a man comes with a right judgment, he will judge his condition to be far worse than the man with the toothache.

So take all the pains in hell: though sense may say they are the greatest that can be, yet discreet judgment can say that the loss of God, the greatest good, is the worst of evils. Now, if you are a firebrand of hell, you must forever be banished from God's presence. You base wretch, do you think heaven is a place for you? Not so. It has no dogs and sorcerers; you are such a dog, therefore you must be put out from God, and from the company of the blessed saints and angels. When Peter saw Moses and Elijah with Christ in His transfiguration, though he had but a glimpse of glory, yet he said, "It is good for us to be here." But how infinitely good will it be to be in heaven! How shall we then be wrapped up with glory when we shall "be forever with the Lord, in whose presence is fullness of joy, and at whose right hand there are pleasures for evermore!" On the contrary, how exceedingly terrible will it be to be shut out from the presence of God, when God shall say, "Depart from Me, ye cursed, into everlasting fire, prepared for the devil and his angels" (Matthew 25:41)! Oh, the unspeakable horror and dread! Oh, the infinite shame of that man who is in such a case!

But this is not all. There is one thing more: the wicked shall not only be banished from God's gracious presence and cast into hell, but this shall be done in the sight of heaven. The glorious saints of God have a continual sight of God's justice upon sinners so that they may glorify His mercy the more. The Scripture speaks much to this purpose. "If any man worship the beast and his image, the same shall be tormented with fire and brimstone in the presence of God and of His holy angels" (Revelation 14:10). This, in verse nine, is "the portion of them that worship the beast" that is, the pope, "and receive the mark of his name." That is, if anyone is an express public or private papist, if any one will be a slave to the pope, see his portion: he shall drink of the wine of the wrath of God, be banished from the society of holy angels, and be tormented with hellfire in their presence. Oh, what a vexation will this be to the damned when they shall see others in heaven and themselves shut out! This will cause weeping and wailing and gnashing of teeth. It will go to their very heart when they shall see Moses and Aaron, the prophets, and the holy saints in joy and glory, and shall consider and remember that if they had made use of these means and opportunities of grace, they might have lived in heaven too, whereas now they must be everlastingly tormented in that lake which burns with fire and brimstone without any hope of recovery. "Punished with everlasting destruction, from the presence of the Lord, and from the glory of His power" (2 Thessalonians 1:9).

By the law of Moses, whenever an offender was to receive his strokes, the judge caused him to lie down and to be beaten about the face, and the judge himself was to see it done (Deuteronomy 25:2–3). So when God comes to give the damned their strokes in hell (for hell is the place of execution, wherein he "that knows his master's will and doth it not shall be beaten with many stripes"), He Himself will see them beaten in the presence of all His holy angels; and if this is so, how shameful will their punishment be when there shall be so many thousands of witnesses of it, when they shall be made, as we say, the world's wonder.

These are they who shall rise to everlasting contempt
(Daniel 12:2). So it is said of the damned that "their worm
shall not die, nor their fire be quenched, but they shall be
an abhorrence to all flesh" (Isaiah 66:24). And the holy
angels and saints shall go forth and look upon them; those
proud ones who scorned God's people here shall then be
abhorred and scorned by them.

Add to all this that he is not only banished from the
presence of God for a while, but from all hope of ever seeing God again with comfort. Your estate is endless and
remediless. While you are here in this life, of a Saul you
may become a Paul; and though you are not yet a beloved
son, yet you may come in favor. While you live under the
means of grace, there is yet hope of recovery left to you. It
may be that this sermon will be the means of your conversion. But among all your punishments, this will be one of
the greatest, that thou shall be deprived of all means of
recovery; and this shall be another hell to you in the midst
of hell, to think, "I have heard so many sermons, and yet
have neglected them. I had so many opportunities of
grace, and yet have slighted them." This will make the sinner rage, bite his tongue, and tear himself, to think that
now all means are past. So the first penalty is the penalty of
loss.

2. Penalties of sense follow. By penalties of loss we are
deprived of all the joys and comforts of heaven and earth,
of Mount Zion, shut out of the city of the living God, the
heavenly Jerusalem, deprived of an innumerable company
of saints, of the general assembly and church of the first-
born, of God Himself, the Judge of all, and the souls of the
saints made perfect. This shall make a sinner curse himself.

Now follows the penalty of torments and sense. When
Adam was banished out of paradise, he had the wide
world to walk in still; but it is not so here. You are not only
cast out of heaven, but cast into hell, and are deprived of
your liberty forever. It is said that Christ preached to the

spirits in prison, them who in the days of Noah were disobedient, and for this cause who are now in prison (1 Peter 3:19). Hell is compared to a prison, and a prison indeed it is, and that an odious one.

Look on your companions. If any man were to be kept a close prisoner, it would be a great punishment. But God says, "Go ye cursed, into everlasting fire, prepared for the devil and his angels." To be among such companions is infinitely miserable; there is no one but devils and damned howling spirits, woeful companions! Here the damned spirits, the filthy and cursed host, must be your yokefellows. Suppose there were no torment to suffer; yet to be banished from heaven, and to be tied and yoked to wicked spirits, would be a torment sufficient to make the stoutest man who ever lived to tremble, quake, and soon be weary of it.

But this is a place of torment too, a prison where there is a rack on which you must be put, and on which you must be tormented. "I am tormented in this flame," said Dives. To speak of these torments would afford matter enough for another hour, but I do not delight to dwell on so sad a subject. But this is that which prepares the way for the glad tidings of salvation, therefore I shall insist a little longer on it.

The body and soul, the whole man, shall there be tormented; not the soul only, but even the body too after judgment. Do you think the members of the body, which have been the instruments of sin, shall escape? Shall they be raised and cast into hell to no purpose? Why should God quicken the body at the last day except to break it on the anvil of His wrath and make it accompany the soul as well in torments as in sinning? It is true that the soul is the fountain of all sense, and the body without it has no sense at all; take away the soul and you may burn the body, and it will not feel it. Now the soul is the fountain of sense, and the body is united to it; so when God shall lay His axe at this root, at this fountain, how dreadful shall it be! How shall the body suffer too! Should any of us be cast into a fire, what a terrible torment would we account it! Fire and water, we say, have no mercy; but, alas, this fire is nothing to the fire of hell; it is but as painted fire to that which burns forever and ever.

The furnace wherein Nebuchadnezzar commanded those to be thrown who did not fall down to the graven image which he had set up was doubtless at every time a terrible place to be. Hell is compared to such a furnace; but what shall we think of it when the King in His wrath shall "command the furnace to be heated seven times hotter than usual!" Nay, what shall we think of hell when the King of heaven shall command it to be heated seventy times seven hotter than before; when there shall be a fire, and a fire prepared; for so is this fire of Tophet: it is a pile of much wood! What will we think when the King of heaven shall, as it were, set to work His wisdom to fit it in the sharpest manner, in procuring such ingredients as may make it rage most and be most violent! It is a fire prepared for the devil and his angels, the strongest of creatures, for the punishment of principalities and powers; and if it can master angels, do not think that God has no fire to roast your soul. It is the soul only that is in hell till the day of judgment; the body is not yet there. A man might think that the soul does not suffer, but philosophy tells us that the soul suffers in and by the body. Therefore it is a rule in divinity that whatever God does by means, He can do without means. Though the body is not there, but the soul only, yet God is able, nay, does make the soul as well feel grief without the body, as He does by means of the body.

But now, besides your fellow prisoners in that cursed jail, consider who are your tormentors, you who continue in impenitency. Your tormentors are the devil, yourself, and God Almighty.

The devil, who is your deadly enemy, a bloody-minded

adversary, a murdering and merciless-minded spirit, a murderer from the beginning, a merciless tormentor who, being in plagues and torments, and thereby even at his wits' end, would fain ease himself by tormenting you. When the devil, as we read, was dispossessed of a child wherein he was, he rent and tore him, leaving him foaming, so that there was little hope of life in him. But when a man is delivered into the hands of this merciless spirit, when God shall say to the devil, "Take him, do what you will with him; do your worst to him"; when you shall be thus put into the hands of one who hates you and delights in your ruin, how will he tear you into pieces! How will he torment you! In how desperate and wretched a case will your soul and body be!

But the tormentor within you is far more heavy, painful, and grievous; it is that never dying worm within, the sting of a guilty and wounded conscience. This, like a sharp dagger, is still stabbing you in the very heart. This, by a reflecting act upon itself, will cause you to revenge God's quarrel on yourself. When a musket is fired, it kicks back on the shooter; and so will your conscience most furiously turn on you. This is that which smote David, when it is said, "David's heart smote him." A man needs no other fire, no other worm to torment him, than what is within him. As worms do on a carcass, this gnaws on a wretched soul.

But there is a greater Tormentor than both these, and that is God Himself. He is highly offended and enraged at you, and therefore comes and takes the matter into His own hands, and will Himself be the executioner of His fury. There is a passage to this purpose, which is more than can be spoken by men or angels: "Who shall be punished with everlasting destruction from the presence of the Lord, and from the glory of His power" (2 Thessalonians 1:9). Mark it: God, whom you have so highly provoked to wrath, has a strong hand and glorious power. He showed the glory of His power in making the world, and all things in it; and all that infinite power which He has manifested in the creation of heaven and earth shall be engaged in the torment of a sinner.

Were there a man who should lay a target of brass or a target of steel on a block, and should then cleave all asunder at a single blow, this would sufficiently manifest his strength. Just so God makes manifest His power in crushing you to pieces. There are still new charges and discharges against sinners to make His power therein manifest. "What if God, willing to make His power known, suffered awhile the vessels prepared to destruction?" (Romans 9:22). God will manifest His power by the strength of His stroke on those who rebel against Him. Hence proceeds "weeping, and wailing, and gnashing of teeth," a metaphor taken from one either that has a great coldness on him or from the symptoms of a fever.

Add to all that has been said these two things:

The torment shall be everlasting; you shall desire to die so that your torments may have end. And here you may expect that I should say something of the eternity of the torments of the damned; but I am not able to sufficiently express it, nor is anyone else. It shall continue ten thousand thousand years, and after that a hundred thousand times ten thousand, and yet be no nearer the end than at the first beginning. You must think of it seriously, and pray to God to reveal it to your soul, for no one else sufficiently can.

And as it is everlasting so is it unabateable. If a man were cast into a fire, the fire coming about him would, in a short time, blunt his senses and take away his feeling; and besides, the materials of the fire would soon spend and waste. But it is not so here: there is not the least abatement of the horror, nor the least inch of torment taken away throughout all eternity. It was a poor request of Dives, one would think, that Lazarus would dip the tip of his finger in water and cool his tongue. All he asked for was but one drop of water for the present, which would soon be dried; and yet that is denied him. He can have no abatement of his torment. Nor is there any abatement of your feeling; but you are kept in full strength, and as long as God is God, Tophet shall burn, and just so long you will feel it.

OBJECTION. This is poor preaching indeed! This will frighten a man and make him out of his senses; this is the way to make him go hang himself sooner than be converted!

ANSWER. True, should God let loose the cord of our conscience, it would be just that way; such would be the terrors of it, to make a man find another cord, did not God restrain him. I do not desire by this to hurt you, but to save you. I am not a messenger sent from Abraham, as Dives entreated, but from the God of Abraham, to warn you so that you do not come to that place of torment.

But now, beloved, there is a way to escape this misery, and that is by Jesus Christ. Matthew 1:21 tells us that He was for this end called "Jesus," because "He shall save His people from their sins," and consequently from wrath. How that is done I shall show in a word, and that is by Christ Jesus offered *for* us, and by Christ Jesus offered *to* us.

We may be saved by Christ offered for us. He must die for us, and if there is any death more cursed than another, that death He must die; if there is anything any more painful, that He must suffer. Thus He undertakes your cause, and suffers what was due to you for sin.

And we may be saved by Christ being offered to us. He is offered to us, as we may see in the sacrament, where there are two acts of the minister: the one the breaking of the bread, the other the offering it to the people. You have as good warrant to take Christ offered as you have to take the bread and wine, which you are commanded to receive. Thus I thought it good to add something to sweeten the rest, so that I might show that there is a way to be freed from the bitter pains of eternal death.

9

The Satisfaction of Christ

"Let this mind be in you which was also in Christ Jesus, who, being in the form of God, thought it not robbery to be equal with God, but made Himself of no reputation, and took upon Him the form of a servant, and was made in the likeness of men; and being found in fashion as a man, He humbled Himself and became obedient unto death, even the death of the cross."   Philippians 2:5–8

You have heretofore heard that point of Christian doctrine which concerns the knowledge of our misery and wretched estate by nature. The substance of all is that we are the children of wrath and disobedience, as well as others. You see then in what state every man stands before he has made his peace with God. You see what the Holy Ghost says, "They are the sons of disobedience, and children of wrath, as well as others." I tell you this not to discourage a sinner or drive him to desperation, but because it is fitting that he should know the estate in which he is. If they will try arguing with God, if they oppose Him, the Lord will come with a bar of iron, and will break them in pieces like a potter's vessel. "Those, mine enemies, that will not have Me to reign over them, bring them and slay them before Me."

It is fitting that every man know this, and it is only to awaken us; otherwise, to what purpose do we preach to you? Till the law awakens us, we sleep securely in our sins till the dreadful trumpet of Mount Sinai comes with thundering and lightning. Ephesians 5:14: "Awake thou that sleepest." Unless this awaken us, in what case are we? We are sleeping men who are dreaming (Jude 8). A sleeping sinner will be a dreaming sinner: he never sees things as they are in their proper shape. He thinks, like the church of Laodicea, that he is rich and lacks nothing, when he is really poor, miserable, blind, and naked. He thinks he shall be admitted into heaven as soon as the best, but this is a dream. "As the hungry man dreameth, and behold he eateth, but when he awakes, behold he is empty; or as a thirsty man that dreams he drinketh, but awakes and behold he is faint" (Isaiah 29:8). Thus it is with us: we think we are entering upon the suburbs of heaven, and yet we are but in a dream and are asleep.

Now being thus awakened, consider what you have to do when the dreadful trumpet of the law has awakened you. Consider your state; if you sleep this night, hellfire will be your portion. It would be better for you therefore to awaken yourself before the flames of hellfire awaken you. Consider likewise that you must not be led by yourself; you must renounce your own will. Our states may be pleasing to us, to enjoy in a dream our heart's lusts here on earth; but consider that unless you cross your will here, it shall be crossed hereafter; yea, it shall be the main cross a man shall have in hell (besides the eternal weight of God's wrath) that he can will or desire nothing but he shall be crossed in it—not the least thing he desires but he shall have the contrary. Learn then what a woeful thing it is to be our own lords, to follow our own lusts and pleasures; see what we shall gain by it. We shall never enjoy the least portion of our will in the world to come; if we would have but a drop of cold water, we shall be crossed in it. We shall have the opposite of everything we desire.

Having truly and plainly showed our sinfulness, wretchedness, and cursedness by nature, I come unto the remedy, our redemption by Christ. And God forbid that He should create man, the best of His creatures, for de-

struction! "What gain and profit is there in our blood?"
(Psalm 30:9). God is full of grace and compassion, and He
considers that we are but dust. And happy are we that we
are but dust. Had we been more glorious creatures, like
angels, we would not have had the benefit of a Savior.
When they rebelled, God considered their makeup; and as
with a high hand they rebelled, "so the Lord reserved
them in everlasting chains under darkness unto the judgment of the great day" (Jude 6; 2 Thessalonians 1:9). They
fell without a Redeemer. It is well for us that God considers that we are but dust. By Jesus Christ He saves us from
the wrath to come. It would have been better for us never
to have been born than to be born firebrands of hell.

But the point is that we are "brands plucked out of the
fire" (Zechariah 3:2). It is fitting, therefore, that we should
know who our Redeemer is. It is Jesus Christ, and here
consider that Christ Jesus offered for us for the satisfaction of God's justice, and this is His priestly office.

Also, as there was no remission without shedding of
blood, therefore after the blood is shed and the priest offered Himself, there comes a second thing, or else we
would never be the better. Christ offered Himself to us,
and this makes up our comfort. Many talk of the extent of
Christ's death and passion, saying that He died sufficiently
for us, which is improper. For what comfort would it be
that Christ was offered for us if there were no more? A
bare sufficiency in Christ does not serve the turn; this
would be a cold comfort. Suppose a man who was in debt,
afraid of every sergeant and every sheriff, should be told,
"Sir, there is money enough in the king's account to discharge all your debts." This may be very true, but what
good is that to him? What comfort does he have by it unless the king offers to come and freely assume his debt?
And it would be a cold comfort to us to know that Christ is
sufficient for us unless He invites us to take freely of the
waters of life. But "Ho, every one that thirsteth, come ye

to the waters" (Isaiah 55:1). Thus, unless Christ is offered
to us as well as for us, we are never the better.

Now to make this more clear. observe that in every sacrament there are two acts of the minister. The first one
has relation to God; it is a commemoration of the sacrifice, in which respects the ancient fathers called it a sacrifice. The other is the breaking of bread and pouring out
of wine, wherein there is a commemoration of the broken
body and the shed blood—not as they are concomitants,
the wine in the bread, as the foolish papists dream, for
that would rather be a commemoration of His life, when
the blood runs in the veins, than of His death. The commemoration of Christ's death is made by separation of the
blood from the body, and as there is one act of the minister in consecrating by breaking the body and pouring out
the blood, so there is a second act that is ministerial. When
the minister says, "Take, eat; this is My body," it is as if
Christ were present, saying, "Come, take My body." You
have as free an interest to it as when you are invited to
your friend's table you have a right to the meat before
you. So that as Christ is offered for you, so He is offered to
you. And what now should hinder you, unless you are one
who will obstinately oppose your own salvation, and say, "I
will not have this Man to rule over me." You cannot miscarry. But if you will be your own lord, then you must perish in your infidelity. Here are the keys of the kingdom of
heaven given unto God's ministers, unless you willfully oppose your own salvation and shut the door of salvation
which Christ has opened so wide for you. The ways of God
are plain. Christ has paid a great price for you, and then,
as great as it is, He offers it to you.

Now for the former of these, which is Christ's satisfaction made unto the Father for us, I made choice of this
place of Scripture, which sets it out particularly. Herein
two things are to be observed:

1. The Person who will thus humble Himself: The apos-

tle grounds his exhortation on the fourth verse, where he tells us that we ought not to look every man on his own things, but on the things of others. "Let this mind be in you which was also in Christ Jesus." If Christ had looked only on His own things, He might have saved Himself a great deal of labor and pains. He, being the Son of God, might as soon as He was born have challenged a seat with God in glory, but He passed on to His journey's end in a thorny and troublesome way. Let then the same mind be in you which was also in Christ Jesus, who did not mind His own things, but the good of others.

2. What form He was in when He humbled Himself: "He took upon Him the form of a servant, and was obedient unto the death of the cross." Is this not the deepest humiliation that can be, that He who is above all praise, whom angels adored, that He should be brought from heaven to earth, and not only be a pilgrim there, but have a sorrowful and pitiful pilgrimage, and at last be cut off by a shameful death from the land of the living? This humiliation has no parallel.

The depth of the humiliation consists in the height of the Person thus humbled; and were not He so high, it would have done us no good. It is no small satisfaction that can appease God's wrath; therefore the apostle to the Hebrews, speaking of Melchizedek, the type of Christ, concludes, "How great this man was!"

Consider the invaluable price when you think of how great He was: "Who, being in the form of God. . . ." He who was a fellow, and fellow-like with God, as good as Himself, as great as Himself, was thus humbled. It was the second Person in the Trinity, He and no other, who was thus humbled for you. He was weary for you and reviled for you. He sweated and fainted for you, went hungry for you, and was buffeted for you. It was He, the second Person of the Trinity, in proper speech, without either trope or figure, who shed His blood for you, died for you, and suffered all these things in His assumed nature, taking on Him the form of a servant, though not in His divine nature. He remained God alone, who could not die, but yet He fain would for you.

Therefore He took your nature on Himself that He might die for you in the assumed nature. He did not take on Himself the nature of angels, but the seed of Abraham. He, being the Fountain of Life and the Prince of our life (and without shedding of blood no redemption could be wrought), having no blood to shed as God, therefore took our nature on Him, as we read in Hebrews 10:5, 7: "Sacrifice and offering Thou wouldst not, but a body Thou hast prepared me. Then said I, 'Lo, I come, in the volume of Thy book it is written of Me, to do Thy will, O God.' " It is as if He had said, "Lord, I am not able to accomplish Thy will, or to be subject to Thee in Thy nature; therefore Thou hast made Me a man so that, in the form of a servant, I might show obedience, which I could not while I was in nature equal unto Thee."

Now consider how great this Person is who has suffered all for you. He is "Jesus Christ, who is the faithful witness, the first begotten of the dead, and the prince of the kings of the earth" (Revelation 1:5). To have a great prince bound like a thief, arraigned and executed, the consideration of this state of the person would move a stony heart. "He is the Lord of lords, and King of kings" (Revelation 17:14).

Among men the father is more honorable than the son, and the son is but a servant until he is emancipated; but it is not so in the Trinity. The Father and the Son are both equally honorable. Among men the son has the same specified nature with the father, but is not the same individual; but it is not so in the Trinity. The Father and the Son there have the selfsame individual nature. "I and my Father are one." Therefore there must be an equality. The Pharisees themselves could draw this conclusion, that if He

were the Son of God, He was equal with God. "Therefore
the Jews sought the more to kill Him because he said God
was His Father, making Himself equal with God" (John
5:18).

A man might ask how that could follow: He was but
God's Son, but God's Son must be equal to the Father. In
making Himself God's Son, He made Himself equal with
God. Know this, because by this stands the point of our
redemption. If a pure and holy angel had suffered ever so
much, it would not have availed for our redemption. It is a
price no man or angel could meddle with; it required a
greater price. It was God Himself who suffered in His assumed nature, He and no other person; for we must understand that, though Christ took on Him the nature of a
man, yet not the person of a man.

Here stands the point: the second Person in the Trinity
sustained all this humiliation. And therefore observe that,
when the point of suffering comes, there is a remarkable
speech in Zechariah 13:7. The Father says to the Son that
it was against His heart to smite Him. The expression is a
lively one; it went to His heart to smite one who was His
equal, who did Him no wrong. "Awake, O sword, against
My Shepherd, and against the man who is My fellow." You
know of whom it is spoken by Matthew 26:31: "I will smite
the Shepherd, and the sheep of the flock shall be scat-
tered." The Lord is ready to break Him (Isaiah 53:10). The
sword was, as it were, unwilling to smite "the man that is
My fellow." A blow that lights on God's fellow, equal with
God, of what value it is!

Consider the difference between a man and a man; the
state of a prince makes great odds between what is done
to him and what is done to another man. When David
would venture himself into the battle, "Thou shalt," they
say, "go no more with us, lest they quench the light of Israel" (2 Samuel 21:17), and more fully, "Thou art worth
ten thousand of us" (2 Samuel 18:3). They would not haz-

ard the person of the king in the battle. Why? Because "thou art worth ten thousand of us." The dignity of a prince is so great that ten thousand will not countervail the loss of him.

If this is the esteem and worth of David, what is the worth of David's Prince? If it is thus with a king, what is it with the King of kings and Lord of lords? This is a great ground of the sufficiency of Christ's suffering. "If the blood of bulls and goats sanctify to the purifying of the flesh, how much more shall the blood of Christ, who through the eternal Spirit offered Himself without spot to God, purge your consciences from dead works to serve the living God" (Hebrews 9:13–14)? It is not the offering of the body only, but He did it "through the eternal Spirit."

When the martyrs and saints offered themselves as a sacrifice, they offered it through the flames of their love, and therefore embraced the stake. Love is described as being as strong as death; but Christ did not offer His sacrifice with the flames of His love, though love was in Him, the greatest that ever was, but with the everlasting flames of His godhead and deity, with that fire from heaven which is a consuming fire. He did the deed that will purge our consciences from dead works. "Take heed unto yourselves, and to the flock, over which the Holy Ghost hath made you overseers, to feed the church of God which He hath purchased with His precious blood" (Acts 20:28). God has purchased the Church with His own blood. Whose blood? God's blood. The blood of God must be shed. "He who thought it not robbery to be equal with God" must shed His own blood. "Had they known, they would not have crucified the Lord of glory," that is, they would not have crucified God.

He who was crucified was the glorious Lord God. "Ye denied the Holy One, and killed the Prince of life" (Acts 3:14–15). Here is the matter: unless the Prince of life had been killed, you could not have life. The apostle sets this down as the ground of all before; he comes to the particulars of His humiliation, and sets down who it was who was thus humbled. He, whom the heaven of heavens could not contain, must descend unto the lowermost parts of the earth—that is a descent indeed. His humiliation appears in that He who was thus high became a man, "and being found in fashion as a man, He humbled Himself and became obedient unto death, even the death of the cross."

Consider the point of His humiliation. Some things have regard to the whole course of His life, others to the conclusion or period of His life. All His life, from His incarnation to His passion, was a continual thread of humiliation; from the manger to His cross, from His birth to His tomb. So here is set down the humbled life of our blessed Savior. For I would not have you think His humiliation consisted only in coming to the cross, where they so mercilessly handled Him. It cost Him more than that. As sinners have the curse of God on them in their life as well as in their death, so Christ must have a miserable life as well as an accursed death. Though the heat came at the end of the tragedy, yet His whole life was a continual suffering. Consider the degrees of it:

"He made himself of no reputation." He emptied Himself. It was the second Person in the Trinity who thus humbled and emptied Himself (not in His divine nature, but His assumed) of all His transcendent endowments.

Consider the particulars of it: He "took on Him the form of a servant." Was not this a great humiliation, that the second Person in the Trinity should stoop so low as to take on Himself the nature of one who is not worth looking on; that He should take dust and ashes upon Himself? God's greatness is thus expressed: "Who is like unto the Lord our God, who dwelleth on high, who humbleth Himself to behold the things in heaven and in the earth" (Psalm 113:5–6). What humiliation is that!

Compare these two humiliations. It is a humiliation to

cast but an eye upon the heavens, to look upon the most glorious of all His works, to look upon the angels; "but what is man that Thou so regardest him?" that Thou should not only look upon him, but take him up, and make him an inmate under Thine own roof? This is a greater abasement, but here is a further degree: Christ, during the time of His pilgrimmage, was content to deprive Himself of the glory that He now enjoys. By reason of His hypostatic union with the Godhead, He deserves all honor and glory: "When He brought His first-begotten into the world He saith, 'And let all the angels worship Him" (Hebrews 1:6). Every knee bows to Him who is thus highly exalted.

We see Christ crowned with glory and honor, all dominion and power being made subject unto Him; yet He for thirty-three and a half years was content to be exiled from His Father's court. "Glorify Thou Me with the glory I had with Thee before the world was" (John 17:5), which is expounded in Proverbs, where the wisdom of God was shown before the world was framed: "Then I was by Him, as one brought up with Him; and I was daily His delight, rejoicing always before Him" (Proverbs 8:30). This was the work before the foundation of the world that God was doing: the Father was glorifying the Son, and the Son was glorifying the Father. The Father took infinite delight in the Son, and the Son took infinite delight in the Father, and the Holy Ghost in them both. To be deprived of such a sight and such a glory as this, and for your sake to be banished from that high court, where not to enjoy that fullness of joy was an emptying of Himself—yet all this He did for you.

He did not mind His own things; if He had, He might have presently sat at God's right hand, where is fullness of joy forevermore. But His bowels yearned over us, and so He took upon Himself the form of a servant and was found in the shape of a man, that is, as an ordinary man.

We know what the nature of servitude is. Every man naturally desires liberty; but Christ, that He might make you free, was content to endure a servile estate. Christ, in both respect of God and man, took on Him the form of a servant.

For Him to be God's servant was a humiliation, though for us it is the greatest honor to be God's servants. Paul called himself "Paul, a servant of Jesus Christ." David called himself the servant of the Lord: "O Lord, I am Thy servant, truly I am Thy servant." But it was a humiliation for Christ to become God's servant. For Him "who thought it not robbery to be equal with God" to become God's servant, and to take a nature on Him that allowed Him to say, "My Father is greater than I; behold My Father and I were one, but now that I have taken on Myself a human nature, I am made inferior to my Father. I have become His servant."

God says, "Behold My servant in whom I am well pleased." And He says in Isaiah 53:11, "By this knowledge shall My righteous servant justify many." There is much difference in a free servant and a bondservant. A very bondman Christ made Himself, being man, and accounts it as great honor as may be, not only to be His Father's servant but His bondman. Can I show that there is any such humiliation as this? Look at Hebrews 10:5: "Sacrifice and burnt offerings Thou wouldst not, but a body hast Thou prepared Me." These words have relation to those of the psalmist: "Sacrifice and burnt-offerings Thou didst not desire, but mine ears hast Thou opened" (Psalm 40:6). In the margin it is, "Mine ears hast Thou digged," or "hast Thou bored." The boring of the ear was an expression of lasting servitude. A servant who had not yet had his ear bored might be freed at the year of redemption, the seventh year; but if not, his ear was bored so that he might be a servant forever according to Exodus 21:6. He who loved his service so well as to have his ear bored was a servant forevermore. "Mine ear, Lord, hast Thou bored. I will be

Thy servant forever."

Christ took on Himself the form of such a servant; nay, Christ was more than an ordinary slave. He was one bound to an everlasting slavery, for He was the Son of a hand-maid. Now the children of a handmaid were not to go forth at the year of jubilee. "The wife and her children shall be her master's, and he shall go out by himself" (Exodus 21:4), meaning that he who was the son of a handmaid must be bound. Now Christ was the son of a handmaid, for which we have Mary's own confession: "Be-hold the handmaid of the Lord," and, "He hath looked upon the low estate of His handmaid" (Luke 1:38, 48). Hence David said, "O Lord, I am Thy servant, and the son of thine handmaid" (Psalm 116:16). I am not only Thy servant, but Thy bond-servant. I am he who was born in Thy house; and out of Thy house I will never go." Thus is Christ a servant in respect of God.

But it is not only thus. He is not only a servant in re-gard of God, but He took on Him the form of a servant in respect of men too. Look what relations are between men who have superiority and subjects. Christ, who was born a free child, yet made Himself a servant unto man. He had a reputed father, but a true and a natural mother; from the twelfth year of His age till the thirtieth He went with them, and was subject unto them (Luke 2:51). No apprentice was more subject to his master in his trade than Christ was to His reputed father; he kept Him close to his trade.

Look on Him out of the family, in the commonwealth. He paid tribute. He might have stood on His privileges. He asked, "Of whom do the kings of the earth exact tribute?" And they answered, "Of strangers. Then are the children free." If the son of a temporal prince is free, how much more shall the Son of God be free! But yet "it behooves us to fulfill all righteousness."

He would be a subject unto Ceasar, and in recognition of His subjection He would pay tribute, though He fetched it out of the fish's belly. Hence the apostle tells us, "For this cause you pay tribute to testify your subjection" (Romans 13:6). Neither was Christ only a servant to those who were in some authority, but generally among men He was in the state of a servant. "The Son of man came not to be ministered unto, but to minister, and to give His life a ransom for many" (Matthew 20:28). Not to be a master to command, and have others to attend Him; but He came to be a servant.

See in what esteem He was had. We account a slave one step above a beast; for liberty is that whereby a man breathes, and a man were better off dead than to have his liberty taken from him. So Christ was not only a bondman in regard of His Father, but in regard of men. In the estimation of men He was vilified as a bondman; and that will appear by the price for which He was sold. It was thirty pieces of silver. To consider what the price was is a considerable part of His passion. There is a prophecy cited out of Jeremiah in your books, but it is Zechariah, though I have seen some copies that mentioned neither, but only, "according to the words of the prophet." The quote is, "Cast it unto the potter, a goodly price that I was priced at of them" (Zechariah 11:13). He speaks it with disdain: "And I took the thirty pieces of silver, and cast them to the potter in the house of the Lord." There is a parallel passage which will expound it clearly: "If an ox shall push a man servant or a maid servant that he die, the owner of the ox shall give to the master of the servant thirty shekels of silver, and the ox shall be stoned" (Exodus 21:32). It was the very price that was paid for a slave, thirty shekels. Such a base estimation they had of Christ, as if He were a bondman; the same price that was given for a slave that was killed by an ox, for this same price was He sold. In the second book of Josephus, chapter 12, when Ptolemy Philadelphus would redeem all the Jews who were bondmen, it was set down what he paid for a slave. There is set down a great sum of money, and the number of the slaves. Here stands the valuation, divide the number of drachmas by the number of slaves, and you shall find the quotient for every man 120 drachmas; four drachmas make a shekel, thirty shekels was the ordinary rate cried in the market for the price of a bondman.

Thus Christ took on Himself the form of a bondman, not only God's bondman, but in the estimation of men so despicable that they valued Him at no higher rate than thirty pieces of silver. This is but the beginning and entrance on Christ's humiliation, to be made in the similitude of sinful flesh, and in the verity of true flesh. Christ had all infirmities, such as weariness, hunger, thirst, which follow a sinful man, which were not sinful; such a nature He took upon Himself, and then He became obedient by both active and passive obedience. That which remains of the pains of His life to the passage of His doleful death we will speak of in the next sermon.

10

The Humiliation of Christ

"And being found in fashion as a man, He humbled Himself and became obedient unto death, even the death of the cross." Philippians 2:8

In these words, and those that went before, there is delivered unto us the point of the humiliation of the Son of God. It stands in this:

He took upon Himself the form of a servant, and was made in the likeness of man. God the Son, the second Person in the Trinity, assumed our dust and ashes unto the unity of His own sacred Person.

This human nature being thus assumed, He was content to deprive Himself for a long time of that beatific vision, which He might have still enjoyed, and in that time was as obedient as the meanest and poorest servant of His Father. Nor was He only actively obedient, but passively obedient. He was obedient unto death. He was content to lay down His life for our redemption. And it was not every death that would serve the turn, but it must be the death of the cross, the most accursed, shameful, and painful death; that death which was most suitable and best able to answer the wrath of God.

He humbled Himself by taking our nature upon Himself: He who thought it not robbery to be equal with God took upon Himself the form of a man. If it were an abasement for God to look upon heaven, the most glorious of His works, how much more to take upon Him a clod or piece of this earth, and unite it to His own sacred person forever. This was a descending indeed. He descended first that He might ascend. "Now that He ascended, what is it but that He also descended first into the lower parts of the earth?" (Ephesians 4:9). That is, He descended into the womb of the virgin; and it was a great abasement indeed for Him thus to descend. Wherefore the psalmist, speaking of the wonderful framing of the babe in the womb, says, "My substance was not hid from Thee when I was made in secret, and curiously wrought in the lowest parts of the earth" (Psalm 139:15).

So we see that God descended into the lowermost parts of the earth, and there was He fashioned. It was a great humiliation for Him! Thus did He humble Himself in taking our nature. Had He taken the form of a king upon Himself, it would have been a great humiliation; how much more when He took on Him the form of a servant! He came not in state to be ministered unto, but to minister. Nor was He only His Father's servant, but a servant of servants, and therein underwent Canaan's curse: "A servant of servants shalt Thou be." Our Savior became such a servant, He who was the author of freedom. "If the Son make you free, then are you free indeed" (John 8:36). He who was the King's Son, and so the most free, the Author of it to all who enjoy any spiritual freedom, became a servant so that we who were servants might be made free.

But besides this, it is added here that He humbled Himself. Having taken on Himself the form of a servant, He humbled Himself. And here we may observe what made the suffering of our Savior so meritorious; it was because it was active, free, and voluntary. Our passions are contrary to our will. We are drawn to it, as it is said of Peter: "When thou art old, they shall lead thee whither thou wouldst not" (John 21:18). Peter died the same death our Savior died, according to the external passions; but they led him where he would not have chosen to go. Our Savior was an actor in it; humbling Himself. God does not re-

gard so much a bare suffering, but when it is done willingly, and in obedience to God, He does.

And as He was obedient in His death, so also in His
other passions. In the gospel, according to John 10:17,
whereas in John 11:33 the text reads, "He was troubled,"
the marginal note has it, "He troubled Himself." He was
the author of his own sufferings. He was not humbled as a
mere sufferer; but He humbled Himself, and so it is said in
Scripture often, "He gave Himself for us." In all His passive
obedience He had an eye to do the will of God. The merit
of His passive obedience arises from a mixture with His
active. His humbling was a great part of His priesthood.
And how did He take His priesthood upon Him? It was by
His Father's call. He was called to it, as was Aaron. "No
man," said the apostle, "taketh this honor upon him, but
he that is called" (Hebrews 5:4). Now Christ, being called
to it, did it to follow His call. And thus He did it actively; it
was not a bare suffering as those in hell suffer, but according to His Father's call. Observe that passage taken out of
the psalms: "I am come to do Thy will, O God" (Hebrews
10:9). What! Was it only in His active obedience? No, it was
God's will that He should suffer; as the words in verse 10
import: "By the which will we are sanctified, and by the
body of Jesus Christ once offered."

So Christ offered Himself up to do His Father's will, so
that His passive obedience was in His active obedience. So
John 10:17: "Therefore doth My Father love Me, because I
lay down My life that I may take it up again; no man taketh
it from Me, but I lay it down." When our Savior laid down
His life, He put it off, as a man who puts off his coat lays it
from him. They wondered that He was dead so soon, but
it was because He Himself laid down His life. His soul was
not dragged or forced out of His body. It was not only
passive, but active obedience. "No man taketh it from Me.
I have power to lay it down, and I have power to take it up.
This had I from My Father."

They are grossly deceived then who say that Christ's active obedience was not free and voluntary because He was commanded; for as well may they say that His passive obedience is not voluntary, and so not meritorious, because it likewise was commanded, which none can deny. Thus Christ's offering was a freewill offering, though it was a most bitter one; yet this being a part of His Father's will, He went as voluntarily to the pains of the cross as you do to your dinner when you are thoroughly hungry. For His meat and drink was to do His Father's will (John 4:34). And what makes it of such worth and efficacy is that He did it willingly.

See it in the type that went before Him, Isaac. Isaac was grown up; he was no babe. He was able to carry enough wood to burn himself when he went to be sacrificed, and therefore surely he had strength. If Isaac had pleased, he might have run away from the old man, his father; yet he allowed himself to be bound and laid upon the wood—a true type of our Savior. His also was a freewill offering, and so a sweet-smelling sacrifice unto God. As the highest active obedience, it presently pacified the wrath of His Father. "He humbled Himself and became obedient." This obedience of our Savior is the matter and ground of our justification. "As by the offense of one judgment came on all unto condemnation; so by the righteousness of one, the free gift came on all to justification of life" (Romans 5:18). By the obedience of this blessed Savior many are made righteous.

Our Savior's obedience was both active and passive.

His active was that whereby He did all the will of His Father. The reason why He came into the world, if we look at the place before alleged, will appear: "Wherefore, when He cometh into the world, He saith, 'Sacrifice and burnt offerings Thou wouldst not have, but a body hast Thou prepared Me. In burnt offerings and sacrifices for sin Thou hast no pleasure.' Then said I, 'Behold I come, in the volume of Thy book it is written of Me that I should do Thy will, O God' " (Hebrews 10:5). When He came into the world He said, "Lo, I come." For what purpose? "To do Thy will, O God." The reason why He came into the world was that He might be obedient unto His Father. "Thus it behoveth us," He said to John, "to fulfill all righteousness." John wondered that He who was pure and spotless should come to him to be baptized. He knew baptism presupposed some sin or blot, some stain or corruption to be washed off, and therefore it is said that "there came unto him all the land of Judea to be baptized, confessing their sins" (Mark 1:5). And surely, if one should come to John and say that he had no sin, and yet desired to be baptized by him, he had no right to baptism. Yet our Savior said, "Let it alone; let it be so, that we may fulfill all righteousness." In other words, "I have no need of it in regard of Myself, but I have taken upon Me the form of a servant; and therefore, what the lowest of them must do, that must I do. Therefore was I circumcised, and therefore am I baptized. I did not come to destroy the law, but to fulfill it." And He fulfilled it to the utmost in both His active and passive obedience.

His active obedience had a double consummation. First, He was actively obedient in the whole course of His life. "I have glorified Thy name, and finished the work that Thou gavest me to do." Would you know what it is to glorify God in this world? It is to finish the work that He gave you to do. Are you a minister? If you would glorify God, finish the work He gave you to do. Then you may say, "Glorify Thou me with Thy glory."

But Christ's work was not all ended when He said that He had finished it; the greatest part was behind, to wit, His passive obedience. All the works of His life were done (of which actions, there Christ is to be understood); but then came His passion, and that being finished, there is something to do yet after that, for He was to rise again for our justification. But as far as the oblation of the sacrifice, it was fully furnished. If we look upon our blessed Savior in the whole course of His life, though He lived in a whole world of sin, yet He was free from all manner of sin, and He was enriched with all manner of good works, graces, and virtue. Christ had both of these. He was free from any spot of sin, though in the midst of a wicked world, and there was nothing in Him that could expose Him to any temptations. He was continually assaulted, and yet He was spotless. The prince of the world came, and yet he found nothing in Him. Satan could find nothing in Him whereon to fasten any temptation. "Such a priest it became us to have, who was holy and harmless, undefiled, separate from sinners" (Hebrews 7:26).

There is the purity of His nature: He is holy and, in His carriage, harmless. He did no man harm. He was undefiled, a pure and innocent Lamb, a Lamb without blemish, separate from sinners, and could not contract any guilt of sin. Though He conversed with publicans and sinners at the table, yet they could not infect Him. "He did no sin, neither was guile found in Him" (1 Peter 2:22). Therefore we see, when it came to the point that the devil tried to tempt Him, yet he said, "What have I to do with Thee, Thou Holy One of God?" He was forced to acknowledge Him to be so.

And so if we look at where He says, "I do the will of My Father always," there likewise He shows Himself to be the Holy One of God. In a word, as He was thus obedient unto God, so was He subject to men too—to His father in the family and to Caesar in the commonwealth. As He taught, He did; subjection towards governors was His doctrine, and rather than not pay tribute, He simply took it out of the fish to show a recognition of His subjection unto higher powers. The text tells us, "He went about doing good." And it was said of Him, "This man hath done all things well." In the end, when all the quarrels and accusations were brought against Him, they could bring nothing that could hold water. He was able to boldly challenge them all, as it were, "Which of you can accuse me of sin?" It was as if He had said, "You who pick so many holes in My coat, come forth; do not spare Me, accuse Me." Yet in the end He was accounted a just man.

Judas himself could acknowledge Him to be blameless, and that he had sinned in betraying His innocent blood. Pilate's wife could say to her husband, "Have thou nothing to do with that just man." Pilate himself washed his hands, and would be free from the blood of that innocent person. The thief crucified with Him acquitted Him. His whole life was a perfect obedience to the law of God. "Christ is the end of the law, that the righteousness of the law might be fulfilled in us"; not by us, for we are not able to fulfill the law, but in us. Christ did it for us, and the Father is more pleased with the thirty-three year's hearty obedience of His Son than if Adam and all his posterity had been obedient throughout the whole course of the world, so acceptable was Christ's obedience to God.

His passive obedience was His suffering. If our Savior will be a sacrifice, He must be used like one. He must be slain if He will make satisfaction to His Father for us. He must, for our eating sour grapes, have His own teeth set on edge. Consider His humiliation both in life and death. If we look on the service of Jacob, under his uncle Laban, his service was a hard service. Fourteen years he served; the drought consumed him by day and the frost by night, and the sleep departed from his eyes; twenty year's hard service, fourteen years for his two wives and six years for his cattle (Genesis 31:41). Our Savior spent thirty-three years in hard service; and often did the sleep depart from His eyes. Jacob's days were few, but as few as they were, they were one hundred and thirty years; but if we look upon our Savior's days, they were scarcely a quarter so many.

A part of our Savior's humiliation is that He was cut off in the midst of His days. If we look into the psalms we shall find it a curse on the "bloody and deceitful man, that he shall not live out half his days." The lively part of a man's age is "threescore years and ten" (Psalm 90:10). Half of this is thirty-five years; and our Savior was taken off before thirty-five had expired. He was to take on Him all the curses due to sinners, to the bloody and deceitful man. He was cut off and cropped off in the midst of His vigor. He who was that Melchizedek, who has neither beginning nor end of days, was cut off like a branch, lopped off as a twig from the land of the living (Isaiah 53). He was pulled out so that His days were few, far fewer than Jacob's. He was not allowed to live out half His days. Yet if we look on His days, they were evil too; evil enough as few as they were; that is, full of trouble, and full of misery: from His first coming into the world to His last going out.

Look at His coming forth into the world. Though His mother was in her own city, yet He was so despicable that there was not room for them in the inn. Our Savior, who would, one would think, have been brought into a stately palace, was fain to have His lodging among the beasts, and a trough for His cradle. When the wise men came to worship Him, they found Him in no better case; and what a disgrace was it that, instead of a palace, the kings of the east should find our Savior in a feeding trough!

And when the eight days were over after His birth, He must be circumcised and give the first payment or earnest of His blood. After the eight days were over, then came the forty days, when He was carried on a long journey to be offered up to the Lord, and His mother, as if she had brought an unclean and impure thing into the world, must be cleansed and purified. Then she came to offer a sacrifice according to the law of the Lord, "a pair of turtle doves, or two young pigeons" (Luke 2:24). But was this the law? It would be good if the law were looked into, so see

Leviticus 12:8. The law was this: "She shall bring a lamb, or if she be not able to bring a lamb, then two turtle doves or two young pigeons." The text reads, "If she be not able," but the original is, "If her hand cannot reach to a lamb," if she is so poor that she cannot offer a lamb. It is as if the text had said, "Alas, poor woman! All she had was not able to reach to a lamb, so poor she was." Doubtless her heart was as large as another's, but she was not able to offer a lamb, and is therefore content with two turtle doves.

Hence we may conceive in what state our Savior lived till He came into the ministry. He lived, no doubt, in a poor house; and He must have gone hungry many times, if His mother was not worth a lamb. All that they had must be by hard labor.

Now our Savior, notwithstanding after He had traveled that weary journey to Jerusalem, must return again and be subject to His parents. But how? Even as a servant in his trade. They had no bread to spare, but only what was gotten by hard, laborious work at His father's trade; for it is said of him, "Is not this the carpenter?" It is put in the nominative case, "the carpenter" (Mark 6:3). And whereas this is cast as a curse on our first parents and their seed, that in the sweat of their brows they should eat their bread (Genesis 3:19), our Savior must undergo this curse too. He must work hard for His living; with His own hands He must get a living for Himself and His poor mother, by a laborious trade. No wonder if He went many a morning without His breakfast, who lived in so poor a house and made his living by so poor a trade.

If we come to the time He lived after He came from His father and mother, that same three years when He showed Himself more publicly in the world, we shall find Him subject to those dangers, difficulties, and distresses that accompany evil days. He was a pilgrim and had no abode. "The foxes have holes, and the birds of the air nests, but the Son of man has not where to lay His head."

He was a diligent preacher of the gospel, although He had neither prebend nor parsonage. He had nothing of His own, but was relieved often by the charity of certain devout and religious women.

Besides this, all the reproaches that could be cast on a man were laid on Him. "This man is a wine-bibber and a glutton, a friend of publicans and sinners." And again, "Do we not say well, thou art a Samaritan?" that is, a heretic. He cast out devils; and therein they did not deny that He did good. But see the villainy of it in that they said it was by the help of Beelzebub. Mark 15:3: "They accused Him of many things." Few things are expressed, yet a great many are comprehended in these words. Those that are expressed are heinous and notorious crimes. First, against the first table of the law, they accused Him of blasphemy, and therefore condemned Him in the ecclesiastical court: "Do you hear His blasphemy?" they said.

Then, against the second table of the law, they posted Him to the civil court, and there they lay to His charge high treason against Caesar: "For he that maketh himself a king is an enemy unto Caesar." And yet the innocent Lamb, for all this, did not open His mouth, insomuch that Pilate wondered that He did not speak a word in His own defense. But the reason was because He came to suffer, and to have all these slanders and reproaches put upon Him, not to excuse Himself.

He led a life subject to dangers; when He went among His own people to preach the acceptable year of the Lord, they brought Him to a high hill, to the brow thereof, to cast Him down and break His neck. Others threatened to kill Him too. The devil followed Him with temptations, even to idolatry itself. The devil himself tempted Him for forty days and then left Him (Matthew 4:11), not as if he would return and tempt Him no more, but as Luke renders it, "The devil left him for a season." He intended to leave Him, but to come and try Him again.

The scribes and Pharisees tempted Him too, and tried Him with hard questions that, if He could not answer, they would proclaim Him an insufficient man, and all the people would have laughed Him to scorn. Nor was this just during His ministry. All His life was, as it were, paved with temptations; every step was, as it were, a trap to ensnare Him.

Add to all this that He was not like us. He knew when and by what death He would die. He knew in all the time of His suffering what He should suffer, and what should come upon Him at His death. If any of us should know that he must die a cursed, shameful, and painful death, and knew when it should be, it would mar all our mirth and put us to grief in the midst of our pleasures. Our Savior, in the midst of all His joy on earth, said, "I have a baptism to be baptized with." He knew the cruel death that He would suffer on the cross. And how He was pained till it was accomplished. The pain of it ran through all His life, and made His whole life uncomfortable to Him. In John 12:23, a little before the Passover, He said, "The hour is come that the Son of man shall be glorified." And then, verse 27: "Now is My soul troubled, and what shall I say? Father, save Me from this hour." When the time was drawing nigh, some five or six days before, the consideration of it troubled Him, though He knew He would be glorified, yet the fright of it enwrapped Him with fear. Such a kind of life did our Savior lead; few but evil were His days. As evil as few, He had no comfort in them.

We now come to the point of His death, the last thing; and those things that touched Him therein were the curse, shame, and pain of it. If there were any death more accursed, He must die that death; if any death more shameful or more painful than another, He must die that. All these concur in the death our Savior suffered on the cross. It was the most accursed, most shameful, and most painful death that could be devised.

As to the accursedness of it, there was no death that had a more peculiar curse on it than this one. All deaths are accursed when they light on one who is without Christ; but this death had a legal curse, for as there was a legal uncleanness, so there was a legal curse, and this was the curse annexed to the cross, a type of that real curse. Now the type of a real curse was hanging on the tree: "Thou shalt bury him that day, for he that is hanged on a tree is accursed by God" (Deuteronomy 21:23). So the Son of God was made a curse for us, alluding to Galatians 3:13. And here we see the blessed Son of God, He in whom all the nations of the earth are blessed, the Fountain of all blessedness. We see Him standing in so cursed a condition to be made, as it were, as an anathema, the highest degree of cursing that may be.

Consider also the shame of this death. There is a place in the best of orators that expresses the detestableness and shame of this death of the cross. It is hardly to be expressed in English; but you may see what a gradation there is: "It is a great fault to bind a citizen of Rome and a gentleman; but what is it to beat him? What is it to crucify him?" His eloquence failed him there, as being not able to express the detestableness of it; and therefore the chief captain was afraid because he had bound Paul, after he had heard he was a free man of Rome. It was worse to beat him; but what was it to crucify him? Our blessed Savior went through all these indignities. First they came against Him with swords and with staves, as against a thief. They sold Him for a base price. They beat Him with rods, pricked Him, and after all, they crucified Him.

Consider then the shame of it. He who was to be crucified was stripped naked. And was not this a shame, to be stripped before thousands? It was a custom among the Romans that the greatest king, if he were baptized, was to be stripped naked, which they did as a memorial of the shame of our Savior. So shameful a thing it was that they thought Him unworthy to suffer within the walls. Christ, that He might sanctify the people, suffered without the walls. Let us go with Him out of the camp bearing our reproach. He was as a man unfit to suffer within the walls. Pilate thought he would meet with them when they were so violent to have Him crucified, and therefore he joined Barabbas with Him, the vilest thief in the country, and a murderer as well. Peter later cast this in their teeth, that they preferred a murderer before Him. He was reckoned with the transgressors, as was prophesied of Him in Isaiah 53:12. They crucified Him between two thieves, as if He had been the captain of them.

Also, consider the pain of the cross. "Whom God raised up, having loosed the sorrows of death." This does not mean that there were sorrows that Christ endured after His death, but that sorrows accompanied His death. It was the most dolorous death that ever could be endured. We scarcely know what crucifying is. The Christian emperors, in honor of our Savior, banished that kind of suffering so that none after Him might suffer it; but it is fitting that we should know what it was, since it was so terrible. And here, as the apostle said to the Galatians, "suppose you see Christ crucified before your face at present."

First, there was a long beam on which the party was to be stretched; and there was a crossbeam on which the hands were to be stretched. They pulled them up on the cross before they fastened them; they pulled him to his utmost length. And this is what the Psalmist speaks of in Psalm 22:17: "You might tell all my bones." His ribs were so stretched that they even pierced the flesh. Conceive of Christ now thus stretched with His hands and feet nailed to the wood; the stretching of Christ on the cross was such a thing as being stretched on the rack. Imagine Him before your eyes thus represented. Your sins crucified Him. Being thus stretched upon the cross to His full length, the hands and the feet were fastened and nailed to the wood.

It is no small torment to have the hands bored, especially if we behold the place; it was through the lower part of the hand where the veins and sinews all meet together. It is a place that is full of sense; consider the size of the nails. "They have digged my hands" (Psalm 22:16), to show the size of the spikes; for the original renders it, "They digged him." Do not believe the painters. Our Savior had four nails, not one through both feet as they describe it, but two through His hands and two through His feet. And that you may the better comprehend it, you must know that toward the lower part of the cross, there went along a ledge or threshold whereto His feet were nailed, otherwise the flesh would have rent by reason of the nails, if He had hung by the hands alone.

Then comes the lifting up: "As the serpent was lifted up, so must Christ be lifted." When a man is stretched to the full length, and should be with a jerk put up; it is like a strappado, as it were, the unjointing of a man; and this is what the Psalmist speaks of, "All my bones are out of joint." Consider how long a time it was. Mark says, "It was the third hour, and they crucified Him" (15:25). In John, it is the sixth hour; but the ancient and best copies have the third hour. "The ninth hour He gave up the ghost," so that for six long hours our Savior hung upon the cross.

It was not with Him as with other men, in whom extremity of pains disannuls sense and blunts pain, because they do not have perfect apprehension; but Christ was in His perfect sense all the while. All that the Jews could do could not take away His life from Him till He was ready to give it up. And therefore it is said in Mark that "immediately before He gave up the ghost, He cried with a loud voice." Others at that time are so weak that they can scarcely be heard to groan; but never was Christ stronger, nor ever cried louder, than when He gave up the ghost (Mark 15:34). This of itself made the centurion, as soon as he heard it, conclude, "Certainly this man was the Son of

God." How does he gather this from His crying? Because for a man to be in his full strength, and cry out so strongly, and immediately to give up the ghost, is a great miracle. Therefore, "Truly this man was the Son of God." This adds unto the greatness of His torment, that He had His full and perfect sense; that He was six full hours thus on the rack, and the extremity of pain did not take away His sense. He was as strong at the last as He was at the first.

These things seriously weighed, oh, how they aggravate the depth of His humiliation! Seriously weigh them: they are miserable and lamentable matters; yet in these lie our comfort. Through these words is there a passage opened for us into the kingdom of heaven. When He had overcome the terrors of death, He opened the kingdom of heaven to all believers. These were now but the external sufferings that belonged to man for his sins. But Christ suffered not only bodily sufferings, but sufferings in soul, and that He did in a most unknown and incomprehensible manner.

QUESTION. But some may ask, "Did Christ suffer the pains and torments of hell?"

ANSWER. No, He suffered those things that such an innocent Lamb might suffer, but He could not suffer the pains of hell. The reason is because one thing that makes hell to be hell is the gnawing worms of an accusing conscience. Christ had no such worm. He had so clear a conscience that He could not be stung with any such evil. Another great torment in hell is desperation arising from the apprehension of the perpetuity of their torments, which makes them curse and blaspheme God, and carry an inexpressible hatred against Him. But Christ could not do so. He could not hate God. God forbid that Christ should be liable to these passions.

But it is certain that God the Father made an immediate impression of pains upon His soul. His soul immediately suffered. Look on Him in the garden, He was not yet touched nor troubled by men, and yet He fell in a sweat. Consider the season of the year; this was when they who were within doors were glad to keep close by the fire. He thus sweat in the garden when others felt cold within. This alone was much, but to sweat blood—thick blood, clotted, congealed blood (for so the words imply), not like that in His veins; and yet it came through His garments, and fell to the ground—this is a thing not to be comprehended.

Our blessed Savior's encountering His Father, He fell a-trembling and was overwhelmed, as it were, with the wrath. He beseeched God intensively: "Father, if it be possible, let this cup pass from Me." He cried, "My God, My God, why hast Thou forsaken Me?" He was content to be forsaken for a time that you might not be forsaken everlastingly.

This was no faint prayer. In the psalm it says, "He cried out unto God." Hebrews 5:7 says, "Who in the days of His flesh, when He had offered up prayers and supplications with strong crying and tears." He cried to the Almighty. He made God's own heart to pity. He was ready to break Him (Isaiah 53), yet He sent an angel to support and comfort Him. In Psalm 22, those strong cries are expressed with a more forcible word: "My God, my God, why hast Thou forsaken me? Why art Thou so far from helping me, and from the words of my roaring?" Consider how it was with Christ before any earthly hand had touched Him, when He sought God for His life; this shows the wonderful suffering of Christ.

And regarding that question, "Why hast Thou forsaken Me?" consider that it was not with Christ as with the fathers. They suffered a great deal of punishment and would not be delivered, yet Christ was more courageous than them all. He had a spirit of fortitude. He was anointed above His fellows, and yet He quivers. "Our fathers cried unto Thee; they trusted in Thee, and were not consumed.

They were delivered; but I am a worm, and no man." It is as if He had said, "I can find no shadow of comfort. Lord, why art Thou so angry with me?" This speech did not come from the upper part of the soul, the seat of reason, but from the lower part, the seat of passion. The words "My God, my God" were not words of desperation. He held fast to God. The words "Why hast Thou forsaken Me?" are words of sense; thus you see the price is paid, and what a bitter thing sin is. God will not suffer His justice to be swallowed up by mercy. It must be satisfied; and our Savior, if He will be a Mediator, must make payment to the uttermost farthing.

Consider what a time this was when our Savior suffered. The sun withdrew her beams; the earth shook and trembled. What ails you, O sun, to be darkened, and you, O earth, to tremble? Was it not to show its mourning for the death of its Maker? The soul of Christ was dark within, and it is fitting that all the world should be dressed in black for the death of the King of kings.

But when He came to deliver up His life and to give up the ghost, the veil of the temple rent in twain, and that was the ninth hour, which in the Acts is called the hour of prayer. It was at three o'clock in the afternoon. Hence it is said, "Let the lifting up of my hands be as the evening sacrifice." The priest was killing the lamb at that time; there was a veil that severed the holy of holies, it was between the place of oblations and the holy of holies, which signifies the kingdom of heaven. As soon as Christ died, the veil rent and heaven was open; the priest saw that which was before hidden. Our Savior, said the apostle, entered through the veil of the flesh into His Father; and it was fitting that the veil should give place when Christ came to enter. But what became of Christ's soul then? His soul and body were pulled asunder, and through the veil of His flesh, as it were, with blood about His ears, He entered the holy of holies unto God, saying, "Lord, here am I in My blood." And here is blood that speaks better things than the blood of Abel, that cries for vengeance, this for blessing and expiation of our sins.

11

The Sacrifice of Christ

"But as many as received Him, to them gave He power to
become the sons of God, even to them that
believe on His name." John 1:12

Having heretofore declared unto you the woeful estate
and condition wherein we stand by nature, I proceeded to
the remedy that God, of His infinite mercy, has provided
for the recovery of miserable sinners from the wrath to
come. And therein I proposed that our Savior was to advance us and raise us out of this condition when we had
lost ourselves in Adam. We had eaten sour grapes, but He
had His teeth set on edge. We accounted Him smitten of
God and buffeted; but we had sinned, and yet He was
beaten. Then, when the Lord in His wrath was ready to
smite us, Christ underwent the dint of God's sword, and
stood between the blow and us; the blow lighted on Him
who was equal with God, and did not deserve to be
beaten. "Awake, O sword, against My Shepherd, and
against the man that is My fellow." The sword was unwilling to strike Him; and thus being smitten, He became a
propitiation for our sins. "The chastisement of our peace
fell upon him." He offered Himself as a sacrifice.

There are two things considerable: how Christ was offered for us, and how He is offered to us.

First, He is offered for us, and so He offered Himself
up as a sweet-smelling sacrifice to God. He was not only
the sacrifice, but the Sacrificer. "He offered up Himself,"
said the apostle. He was the Priest, and it was a part of His

priesthood to offer up Himself. The sacrifices in the old law that typified Him were only sufferers. The poor beasts were only passive; but our Savior was an actor in the business. He was active in all that He suffered. He did it in obedience to His Father's will, yet He was an agent in all His passion. "He groaned in spirit, and was troubled" (John 11:33). The Greek is as it is in the margin: "He troubled Himself."

With us in our passions it is otherwise; we are mere sufferers. Our Savior was a conqueror over all His passions, and therefore, unless He would trouble Himself, no one else could trouble Him; unless He would lay down His life, none could take it from Him; unless He would give His cheek to be smitten, the Jews had no power to smite it. "I gave my back to the smiters, and my cheek to them that plucked off the hair, and hid not my face from shame and spitting" (Isaiah 50:6). In all these we should consider our Savior not as a sacrifice only, but as the Sacrificer also, as an actor in all this business. Their wicked hands were not more ready to smite than He was to give His face to be smitten—and all to show that it was a voluntary sacrifice. He did it all Himself. "He humbled Himself unto death." And now, by all this, we see what we have gotten: we have gotten a remedy and satisfaction for our sins. That precious blood of that immaculate Lamb takes away the sins of the world because it is the blood of the Lamb of God, under which else the world would have eternally groaned.

QUESTION. But does this Lamb of God take away all the sins of the world?

ANSWER. It does not actually take away all the sins of the world, but virtually. It has the power to do it, if it is rightly applied; the sacrifice has such virtue in it that if all the world would take it and apply it, it would satisfy for the sins of the whole world. But it is here as with medicines: they do not help because they are prepared, but because they are applied. In Exodus 39:38 there is mention made of a golden altar. Christ is this golden altar, to show that His blood is most precious: "We are not redeemed with silver and gold, but with the precious blood of Jesus Christ." He is that golden altar mentioned in Revelation that stands before the throne. He was likewise to be a brazen altar; for so much was to be put upon Him that, unless He were made of brass and had infinite strength, He would have sunk under the burden.

In his passion Job uses this metaphor: "Is my strength the strength of stones? Or is my flesh of brass?" (Job 6:12). If Christ's flesh had not been brass, if He had not been this brazen altar, He could never have gone through these. But He is prepared for us as a sacrifice for sin. "For what the law could not do, in that it was weak through the flesh, God sending His own Son in the likeness of sinful flesh, and for sin . . ." (Romans 8:3). "For sin" has no reference to "condemned." To condemn sin for sin does not make good sense; but the words depend on this: "God sent His Son," that is, God sent His Son to be a sacrifice for sin, which is how the word is translated in Hebrews 10:6: "a sacrifice for sin." It is impossible the law should save us; not because of any transgression or failing in the law, but because our weakness is such that we could not perform the conditions; therefore God was not tied to promises. By reason, then, of the weakness of our flesh, rather than that we should perish, "God sent His own Son in the likeness of sinful flesh, and in that flesh of His, condemned all our sins."

We need not look that sin should be condemned in us. When He bore our sins on the tree, then were our sins condemned. Therefore Isaiah 53:10 says, "When He had made His soul an offering for sin." In the original it is "when He had made His soul sin," then He "saw his seed."

We come now to the second thing. If Christ is offered for us, unless He offers Himself to us, unless any man has an interest in Him, it is worth nothing. Here then stands the mystery of the gospel. When Christ offers Himself to us, He does not find a wit in us that is to be respected— nothing. And that is the ground of all the disturbance to ignorant consciences; for there is naturally in men pride and ignorance. They think they may not meddle with Christ, with God's mercy, unless they bring something of their own to lay down. This is to buy Christ, to barter between Christ and the soul. But salvation is the free gift of God. As the apostle says, Christ is freely given unto you when you had nothing of worth in you. When faith comes, it empties you of all that is in you. To whom is the gospel preached? To the dead. Now before Christ quickens you, you are stark dead, rotting in your sins. Here is the point then: when there is no manner of goodness in you in the world; when you realize that you have been the most outrageous sinner, then you may lay hold of Christ. Christ then comes and offers Himself to you.

Now when Christ offers, the other part of the relationship is that we may take. We have an interest to accept what He offers. Take this for an example: if someone gives me a million pounds and I do not receive it, I am never the richer; and so if God offers me His Son, and with Him all things, I am none the better if I do not receive Him. That He is born and given, what is that to me, unless we can say, "To me a child is born, to me a Son is given"? Faith comes with a naked hand to receive that which is given; we must empty ourselves of what is in us.

Consider your estate. The Lord sets down how it is with us when He comes to look upon us: "And when I passed by thee and saw thee polluted in thy blood, I said unto thee, when thou wert in thy blood, 'Live' " (Ezekiel 16:6). This is set down to show how God finds nothing in us when He comes to show mercy. He finds nothing in us that is lovely when He comes to bestow His Son upon us. For it is said that Christ loved us, and washed us from our sins in His own blood (Revelation 1:5). He first casts His love upon us when we are unwashed (and, I may say, unblessed): "When no eye pitied thee, and thou wast cast out in the open field; when thou wast in thy blood, I said unto thee, 'Live.' " Then He comes to make up the match: "Then I washed thee with water, yea, I thoroughly washed away thy blood from thee, and I anointed thee with oil. I clothed thee also with embroidered work, and shod thee with badgers' skins" (Ezekiel 16:9–10). That is, when Christ comes to cast His affections on us, and to wed us unto Himself, He finds us polluted, with not a rag on us. We are full of filth and have just nothing. He takes us with nothing; nay, we are worse than nothing. So here is the point: what ground is there whereby a man who is dead and has no goodness in him (make him as ill as can be imagined) may receive Christ? "As many as received Him, to them gave He power to become the sons of God." First comes receiving Christ, and then comes believing. It is the receiving of this gift that is the means whereby Christ is offered to us. The apostle, joining the first and second Adam together, makes the benefit we have by the second to lie in the point of receiving (Romans 5).

OBJECTION. If it is a free gift, why is faith required?

ANSWER. Because faith takes away nothing from the gift. If a man gives a beggar an alms, and he reaches out his hand to receive it, his reaching out the hand makes the gift none the less because the hand is not a worker, but an instrument in receiving the free gift. "If through the offense of one many be dead, much more the grace of God, and the gift by grace hath abounded unto many in Jesus Christ" (Romans 5:15). And "if by one man's offense death reigned by one, much more they that receive abundance of grace shall reign in life by one, Jesus Christ" (verse 17). Here is the point then. God is well-pleased, and therefore sends this offer to us: "Will you have My Son? With Him you shall have abundance of grace, everlasting life, and My love too."

There is no creature in this place but this shall be made good unto if he can find it in his heart to take Christ. You shall have a warrant to receive Him. Now to receive Christ, is to believe on His name and to draw near unto Him. The word "receiving" means "taking with the hand with free entertainment." It is not so much "receiving" as "entertaining." "He came to His own, and His own received Him not." They were like the foolish Gadarenes, who preferred their pigs before Christ. They would rather have His room than His company. So when Christ comes, and you would rather be a free man, as you think, and will not have Him to reign over you, then your case is lamentable; then self-will self can have. Whether we come to Christ or He comes to us, there is a drawing near. If you come to Christ, He will not turn you away; if Christ comes to you by any good motion, if you do not shut the door against Him, you shall not miss Him. "Behold, I stand at the door and knock; if any man hear My voice and open the door, I will come in unto him, and sup with him, and he with Me" (Revelation 3:20). The Lord, by the knock of His mouth, by the sword that comes out of His mouth, would fain come in, be familiar with you, and be friends with you. If you will not let Him in, is there not good reason that He withdraw Himself? If He see your sins, and would fain come in, what an encouragement you have to open! "He that cometh unto Me, I will in no wise cast out" (John 6:37).

Can you have a better word from your Prince than this? When He holds out His golden scepter, if you take hold of it, you are safe; otherwise you are a dead man. You cannot have a greater security.

The point is, faith is drawing near to Christ, and unbelief is going from Him. The gospel is preached to those who are afar off and to those who are near. "He came and preached peace to you that were afar off, and to them that were nigh" (Ephesians 2:17). Who were they who were afar off? They were those who had "uncircumcision in the flesh, without Christ, aliens to the commonwealth of Israel, those that had no hope." To these Christ came, these who were afar off by faith drew near. That expression is a singular one. Hebrews 10:38: "Now the just shall live by faith." What is that? "But if any draw back," that is, if any man is an unbeliever, "My soul shall have no pleasure in him." Faith makes a man come and draw near to Christ. It is a shamefaced bashfulness that makes a man draw back; it is unbelief if any draw back, and to believe is to go on with boldness. "We are not of them which draw back unto perdition, but of them. . . ."

What an excellent encouragement this is to come with boldness unto the throne of grace, that we may find help in time of need! So that now, let your state be what it will, if you will not hold off, but will "entertain" Christ, "though your sins be as red as scarlet," do not be discouraged, "they shall be made as white as snow."

The very sinner against the Holy Ghost is invited; and why is that unpardonable? Can any sin be so great as to overtop the value of Christ's blood? There is not so much wretchedness in the heart of man as there is grace, goodness, and merit in Christ. But why is that sin unpardonable? Because it is the nature of the disease that will not suffer the plaster to stick on. It counts the blood of the covenant, wherewith we should be sanctified, an unholy thing. If this sinner would not pluck off the plaster and tread it under foot, he would be saved. But this is the sin: when God is liberal and Christ is free, we do not have the heart to take Him at His Word and come.

This is the free preaching of the gospel indeed. When a man has nothing desirable in him, but is stark naught, stark dead, and is not worth the taking up, then he may challenge Christ and be sure of all. Unless you have Christ, you have nothing by promise, not so much as a bit of bread by promise. If you have it, it is by Providence. "All the promises of God are in Him," that is, Christ, "yea, and amen. Ye are the children of the promise in Christ," but you have nothing till you are in Christ.

QUESTION. What must I do in this case? What encouragement shall I have in my rags, when I am abominable and worth nothing?

ANSWER. There are certain things that are preparations to a promise, such as commands, precepts, and entreaties, which encourage them to it, and then comes a proposition: "I, being a believer, shall have eternal life. If Christ is mine, I may challenge forgiveness of sins, the favor of God, and everlasting life."

But how is faith wrought? Do not believe that foolish conceit which is too common in the world, that faith is only a strong persuasion that God is my God and that my sins are forgiven. This is a foolish thing, a fancy; a dream, unless it is grounded on the Word of God. It is but a dream that will lead you to a fool's paradise. Nothing can uphold faith but the Word of God.

Your question was this: I am as bad as bad can be, so what ground do I have out of the Word of God that, of an unbeliever, I can be made a believer?

Now we must not take every text, but such only as may be applicable to a dead man, one who has no goodness in him, who is yet outside of Christ. The first word is a general proclamation, whereby Christ gives anyone leave to come and take Him. Christ is not only a "Fountain sealed," as in the Song of Solomon, but a "Fountain open for sin and for uncleanness," as in Zechariah. So now, when He keeps open house, He makes proclamation that none shall be shut out. He puts none back; not even the greatest sins that can be can keep you from Him.

To confirm this, we have our Savior's own proclamation: "Ho! Everyone that thirsteth, come ye to the waters; and he that hath no money, come ye, buy, and eat; yea, come, buy wine and milk without money, and without price" (Isaiah 55:1). A strange contradiction, one would think. What! Buy without money and without price? The reason is because there is a certain thing that fools esteem, a price which is none, something that is free. "I counsel thee to buy of Me gold tried in the fire" (Revelation 3:18). Why? How must this be done? Whenever you as a sinner come to Christ to have your sins pardoned, and to be a subject of Christ's kingdom, you must not then be as you were, but you must be changed. You must not live as you did before, in a state of rebellion.

Now to leave sin is not a sufficient price; yet we see a fool will esteem his own baubles: "I must lay down my lusts. I must lay down my covetousness, intemperance, and the like." And a man thinks it a great matter thus to do, and to leave the freedom he had before, though it is a matter of nothing. When a rebel receives his pardon, is the king's pardon abridged because he must live like a subject hereafter? Why else should he seek for the benefit of a subject? This is said in respect of the foolish conceit of man, who thinks it a great price to forsake his corruptions.

Again, with the same loud voice Christ cried when He offered Himself a sacrifice for sin. He cried at the time of the great feast that all should come. "In the last day, the great day of the feast, Jesus stood, and cried, saying, 'If any man thirst, let him come unto Me and drink' " (John 7:37). In the last of Revelation, there is a "whosoever will" that is pressed; it is a passage worth gold. And these are the passages that, if applied, will make you strangers to draw near. But these are not applicable to a man before He has grace; everyone cannot apply them. Never forget that place while you live; it is at the close of God's holy book, and the sealing up of His holy book. It is in Revelation 22:17: "And the Spirit and the bride say, 'Come.' And let him that is athirst come, and drink of the water of life freely. Whosoever will, let him come." What more would you have? Have you no will to come to Christ? No will to receive salvation? Then it is a pity that you should be saved. No man can be saved against His will, nor blessed against His will. If you will not have Christ, if you will try arguing with God, then go further and fare worse—but "whosoever will, let him come."

And if you say, "Oh! But I have a will," why, then, you have a warrant to take Christ.

OBJECTION. But O sir, you sound like a great patron of freewill. Does it all lie in a man's will? Will you make the matter of taking Christ lie there?

ANSWER. I say, if you see that you have a will, then you have a warrant. I do not say that this will comes from yourself. It is not a blind faith that will do you good; the Word of God works faith in you. You do not have a will to it born in you. It is not a flower that grows in your own garden, but one that is planted by God: "No man can come unto Me except the Father which hath sent Me draw him" (John 6:44).

What! Will Christ offer violence to the will and draw a man against his will?

No, there is no such meaning here. It is expounded in verse 65: "No man can come to Me except it were given him of My Father." By this Christ shows what He means. If you have a will to come, thank the Father for it; for of Him, as in Philippians, we have both the will and the deed.

For example, take that general proclamation in Ezra 1:3. The king who had power to make them free said, "Who is there among you of all his people, his God be with him, and let him go up to Jerusalem which is in Judah, and build the house of the Lord God of Israel." Then we read, "Then rose up the chief of the fathers of Judah and Benjamin, and the priests, and the Levites, and all them whom the Spirit of God had raised to go up" (verse 5). Observe here, though the proclamation was general, yet the raising up of the will was from the Spirit of the Lord. We must not by any means take our will to be a ground; the will comes from God. But if you have a will, you have a warrant. Whosoever will, let him take the water of life freely without covenanting.

Do not say that if you had but a measure of faith, and such a measure of humiliation; for that would be to compound with Christ. Away with that! Rather, "Whosoever will, let him come." Christ keeps open house, so "Whosoever will, let him come." Whosoever comes to Him, He will not shut out (John 6:37). If you have a heart to come to Him, He has a willing heart to receive you. As it was with the prodigal son, the father did not wait till he came home, but ran to meet him. Christ is swift to show mercy and to meet us, though we come slowly towards Him.

But this is not all, there is a second gracious word that is preached to a man who is not yet in the state of grace. A man who keeps open house seldom invites any particularly; but if he comes, he shall be welcome. Christ keeps open house, but some are so fearful and so modest that, unless they have a special invitation, they are ashamed to come to Christ. They reason thus: "If my case were an ordinary man's, I should come. But I am so vile and wretched that I am ashamed to come; my sins have been so many and are so heavy that I am not able to bear so great a weight. They are more in number than the hairs of my head; and, alas, they are crying ones too."

But hearken here to a second word. Do you think your case is more heavy because you are sinful beyond measure? Lo, it pleases God to send you a special invitation, you who find yourself discouraged with the great bulk and burden of your sins. It pleases God, I say, to send you a special invitation (see Matthew 11:28), though all do not apply it to this use: "Come unto Me, all ye that labor and are heavy laden, and I will give you rest." You, of all others, are they whom Christ looks for. Those who can walk upright in their sins, who desire to live and die in them, will not look upon Christ, and He will not look upon them.

They scorn Him and He scorns them. But you who are
heavy laden and feel the burden of your sins are invited by
Christ.

Do not let Satan then deceive you of the comfort of
this word. That which Christ makes the latch to open the
door to let Himself in, we usually, by our foolishness, make
the bolt to shut Him out. Let your wound be ever so great,
you have a warrant to come and be cured. Be of good
comfort then. As it was said to blind Bartimeus, so it is said
to you, "Lo, He calleth thee." When Christ bids you come,
and gives you His Word that He will heal you, then come.
Do not let the devil or your corruptions hinder you or
make you stay back. Hasten to this city of refuge. He has
engaged His Word for you, and He will ease you.

But now, after all this, there is a third word. Though
Christ keeps open house so that whosoever will may freely
come; and though He sends special invitations to them
who are most bashful because their case is extraordinary,
do you think now that Christ will come with His soldiers
and destroy those who do not come in? He might do it,
when He so freely invites you, and you turn His offer back
again into His hand. But yet here is another word of comfort: Christ not only sends a messenger to invite you, who
have no goodness in you, but He beseeches and entreats
you. And that is a third word whereby faith is wrought in
an unbeliever. "Now then, we are ambassadors for Christ,
as though God did beseech you by us." Observe this passage: "We pray you in Christ's stead, be ye reconciled unto
God" (2 Corinthians 5:20). This is the most admirable
word that ever could be spoken unto a sinner!

"Alas," you may say, "I am afraid that God will not be
friends with me!" Why not? He would have you to be
friends with Him. Do not do what the papists do, and
make God so austere that He might not be spoken unto,
as though you might not presume to make friends with
Him. "We have not a High Priest that is not touched with

our infirmities." Will the papists tell me that I am too bold
if I go to God, or lay hands on Christ? I am not more bold
than I am welcome. Let us go with boldness to the throne
of grace. We are commanded to do it. Do not think that,
though He had bowels to weep over Jerusalem, and He
carried the same with Him into heaven, when you lie
groaning before Him, He will spurn you. It is God's good
pleasure to entreat you, and therefore you have warrant
enough. Christ wept over Jerusalem, and He is as ready to
embrace you.

You have now three words to make a man a believer of
an unbeliever. Is there, or can there be more than these?
Open house-keeping, special invitations, entreaties, and
beseechings; yet there is more than all this which, if you do
not have a heart of stone, will make you believe, or make
you rue that you do not.

When God sees all these things will not work with us,
but we are slow of heart to believe, then He quickens us;
and then comes a word of command. God charges, and
commands you to come; and then, if you break His command, you do it to your peril. It is the greatest sin that can
be committed. You will not draw near to God because you
are a sinner; you now commit a greater sin than before,
for you send Christ back to God; you bid Him take His
commodity back into His hand again. You will not believe,
and this is a heinous crime. "And when the Spirit shall
come, it shall reprove the world of sin, of righteousness,
and of judgment: of sin, because they believe not in Me"
(John 16:8–9). This is that great sin He shall convince the
world of, that they do not believe in Him. Of all sins, this is
the most notorious; this makes us keep all other sins in
possession. It is not only one particular sin, but it fastens all
other sins upon us, be they ever so many. When faith
comes, it will turn them out; but till then they remain in
you.

Where there is no commandment, there is no sin. How

could it be a sin in not believing if we were not commanded so to do? But you shall hear more than so. The apostle speaks of excluding rejoicing under the law: "Where is boasting, then? It is excluded. By what law? By the law of works? No, but by the law of faith" (Romans 3:27). There is a law of works and a law of faith. God not only gives you leave to come and take Him, and draw near unto Him, but He commands you to do it. There is a law, and by the breach of that law of faith you are made guilty of a high sin. There is a full testimony of this in 1 John 3:23: "And this is the commandment, that we should believe in the name of His Son, Jesus Christ."

If a man should ask, "May I love my neighbor?" would you not think him a fool? He must do it; he is commanded to do it.

So if a poor soul came and said to me, "May I believe?" I would say, "You fool, you must believe!"

God has laid a command upon you; it is not left to your choice. The same commandment that bids you to love your brother bids you to believe on Christ. To entreaty is added God's command; and therefore, if you argue, "What warrant do I have to believe?" Why, God enjoins it upon you and commands it. As the impotent man said, so may you, "He that healed me said unto me, 'Take up thy bed and walk.' " This is the very key of the gospel, and this is the way to turn it right.

The last thing is, if keeping open house, special invitations, entreaties, and commands will not serve the turn, then Christ waxes angry. What! To be scorned when He offers mercy and, as it were, invites all sorts, and compels them to come in by His preachers, and by a peremptory command? Then He falls to threatening. If you will not come upon this command, you shall be damned. "He that believeth not shall be damned" (Mark 16:16). Christ commands men to go into all the world "and preach the gospel to every creature." Speak unto every soul this gospel that I speak to you. If you will not hear and believe, if you will not take God at His Word, you shall be damned. "He that believeth not shall not see life, but the wrath of God abideth on him" (John 3:36). Here is an iron scourge to drive you, you who are so slow of heart to believe. In Psalm 78, God's mercy unto the Israelites is set down. Afterwards comes one plague upon another. It is said of the Israelites that "they hardened their hearts as in the day of provocation" (verse 21). This is applied to unbelievers. "The Lord heard this and was wroth, a fire was kindled against Jacob and against Israel." Why was this? Because they did not believe in Him, because they did not trust in His salvation. Nothing will more provoke God to anger than when He is liberal and gracious, and we are straitened in ourselves, harden our hearts, and do not trust Him. Never forget this sermon while you live; this is the net that Christ has to draw you out of the world. I shall next tell you what faith is, which is to receive Christ and to believe in His name.

12

Faith

"In whom ye also trusted, after that ye heard the word of truth, the gospel of your salvation: in whom also after that ye believed, ye were sealed with that Holy Spirit of promise." Ephesians 1:13

The last time I entered on the declaration of that main point and part of religion, which is the foundation of all our hopes and comfort, namely the offering of Christ unto us; that as He offered Himself a sacrifice to His Father for us upon the cross, so, which is the basis, ground, and foundation of our comfort, He offers Himself to us. And here comes that gracious gift of the Father which closes with God, that as God says, "To us a child is born, to us a Son is given," so grace is given to us to receive Him. And as the greatest gift does not enrich a man unless he accepts it and receives it, so this is our case. God offers His Son unto us as an earnest of His love; if we will not receive Him, we cannot be the better for Him. If we refuse Him and put God's commodity which He offers us back in His hand, then God storms, and His wrath abides on us forevermore. That it is His good pleasure that we should receive Christ, it is no doubt; we have His Word for it. Our present point is how we may receive Him, and that is by faith.

In this text is declared how faith is wrought, and that is by the Word of truth: "In whom also ye trusted, after that ye had heard the word of truth." Now after this faith, there comes a sealing by the Spirit of God: "In whom also

162

after that ye believed, ye were sealed with that Holy Spirit
of promise." Now lest a man, through ignorance and in-
discretion, should be misled and deceived, there is faith
and there is feeling. Where this is not the case, I do not say
that there is no faith; no, for feeling is a later thing, and
comes after faith. If we have faith, we live by it; but "after
ye believed, ye were sealed." You see, then, faith is that
whereby we receive Jesus Christ: "To as many as received
Him, to them gave He power to become the sons of God,
even to them that believe on His name."

The blood of Christ is that which cures our souls, but,
as I told you, it is by application. A medicine does not heal
by being prepared, but by being applied. So the blood of
Christ shed for us, unless applied to us, does us no good.
In Hebrews 12 it is called "the blood of sprinkling." Psalm
51 has relation to it, where he says, "Purge me with hyssop." In the Passover there was blood to be shed—not to
be spilt, but to be shed—and then to be gathered up again
and put into a basin. And when they had so done, they
were to take a bunch of hyssop and dip and sprinkle.

Faith is this bunch of hyssop that dips itself, as it were,
into the basin of Christ's blood, and our souls are purged
by being sprinkled with it. In Leviticus 14:6, there was a
bird to escape alive; but see the preparation for it: "You
shall take it, and the scarlet, and the cedar wood, and the
hyssop, and shall dip them, and the living bird in the blood
of the bird that was killed . . . and then you shall sprinkle
on him that had the leprosy seven times, and shall pro-
nounce him clean, and shall let the living bird loose into
the open field." We are thus let loose, cleansed, and freed.
But unless we are dipped as the living bird was in the
blood of the dead bird, there is no escaping; unless we are
dipped in the blood of Christ Jesus, this dead bird, and
sprinkled with this hyssop, we cannot be freed.

Now we come to that great matter, without which
Christ profits us nothing, which is faith. The well is deep,

and this is the bucket with which we must draw. This is the hand by which we must put on Christ. "As many as are baptized, put on Christ." Thus must we be made ready: we must be thus clothed, and by this hand attire ourselves with the Sun of Righteousness. I declared unto you that this faith must not be a bare conceit floating in the brain, not a device of our own. The devil, taking hold of this, would soon lead a man into a fool's paradise. To say, "I am God's child, and surely I shall be saved because I am persuaded so," this the devil would say amen to, and would be glad to rock men to sleep in such conceits. Such are like the foolish virgins, who went to buy oil for their lamps, and were persuaded that they would come soon enough to enter with the bridegroom. But their persuasion was groundless, and they were shut out.

So such groundless persuasions and assurances in a man's soul, that he is the child of God and shall go to heaven, is not faith. You may carry this assurance to hell with you. This faith is not faith; for faith comes by hearing, and that not of every word or fancy, but by hearing the Word of truth. Faith must not go a jot further than the Word of God goes. If you have an apprehension, but no warrant for it out of the Word of God, it is not faith; for the text says, "After ye heard the word of truth, ye believed." So we must have some ground for it out of the Word of truth, otherwise it is presumption, mere conceits and fancy, but not faith.

I showed you the last time how this might be; for while a man is an unbeliever he is wholly defiled with sin; he is in a most loathsome condition; he is in his blood, filthy, and no eye pities him. And may one fasten comfort on one in such a condition, on a dead man? I showed you that this was our case. When faith comes to us, it finds no good thing in us; it finds us stark dead and stark naught. Yet there is a word for all this to draw us unto Christ from that miserable ocean in which we are swimming unto perdition, if God does not catch us in His net. Hearken therefore to God's call; there is such a thing as this calling. God calls you and would change your condition, and therefore offers you His Son. "Will you have My Son? Will you yield unto Me? Will you be reconciled unto Me? Will you come unto Me?" And this may be preached to the worst rebel there is. It is the only word whereby faith is wrought. It is not by finding such and such things in us beforehand; no, God finds us as bad as bad may be when He offers Christ to us. He finds us ugly and filthy, and afterwards washes us and makes us good. It is not because He found this or that good thing in you that He give you interest in His Son. No, He loved us first; and when we were defiled, He washed us with His own blood (Revelation 1:5).

Now there is double love of God towards His creatures, a love of commiseration and a love of complacency. Commiseration is a fruit of love which tenders and pities the miserable estate of another. But there is a love of complacency, which is a likeness between the qualities and manners of persons: for like loves like, and this love God never has but to His saints after conversion, when they have His image stamped on them, and are reformed in their understandings and wills, resembling Him in both. Then, and not until then, He bears this love towards them. Before He loves them with the love of pity; and "so God loved the world," that is, with the love of commiseration, "that He gave His only begotten Son, that whosoever believeth in Him might not perish, but have everlasting life."

The Word is free, and requires nothing but what may consist with the freest gift that may be given. Although here may be something that a man may startle at.

QUESTION. Is there not required a condition of faith and a condition of obedience?

ANSWER. Neither of these hinders the fullness and freedom of the grace of the gospel. Faith does not, because faith is such a condition as requires only an empty hand to receive a gift freely given. Now, does that hinder the freeness of the gift to say that you must take it? Why, this is required to the freest gift that can be given. If a man would give something to a beggar, if he would not reach out his hand and take it, let him go without it; but it is a free gift still. So the condition of faith requires nothing but an empty hand to receive Christ.

Obedience does not hinder it.

OBJECTION. But I am required to be a new man, a new creature, to lead a new life. I must alter my course; and is not this a great clog and burden? Do you account this as free, when I must crucify lusts and mortify passions? Is it free when a man must renounce his own will?

ANSWER. Yes, it is as free as free may be, as I showed you the last time. The very touching and accepting of Christ implies a renunciation of former sinfulness, and going off from other courses that are contrary to Him. Suppose a king gives a pardon to a notorious rebel for treason, so that now he must live obediently as a subject; the king did not need, in regard of himself, to have given the pardon. If he gives it, he does not take from its freeness by insisting that the pardoned man live like a subject afterwards; the very acceptance of the pardon implies it.

Now let me open the mystery of faith. Faith is a great thing; it is our life; our life stands in the practice of it. In the offering of Christ for us, there is given to Him a name that is above every name. And as it is in the purchasing of redemption, so it is in the point of acceptance: God has given unto this poor virtue of faith a name above all names. Faith indeed, as it is a virtue, is poor and mean, and comes far short of love; and therefore the apostle says that love is many degrees preferred before faith, because love fills the heart, and faith is but a bare hand. It lets all things fall so that it may fill itself with Christ. It is said of the Virgin Mary that God respected the low estate of His handmaid. So God respects the low estate of faith, so that nothing is required but a bare, empty hand which has nothing to bring with it. Though it is ever so weak, yet if it has a hand to receive, the faith of the poorest believer and the faith of the greatest saint are equally precious.

In our text, there is the point of faith, and then there is a thing God confirms it with, a seal. "In whom also after that ye believed, ye were sealed." Faith is of itself a thing unsealed; the sealing with the Holy Spirit of promise is a point beyond faith. It is a point of feeling and not only of believing of God's Word, but a sensible feeling of the Spirit; a believing in my soul, accompanied with joy unspeakable, and full of glory. Of this sealing we shall speak more hereafter.

1. Observe here the object of faith: "In whom ye trusted." We speak of faith now as it justifies, as it apprehends Christ for its object; for otherwise faith has as large an extent as all God's Word. Faith has a hand to receive whatever God has a mouth to speak. What is the object? "He in whom ye trusted." It is a wonder to see how many are deceived, who make the forgiveness of sins to be the proper object of faith. A man may call as long as he lives for forgiveness of sins; yet unless there is the first act to lay hold on Christ, in vain will he expect forgiveness of sins. Until you accept Christ as your King and Savior, you have no promise. We are never children of the promise till we are found in Him.

The proper and immediate object of faith is, first, Christ, and then God the Father by Him; for faith must have Christ for its object. I must believe in none else but God in and through Christ. Now that this is so, we may see in that famous passage in 1 Peter 1:20–21. When he had spoken of the precious blood of Christ, the Lamb without blemish, he went on and showed that He was "manifested in these last times for you, who by Him do believe in God, that raised up Christ from the dead, and gave Him glory, that your faith and hope might be in God." There is no true believing in God the Father but by the Son. The proper object of hope and faith is God, and he who believes, hopes, or trusts in anything else is an idolater. We believe in God by Christ, so the primary object of faith is Christ. "Ye are all the children of God by faith in Jesus Christ" (Galatians 3:26). What is my faith in then? If you will be the child of God, receive Christ Jesus; accept Him as your Savior and as your Lord. He is the proper object of your faith.

You must know Christ Jesus and Him crucified; that should be the highest knowledge in your account. Hereupon the apostle to the Romans, when he speaks of faith, makes the object of it Christ, and Christ crucified. "Whom God hath set forth to be a propitiation through faith in His blood; to declare His righteousness for the remission of sins that are past, through the forbearance of God" (Romans 3:25). Whatsoever then that you find in Christ is an object of your faith. The point is, "He who eats My flesh and drinks My blood" (John 6:54), that is, he who receives Me and makes Me his meat and drink, shall be partaker of Me. Compare Romans 3:25 with Romans 5:9, for it is worth comparing. We are said to be "justified by His blood" (Romans 5:9), "by faith in His blood" (Romans 3:25). Now both these come to one thing, and they resolve the point and clear the question whether faith in itself as a virtue justifies, or in respect of its object. Surely it is in respect of the object.

You who have skill in philosophy know that heat, if considered as a quality, its effects are not so great; but considered as an instrument, it transcends the sphere of its own activity. It does wonders, for it is the principle of vegetation, and many other strange effects. So it is here. Take faith as a virtue, and it is far short of love; but consider it as an instrument whereby Christ is applied, and it transcends, it works wonders beyond its proper sphere; for the meanest thing it lays hold on is the Son of God. "He that hath the Son hath life." When we are justified by faith, we are justified by Christ. To be justified by His blood and by faith in His blood is the same thing.

It is as if a man should say, "I was cured by going to the physician." A man is not properly said to be cured by going to the physician, nor is justified by coming to Christ by the legs of faith. But the applying of the physician's prescription, the coming to Christ and applying His virtue, to make Him the object of my faith, this is the way to be justified. It is not making and preparing a plaster cast that cures, but applying it.

So the true object of faith is Christ crucified, and God the Father, in and by Him. Here then is the point: you must not look for any comfort in faith till you have Christ. If you think that you shall ever have any benefit by God till you have Christ, you deceive yourself. It is impossible for a man to receive nourishment by his bread and drink till he partakes of it; so you must partake of Christ before you can receive any nourishment by Him. Christ does not say, "You must have forgiveness of sins," nor, "You must have My Father's favor," but, "Take My body and blood; take Me crucified."

Buy the field and the treasure in it is yours; but you have nothing to do with the treasure till you get the field. This is preferment enough, to have the Lord's promise to Abraham: "I am thy exceeding great reward." God is His well-beloved's, and His well-beloved is His. There is a spiritual match between Christ and you. There are many who are matched with Christ, and yet do not know how rich they are. When a man only reckons what he shall get from Christ, when all his thoughts are on that, he marries the portion and not the Person. You must set your love on Christ's person, and then, having Him, all that He has is yours. However rich Christ is, so rich you are. He must first be yours. "He that hath the Son hath life," but the Son must first be had.

Are there any now in this congregation who are so hard-hearted as to refuse such a gift as this? When God will give you His Son, if you will take Him, is there any so profane as, with Esau, to sell his birthright, to pursue the poor, peddling things of this life and refuse so high a gift as salvation? This is a gift that is not given to angels; they think it is an honor to wait at the Lord's table; they do not have this precious food given to them; they never taste it. And therefore many Christians, on serious consideration, would not change their estate for the estate of angels. Why? Because Christ is my Husband. I am wedded to Him. He is bone of my bone and flesh of my flesh, which the angels cannot say. Our nature is advanced above the angelic nature; for we shall sit and judge the world with Christ; we shall judge the twelve tribes of Israel. And what a high preferment is this!

Nay, observe this, and take it for a rule. Never beg God to pardon your sins till you have done this one thing, accepted Christ from God's hands. For you never can confidently ask anything till you have Him. "For all the promises of God are in Him yea and amen." This may serve to show that the primary object of faith is Christ crucified, and God by Him.

2. I come now to declare what the acts of faith are, and there is some intricacy in that too. There is much ado made in what part and power of the soul faith is. We must not proportion the act of faith according to our own fancy. For it is not faith, but only as it has relation to the Word. Look how the Word is presented: "After you heard the word of truth, the gospel of your salvation."

Now the Word is presented under a double respect:

First, it is presented as truth. "After you heard the word of truth," and there is where the understanding comes in.

Second, it is presented as a good Word, so that we should lay hold on it, and here is where the will comes in; for the will, we say, challenges that which is good for its object. Now the gospel of salvation is a good Word; it is glad tidings "worthy of all acceptation, that Christ Jesus came into the world to save sinners." And now, as the Word is presented as a good Word, so must my act of faith be answerable unto it. See in Hebrews 11:13 the act of faith answering hereto: "These all died in faith, not having received the promises." What did their faith do for them? It made them "see the promises afar off, and they were persuaded of them, and embraced them, and confessed that they were strangers and pilgrims in the earth."

So by comparing passage with passage, it appears that first this gospel was presented as the Word of truth, and they were persuaded of it. It is the first act of faith to persuade men of the truth of the Word; and then, since it is a good Word, they embrace it. These are the two arms of faith. As it is true, it persuades me; as it is good, I embrace it.

We must not now be too curious in bringing in philosophical disputes, whether one virtue may proceed from two faculties; whether faith may proceed from the understanding and the will. The truth is, these things are not yet agreed upon; and shall we trouble ourselves with things not yet decided in the schools, such as whether the practical understanding and the will are distinct faculties or not? The Word of God requires that I should believe with my whole heart. As Philip told the eunuch, "If thou believest with all thy heart, thou mayest" (Acts 8:37). Believe with your whole heart. Shall I piece and divide the heart when the whole heart is required?

So the Word is presented as a true Word, and then as a good Word.

It is presented as a true Word. And the act of faith answering thereto is called in Scripture "knowledge" and "acknowledgment" (Titus 1:1; 1 Peter 3:1).

Knowledge is a thing that is required. Why? Because if there is a remedy able to cure a man's disease, and he does not know about it, how is he the better for it? Knowledge is so essential to faith that without it there can be no faith. In John 17:3, the terms are interchangeable: "This is life eternal, to know Thee the only the true God, and Jesus Christ whom Thou hast sent." To know God is to believe in God, because knowledge is so essential to belief that one cannot be without the other. You cannot believe what you have never heard of. "I know," said Job, "that my Redeemer liveth," that is, I believe that He lives. And hereupon it is said in Isaiah 53:11, "By His knowledge shall My righteous Servant justify many." Knowledge is an act primarily requisite to faith. To be justified by His knowledge is to be justified by faith in His blood. This, then, is the first thing, that I know something to be as true as gospel; and then comes the acknowledgment.

The acknowledgment is this: "We believe, and are sure that Thou art that Christ" (John 6:69). This is an assurance, not the assurance of my salvation, for that is another kind of thing, but an assurance that God will keep His Word with me, will not delude me; but that if I take His Son I shall have life. I shall have His favor. When God illuminates me, I find all things in Him. When the understanding clearly apprehends this, then comes the next word, it is the gospel of salvation, there being a knowing and acknowledging, the act of the understanding.

Then comes the will, and it being propounded as a good Word, then follows acceptance and affiance.

Acceptance receives Christ. "As many as received Him, to them gave He power to become the sons of God, even to as many as believed on His name" (John 1:12). Then a man resolves, "I will take God at His Word."

Thereupon follows a resting or relying on God, which is a proper act of faith. I need no other place than Romans 10:13–13: "Whosoever shall call on the name of the Lord shall be saved. But how shall they call on Him in whom they have not believed?" that is, "on whom they have not reposed their confidence." Mark what the apostle says, "How shall they call on Him in whom they have not believed?" That faith which was in the antecedent must be in the conclusion; therefore our faith is a relying on God. And so in this passage this trust is made the same as faith, as it is in the text: "In whom you trusted, after you had received the word of truth"; for our trust and belief there is the self-same word. I have a knowledge of God, and I acknowledge Him; and from my knowing, my will is conformed to accept Christ; and if, when I have accepted Him, I will not part from Him, this is faith. And if you have this faith, you will never perish.

Even if you never have one day of comfort all your life long, yet, my life for yours, you are saved. Perhaps by reason of your ignorance you have no feeling; yet if you consent, you are justified; the consent makes the match. If you consent to the Father and take Christ the Son, whether you know it or not, you have Him.

Though you do not know whether your sins are forgiven, yet as long as you keep your hold, all the devil's temptations shall never drive you from Him. You are justified and in a safe case, though ignorance and other things in you cause you not to feel it. If you lay hold on Him for His sake, you are apprehended.

OBJECTION. It is an easy matter to believe.

ANSWER. Not as easy a matter as you guess it to be. It would be easy indeed, were there nothing but saying the words. To make you and Christ to be as husband and wife, there are terms and conditions to be agreed upon. God does not just cast His Son away, but there shall be conditions on your side. He must be your King and Head if you will have Him to be your Husband.

"But what shall I get by Him then?" says the wife. What shall you get? There is no end of your getting. "All is thine, Paul, Apollos, Cephas, life. . . . Thou art Christ's, and Christ is God's."

Every man will take Christ thus for the better; but there is something else in the match. If you will have Him, you must take Him for better, for worse, for richer, for poorer. Indeed, there are precious things provided for you. "It is your Father's good pleasure to give you the kingdom." You shall be heirs with Christ; but for the present, while you are in the church militant, you must take up your cross; you must not look for great things in this world. In this world you must have tribulation, you must deny yourselves and your own wills. Would you have Christ be the wife and you be the husband? No, and if you think so, you mistake the match. Christ must be the Husband and the Head; and as the wife promises to obey her husband, to cleave to her husband in sickness and in health, and to forsake all others, so Christ asks, "Will you have Me? If you will, you must take Me on these terms. You must take My cross with Me. You must deny you own will, yea, perhaps even your own life also."

Let a Christian consider all these things. If you can say, "I will have Christ, however, for I shall be a gainer by Him. I will take Him with all conditions, and I know I shall make a good bargain; therefore I will have Him on any terms, come what will." When a man can have his will so perpendicularly bent on Christ that he will have Him, though he leaves his skin behind him, there is a true acceptance of Him. We must not here distinguish with the schools about velleities, "wishing and would-ing," and true desires after Christ (wishers and woulders never thrive); but there must be a resolution to follow Christ through thick and thin, never to part with Him. A direct will is here required. And therefore Christ bids us consider beforehand what it will cost us. "If any man come to Me, and hate not father and mother, wife and children, and his own life also, he cannot be My disciple."

Do not think that our Savior here would discourage men from love. Does the God of love teach us hatred? The phrase in the Greek is "loving less." So "if any man come to Me, and hate not father and mother," that is, "if he does not love all those less than Me." And that it is so we may see expounded by our Savior: "He that loveth father or mother more than Me is not worthy of Me" (Matthew 10:37). He who will follow Christ in calm weather and not in a storm is not worthy of Him. "Which of you, intending to build a tower, sitteth not down first, and counteth the cost, whether he have sufficient to finish it" (Luke 14:28)? What does that have to do with our purpose? See verse 33: "So likewise, whosoever he be of you that forsaketh not all that he hath, cannot be My disciple."

It is a small matter to begin to be a Christian, unless you consider what it will cost you. Do you think it is a small matter to be the King's son? Do not think on so great a business without considering what it will cost you. It will mean denying your own will. You must be content to follow naked Christ nakedly, follow Him in His persecution and tribulation, in His death and suffering, if you will be conformable to Him in glory. When this case comes, it makes many draw back. When the rich man in the gospel heard that he must forsake all, he drew back. When troubles arise, many are offended; so when it comes to a point of parting, they go back.

Now we come to speak one word regarding the sealing mentioned in our text: "After that ye believed, ye were sealed with the Holy Spirit of promise." This sealing, which is a point of feeling, is a distinct thing of itself from faith; it is no part of faith. If I have faith I am sure of life, though I never have the other; these are two seals. We put our seals to the counterpart that is drawn between God and us.

The first seal is our faith. I have nothing but God's Word, and indeed I have no feeling, yet I venture my salvation and trust God upon His bare Word. I will pawn all upon it. "He that believeth," said John, "hath set his seal that God is true." If men doubt, and trust God no further than they see Him, it is not faith. But when God gives me a good Word, though I am in as much distress as ever, yet I trust; though it is contrary to all sense or outward seeming, yet I put my seal to it and trust Him still.

Then comes God's counterpart. God is honored that I believe His Word, though contrary to all sense and feeling, even His bare Word. Then God sets His seal, and now the Word comes to particularizing. Before it was in general, now it comes and singles out a man. "Say thou unto my soul, 'I am thy salvation' " (Psalm 35:3), that is, as I applied the generality of God's Word to my own case to bear me up against sense and feeling. Then comes the Spirit of God and not only delivers generalities, but says unto my soul, "I am thy salvation." This is called in Scripture a manifestation, when God manifests Himself unto us. Isaiah 60:16: "Thou shalt suck the milk of the Gentiles, and shalt suck the breast of kings; and thou shalt know that I the Lord am thy Savior and thy Redeemer." That is, when we have made particular application by faith, God will put His seal to it so that I shall know that God is my strength and my salvation. "He that loveth Me shall be loved of My Father, and I will manifest Myself unto him" (John 14:21).

Christ comes and draws the curtains, and looks on with the gracious aspect of His blessed countenance. When this comes, it cheers the heart, and then there are secret love tokens passed between Christ and His beloved. "To him that overcometh will I give to eat of the hidden manna, and will give him a white stone, and in the stone a new name written, which no man knows, save he that receives it" (Revelation 2:17). That is, there is a particular intimation that I shall know of myself more than any other, more than all the world besides. It is such a joy as the stranger is not made partaker of, such joy as is glorious and unspeakable, such peace as passes all understanding. One minute of such joy overcomes all the joy in the world besides.

Now, surely there is such a thing as this joy, or else why

do you think the Scripture would talk of it, and of the Comforter, the Holy Ghost, "by whom we know the things that are given us of God." There is a generation in the world that has this joy, though you who do not know it do not and cannot believe it; there is a righteous generation who has it—and why do you not try to get it? Do as they do, and you may obtain it likewise. "The secrets of the Lord are revealed to them that fear Him." These are hidden comforts; and do you think God will give this joy to those who do not care for Him? No, the way is to seek God, and to labor to fear Him. The secrets of the Lord are revealed to such, and such only, as fear Him. Do as they do, and follow their example, and you may have it likewise.

OBJECTION. But many have served Christ a long time and have not found it.

ANSWER. It must be owing to themselves; they must be straitened in their own bowels. For God has said, "Open your mouths wide, and I will fill them." No wonder that we are so barren of these comforts when we are straitened in ourselves. There is a thing wondrously wanting among us, and that is meditation. If we would give ourselves to it and go up with Moses to the mount to confer with God, and seriously think of the price of Christ's death, of the joys of heaven, and the privileges of a Christian—if we could frequently meditate on these, we would have these sealing days every day, or at least more often than we do now. This needs to be pressed upon us; for the neglect of this makes lean souls. He who is frequent in that has these sealing days often. If you could have a parley with God in private, and have your heart rejoice with the comforts of another day even while you are thinking of these things, Christ would be in the midst of you. Many of the saints of God have but little of this because they spend but few hours in meditation.

13

Come to the Throne of Grace

"Let us therefore come boldly unto the throne of grace,
that we may obtain mercy, and find grace to help in
time of need." Hebrews 4:16

In handling the doctrine of the conversion of a sinner,
I declared and showed you what man's misery was, and
what that great hope of mercy is which the Lord proposes
to the greatest sinner in the world. I showed you the
means whereby we may be made partakers of Christ, and
that was by the grace of faith, which lets fall all other
things in a man's self and comes with an open and empty
hand to lay hold on Christ and fill itself with Him. I also
showed you the acts of faith as it justifies.

And now, because it is a point of high moment,
wherein all our comfort stands and in which it lies, I
thought good to see what the work of God's Spirit is from
the first to the last in the conversion of a sinner from the
corruptions and pollutions of the flesh in which he wal-
lowed. And to this purpose have I chosen this passage of
Scripture, wherein we are encouraged by God's blessed
Word that whatever we are, though accursed and the
greatest sinners in the world, and that whatever we want,
we should come to God's throne of grace.

Whatever sins are or have been committed, and
though our sins are ever so great, yet they are not so great
as the infiniteness of God's mercy; especially having not
only such an Intercessor, but an Advocate to plead the
right of our cause. Christ comes and He makes payment;

and however great our debts are, yet He is our ransom. Therefore, God's justice being satisfied, why should not His mercy have place and free course? This is the great comfort that a Christian has, that he may come freely and boldly to God because he comes but for an acquittance of what is already paid. A man will appear boldly before his creditor when he knows his debt is discharged; he will not then be afraid to look him in the face. Now we may come and say, "Blessed Father, the debt is paid. I pray, give me pardon of my sins; give me my acquittance." This is the boldness and access spoken of in Romans 5:2: "In whom we have access by faith."

We now come to the ground and matter in the words. Herein there is:

1. The preparatives for grace.

2. The act itself whereby we are made partakers of the grace of God.

1. The preparatives are two, the law and the gospel. The law works in a time of great need. This is the first preparative, whereby a man is brought to see that he stands in great need of God's mercy and Christ's blood, so that the sinner cries out, "Lord, I stand in great want of mercy!" His eyes being thus opened, he is no longer a stranger at home, but he sees the case is wondrously hard with him, and thus concludes, "Unless God is merciful to me in Christ, I am lost and undone forever." Until we come to this place, we can never approach the throne of grace.

The second preparative is the gospel. I see that I stand in great need; but by this second preparative I see a throne of grace set up, and that adds comfort unto me. If God had only a throne and seat of justice, I would be utterly undone. I see my debt is extremely great; but the gospel reveals unto me that God, of His infinite mercy, has erected a throne of grace, a city of refuge. Finding myself in need, my soul may flee to it.

And now to fit us for this, God's blessed Spirit works by
His Word to open unto us the law and our wants; to en-
lighten our understandings to see that we stand in great
need; to win our affection, and open the gospel and its
comforts.

Therefore, for the time of need, the law reveals unto
us our woeful condition, to be born in sin, as the Pharisee
said, and yet not able to see it. Every man may say in general, "I am a sinner." Yet to say and know himself to be
such a sinner as indeed he is, to stand in such need, that
he cannot do. This one would think to be a matter of
sense; but unless God's Spirit opens our eyes, we can never
see ourselves to be such sinners as we are. Or else what is
the reason that the child of God cries out more against his
sin and the weight thereof after his conversion than he did
before? What! Are his sins greater or more than they were
formerly? No, but his light is greater; his eyes are opened
and now he sees more clearly what sin is. When the sun
shines and its rays come in, what a number of motes do we
discover which before we did not see! It is not as if the
sunbeams made them, or the sun raised the dust; no, there
are as many motes and as much dust flying about whether
the sun shines or not. What is the matter then? The sun
discovers them to us.

So here is the point: the sins in our souls are as motes
in the air, and are not more than they were before conversion; but we cannot see them till the glorious beams of
God's Spirit shines upon us. The sight of sin, and of the
danger that comes by it, is the work of God's Spirit. The
Spirit discovers sin unto us: "When the Spirit cometh, He
shall convince the world of sin" (John 16:8). The words are
literally, "The Spirit shall convince them." The same word
is used in Hebrews 11:1, where faith is said to be "the evidence of things not seen." Heretofore we had a slight
imagination of our sins; but to have our mouths stopped

and to be convinced of sin is not a work of flesh and blood, but of God's Spirit (Romans 3:19). Till we are awakened by His Spirit, we cannot see or feel the mountains and heaps of sins that lie upon our souls. You are dead in sin. You are in bondage; and to know it is a work of the Spirit, not of nature.

The spirit of bondage, what is that? Why, however we are all bondmen until the Son has made us free, in a woeful estate, slaves to sin and Satan, yet till God's Spirit convinces us, shows it to us, and makes us know it, we sleep securely and are not afraid. Rather we think ourselves the freest men in the world, and do not see this to be a time of need.

This, therefore, is the first preparative, when God brings His people to Mount Sinai: "For ye are not come unto the mount that might be touched, and that burned with fire, nor unto blackness, and darkness, and tempest" (Hebrews 12:18, and so Galatians 4). Mount Sinai is made a figure of the law, which begets bondage. Not that mount which might be touched, and that burned with fire, where was the sound of the trumpet, and voice of words, such a sound as never before was heard, nor ever will be one day we shall hear the same. The sound of the trumpet which sounded at the delivery of the law (Exodus 19:19), where it is described; for when the voice of the trumpet sounded long, and waxed louder and louder, that Moses heard, it was such a noise, a great noise at first, but it grew higher and higher, and at last it came to that height that it was almost incomprehensible; and then Moses spoke. And what did he say? The Holy Ghost does not set down what He spoke in that place. Look at Hebrews 12:21: "So terrible was the voice that Moses said, 'I exceedingly fear and quake.' "

Such a kind of lightning and loud voice this was. The Lord commands such a voice as this: "Cry aloud, spare not, lift up thy voice like a trumpet, and show My people

their transgression, and the house of Jacob their sins"
(Isaiah 58:1). When God shall sound with the voice of the
trumpet of His holy Word, of His law, and show you that
you are a traitorous rebel, and that there is a death sentence gone out against you, body and goods; when God
sounds thus to the deaf ear of a carnal man, then comes
the Spirit of bondage of necessity on him, which shows
that we have a time of need. The law must have this operation before you come to the throne of grace. None will fly
to the city of refuge till the revenger of blood is hard at his
heels, nor any to Christ till he sees his want.

Thus the Lord makes us know our need by turning the
edge of His axe towards us. When offenders are brought
to the bar at Westminster for treason, they have the edge
of the axe turned from them; but when they have received
the sentence of condemnation and are carried back to
the Tower of London, the edge of the axe is turned towards them. Thus is it here: the law turns the edge of
God's axe towards us. Therefore it is said of St. Peter's
hearers that they were pricked to the heart (Acts 2:37).
The law puts the point of God's sword to our very breasts,
as it were, and brings us to see that we stand in great need
of heaven.

This is the first preparative, when God enlightens our
minds to see our dangerous estate. Then there must necessarily follow fear, and a desire to be rid of this condition;
for the will and affections always follow the temper of the
mind. And hence, when a man has a false persuasion that
he is in a good case, that he is safe and well, what works it
but pride, presumption, confidence, and security? So on
the contrary, contrary effects must follow. If a man is in
health and jollity, and suddenly is proclaimed a traitor, so
that he must lose his life and goods, is it possible it should
be thus, and he not be wrought on or have any alteration?
So when news comes from the law that you are a dead
man and must everlastingly perish, the law then works

wrath, that is, it manifests unto us the wrath of God. When it is thus, there follows a shaking and a trembling, and it is impossible but that, with Moses, you should exceedingly quake and tremble.

For all this there is a throne of grace erected. God has not forgotten to be merciful, though your sins be ever so great. This is the next preparative for faith, namely, the discovery and acknowledgment of the gospel of Christ Jesus. We see in Ezra 10:2, "We have trespassed against our God, and have taken strange wives of the people of the land; yet now there is hope in Israel concerning this thing." We have trespassed; what then? Must we be the subjects of God's wrath? No, "Yet notwithstanding," though we have committed this great offense, "there is hope in Israel concerning this thing." What if we have provoked God to indignation, must we be the matter for His wrath to work on? No, there is a balm in Gilead. "Is there no balm in Gilead? Is there no physician there? Why then is not the health of the daughter of My people recovered" (Jeremiah 8:22)? What if we are sick to death? Yet there is a help in time of need. And this knowledge of the people, that there is a throne of grace, is the first comfort that comes to a miserable and sinful soul.

A man who has a deadly disease, though the physician does him no good whom he has made use of, yet he comforts himself when he sees a physician who has cured the same disease; he sees then there is some hope.

Thus it is with a sinful soul. When the welcome news of the gospel comes, after the law has discovered his disease, it says, "Do not be discouraged; there is a throne of grace prepared for you. God has a seat of justice to deal with rebels and open traitors; but if you are weary of your state, if you will submit to God, take Christ for your King and cast down all your weapons, if you will live like a subject, He has prepared a throne of grace for you." Christ is your attorney in the court to plead for you. He is not, as the papists make Him, so stout, and one who takes such state on Himself that a man may not come near Him. This is the highest injury that can be offered to Christ, to think that any creature has more mercy and pity than He has. It is to rob Christ of the fairest flower in His garden, when we rob Him of His mercy and pity. Mark Hebrews 4:15, so that we may not think Him to be austere: "We have not a high-priest that cannot be touched with the feelings of our infirmities."

Christ is no hard-hearted man; when you were His enemies, He loved you insomuch that He humbled Himself and suffered death, even the death of the cross for you. And He has the self-same compassion in heaven that He had on earth. He wept over Jerusalem, and He carried the self-same weeping heart to heaven with Him, the self-same weeping eyes. Do not believe then the papists, who say that He is so hard-hearted or so stately, and that His mother is more ready to speak for us than He is. Away with such lies! This is to pervert the gospel, and make Christ no Christ. "We have not a high priest that cannot be touched with the feelings of our infirmities." And "In all things it behooved Him to be made like unto His brethren, that He might be a merciful and faithful high priest" (Hebrews 2:17).

"Alas, poor soul," says Christ, "what the malice of the devil is I know by my own experience in the flesh." For Christ was tempted in all things according to us, sin alone excepted. "I know what the temptations of the world are." But whereas we have three enemies—the devil, the world, and the flesh—only the two former ones were His. Christ had the temptations of the world and the devil, not those of the corrupt flesh, for He had no corrupt flesh. A man who has himself been in terrible tempests on the sea, when he sees a storm, out of his own experience, he pities those who are in it; for he has seen that consternation of mind which on every side appeared whereas others, having not been there, do not lay their miseries to heart. Christ, having suffered Himself, and being tempted as we are, is sensible of our miseries; and therefore never count it boldness to come boldly to Him who gives you this encouragement: "Come boldly to the throne of grace."

We must understand that all this is before faith; we must know that we have a need, that there is a throne of grace, to which God enlightens my conscience and encourages me to come.

2. And thus, having spoken of the preparatives, I come to the work, the main thing itself, which is coming. This coming is believing. It is like the feet which carry a man to the place he would be in; his feet carry him nearer and nearer. If a man cannot be cured but by the bath, his feet must carry him there. Now faith is the legs of the soul; the feet of that carry us unto Christ. We were afar off and all drew back as unbelievers; but now by believing we draw near. As unbelievers draw back, so believers draw forward. And therefore to come to Christ and to believe in Him are the self-same thing (John 1:12 and John 6:35). "He that cometh to Me shall never hunger, and he that believeth on Me shall never thirst." Coming is there made an act of faith, and the same thing with it. The one is the explication of the other: your coming to Christ is your believing in Him. When you hear of a throne of grace, and see the Lord of glory stretching out His golden scepter, come and touch it; take the benefit of the King's pardon. If a man knows there is such a throne of grace, he must come to it; and then it is that faith begins to work.

Faith first begins to work when you take the first step towards the throne of grace. And this is the hour in which salvation has come to your house. "None can come to Me," said Christ, "except My Father draw him." If you see a virtue to come to Christ, and to draw you as an adamant, and you feel that loadstone working on you, then faith begins. It makes you draw near to Christ, whereas before you were a stranger. Till then you were like your grandfather Adam: you ran away and thought yourself most secure when you were farthest from God. But now you see no comfort unless you draw nigh to Him.

Now, as the apostle says, "It is He that worketh in you both to will and to do" (Philippians 2:13). These must both be wrought in us by God: first, a will, and then the deed. And then it is not only "I would do such a thing," but "I do it." God works not only the will of coming, but the deed of coming; and all His acts are acts of faith, and have a promise. God makes no promise till we are in Christ; till we have faith, we are no heirs of the promise. When a man sets his face towards Jerusalem, and begins to set himself to go to Christ, all he does then has the promise; there is now not a tear that he sheds but is precious. God puts it into His bottle. There is not a cup of cold water that now he gives but shall have a great reward. It is a blessed thing when everything we do has a promise annexed to it, when every step we take has a promise made to it.

Now then, the will is the first thing that is wrought in us. This is that which makes the act of faith, that I have a will, a resolution to do this. And the apostle makes it more than the very deed itself, as I may so say: "For this is expedient for you, who have begun before not only to do, but to be forward" (2 Corinthians 8:10). So we translate it. But if you look in the margin "to be forward" is rendered "to be willing," as the Greek has it—as if the will were more than the deed itself. For a man to come unwillingly is worth nothing. The groundwork is the will, which is a greater matter than the deed. Nothing more separates a man from Christ than to say, "I will not have this Man to reign over me." But if you can frame your will so that it goes perpendicularly on the object, and accept Christ on the terms offered, that is, faith, that has the promise. Therefore the Scripture compares it to conjunction with Christ. In the sacrament we spiritually eat His flesh and drink His blood; the conjunction is between Christ and His Church. And therefore the Scripture compares our conjunction by faith to the mystery of marriage. What makes a marriage? It is consent. "Will you have this man to be your husband?" And there the woman answers, "I will." That expression makes the marriage. The knot is knit by this mutual pledging of troth; all other things are but subsequents of it. So God says, "Will you have My Son? You shall have with Him all His wealth; though for a time you must go bare and fare hard, yet you shall have a kingdom."

When a man considers, "Here is the cost: I must deny myself and obey Him, but I shall have a kingdom, God's blessing, and peace of conscience." All things considered, casting the best with the worst, then the resolution is, "This is a true saying, worthy of all acceptance, I will take Him on any terms, be they ever so hard, for I shall be a gainer in the end." When we can take Christ no matter the cost or the loss, this is the will which God requires.

There is another comparison in Scripture. John 6:35 compares believing to hunger and thirst. Believing was expressed by coming, and believing is expressed by hungering and thirsting. So when I see such a will and desire after Christ that I hunger and thirst after Him, so that a hungry man does not long more for bread, nor does a deer thirst more for water, than my soul does for Christ—then a promise is made unto us, but that promise is never made unto us till we are in Christ. In Matthew 5, Revelation 22, and Isaiah 55, we find promises. Matthew 5:6: "Blessed are they that hunger and thirst after righteousness; for theirs is the kingdom of heaven, they shall be filled." Consider here what the nature of hunger and thirst is; they shall be filled, which implies that they were empty before, but now they shall be filled. Suppose now I am not filled with Christ. What! Am I without Him? No, I want Him; yet there is a blessing to the hungry and thirsty, and there is no blessing without faith. If we are not heirs of the faith, we cannot be heirs of the blessing. Do you find in yourself a hungering and thirsting after Christ? You are blessed, and this faith will save you.

Now faith will say, "I am wonderfully in pain, I am faint, and even starved, and I cannot be filled without Christ." Yet be content, man, you shall be filled with Him. In the meantime you have Him, and you have blessedness, and you shall be blessed. It is said in 1 John 5:13: "These things have I written unto you that believe in the name of the Son of God, that you may know that you have eternal life, and that you may believe on the name of the Son of God." Mark how the apostle distinguishes these two things. You believe on the name of Christ, yet you say, "Though I believe, I am not sure of my salvation, I do not know it." Why, do not let that much trouble you; that is a consequence of it, and that assurance will follow after. Therefore you should not confuse assurance with believing. "These things have I written unto you that ye might know." So there is a conclusion to be deduced from the promises, so that a man may have full hold of Christ and yet not be fully assured of his salvation. So then here is the will, which is the first thing.

But the Lord works the deed also. And whereas it is said that God takes the will for the deed, the place needs to be well understood. When we say that God takes the will for the deed, it is not always true unless it is understood properly. When a man has done to the utmost of his power what he is able, has endeavored by all means, *then* God will take the will for the deed; but if there is ability in me, and I do not as much as I am able, if I do not my utmost endeavor, then God will not take it. But my point is that God works the will and the deed.

When a man comes to the throne of grace, and sets forward in his journey towards God, the first thing he does is to come to the throne of grace with Christ in his arms, and then, having fast hold on Christ, he hastens and does

not delay, having hold as Joab on the horns of the altar.
He hastens, he sees it is no time to delay, he sees it is now a
time of need. Is it not needful to make haste (when the
pursuer of blood follows) to the city of refuge? Who
would make delay, and not run as fast as his legs would
carry him? As soon as I apprehend my need, and see the
golden scepter stretched out, then I come with Christ in
my arms, and present Him to the Father. This is the ap-
proaching and drawing near to the throne of grace im-
plied in the text.

But when I have come there, what do I say? Shall I
come and say nothing? The prodigal son resolved to go to
his father, and say, "I will up and go (there is the will), and
say (there is his speech)." The believer is not like the son
who said to his father, "I will go," but did not. He will not
only say so, but will draw near. And then he has a promise:
"Him that cometh unto Me, I will in no wise cast out."

But when we come, what must we do? We must take
unto ourselves words, according to the prophet's expression: "Take with you words, and turn to the Lord; say
unto Him, 'Take away all iniquity, and receive us gra-
ciously; so will we render the calves of our lips' " (Hosea
14:2). When we come to the throne of grace, the thing
that we do is to present unto the Father Christ bleeding,
gasping, dying, buried, and conquering death. And when
we present Christ to Him, we open our case and confess
our sin to the full, saying, "Lord, this is my case."

When a beggar comes to ask alms of you, he makes a
preface and tells you his extremity: "Sir, I am in great want.
I have not tasted a bit of bread in so many days, and unless
you help me by your charity, I am utterly undone." Now
when these two concur, that there is true need in the beggar, and liberality in him of whom he begs, it encourages
the beggar to be importunate, and he prevails; you can tell
when the beggar has a real need by his tone, accent, or
language. The needy beggar's tone and accent is different

from the sturdy beggar's who has no need. But yet, though the beggar is in great misery, if he sees a churlish Nabal go by him, he has no heart to beg nor follow him, nor does he beg hard because he has but little hope of attaining anything from him.

But let both these meet together, that the beggar is in great need, and that he from whom he begs is very liberal, and it makes him beg hard. A beggar's need will make him speak, and he will not hide his sores; but if he has any sore more ugly or worse than another, he will uncover it: "Good sir, behold my woeful and distressed case." He will lay all open to provoke pity.

So when you come before God in confession, can you not find words to open yourself to Almighty God? Is there not one word whereby you may uncover your sores and beseech Him to look on you with an eye of pity? We must not mince our sins, but amplify and aggravate them so that God may be moved to pardon us. Till we do this, we cannot expect that God will forgive us. There is a great ado made about auricular confession, but it is mere babble. It would be better to cry out our sins at the high cross than to confess in a priest's ear. You whisper in the priest's ear, and how are you the better for it? Come and pour your heart and soul out before Almighty God; confess yourself to Him as David did, for that has a promise made to it: "Against Thee, Thee only have I sinned, and done this evil in Thy sight, that Thou mightest be justified when Thou speakest, and be clear when Thou judgest" (Psalm 51:4).

Why should we confess sin? One main reason is to justify God. When a sinner confesses, "I am a child of wrath and of death; and if Thou dost cast me into hell, as justly Thou may, I have received but my due." When a man does this (as the king's attorney may frame a bill of indictment against himself) he justifies Almighty God. Thus did David: "Against Thee, against Thee." Now when we have thus aggravated our misery, then comes the other part of begging, to cry for mercy with earnestness. And this takes the power of the Spirit.

It is one thing for a man to pray, and another thing for a man to say a prayer. It is the easiest thing for a man to say a prayer. It is the easiest thing in the world to say a prayer, but to pray and cry for mercy, as David did, in good earnest to wrestle with God and say, "Lord, my life lies in it. I will never give Thee over. I will not go with a denial"—this is the work of God's Spirit. In Jude 20, the apostle exhorts: "But ye beloved, build up yourselves in your most holy faith, praying in the Holy Ghost." There is the prayer of the faithful, to pray in the Holy Ghost. In Ephesians 6 we read of armor provided for all the parts of a man's body, yet all that will not serve the turn unless prayer comes in as the chief piece of armor. "Praying always with all prayer and supplication in the Spirit, and watching thereunto with all perseverance" (Ephesians 6:18). This is the prayer of faith that procures forgiveness of sins; we must pray in faith and in the Spirit; that is the language that God understands. He knows the meaning of the Spirit, and knows none else but that.

Many men are wondrously deceived in what they call the spirit of prayer. One thinks it is a faculty to set out one's desires in fair words, showing earnestness, and speaking much in an extemporary prayer. This I think is commendable, yet this is not the spirit of prayer. One who shall never come to heaven may be more ready in this than the child of God; for a prayer is a matter of skill and exercise, but the spirit of prayer is another thing. "The Spirit helpeth our infirmities, for we know not what we should pray for as we ought; but the Spirit itself maketh intercession for us with groanings that cannot be uttered" (Romans 8:26).

What! Shall we think then that the Holy Ghost groans or speaks in prayer? No, but it makes us groan, and though we do not speak a word, yet it so enlarges our hearts that we send up a volley of sighs and groans which fit the throne of grace. And this is the spirit of prayer, when with these sighs and groans I beg as it were for my life. This is that ardent affection the Scripture speaks of. A cold prayer will never get forgiveness of sins; it is the prayer of faith that prevails. The prayer of the faithful avails much if it is fervent. Prayer is a fire from heaven which, if you have it, will carry all heaven before it; there is nothing in the world so strong as a Christian thus praying.

Prayers that are kindled with such a zeal are compared to Jacob's wrestling with the angel (Hosea 12:4), whereby he "had power over the angel." The prophet expounds what this wrestling was: "he wept and made supplication unto him; he found him in Bethel, and there he spake unto us." This is wrestling with God, when you fill heaven with your sighs and sobs, wet your couch with tears as David did, and have this resolution with Jacob: "I will not let thee go except thou bless me." God so loves this kind of boldness in a beggar, that he will not go away without an answer. The poor widow in the parable would not quit asking until the judge, though he did not fear God or care for man, by reason of her importunity, granted her desire.

Mark the other thing in the apostle: he bids us pray with the Spirit and with perseverance. And he who comes thus has a promise: "He that calleth on the name of the Lord shall be saved. Call on Me in the day of trouble, and I will hear thee." It is set down fully in Matthew 7:7–8: "Ask, and it shall be given you; seek, and ye shall find; knock, and it shall be opened unto you: for every one that asketh receiveth, and he that seeketh findeth, and to him that knocketh it shall be opened."

There is a promise annexed to asking, seeking, and knocking, but it is also proved by universal experience: "for every one that asketh receiveth." It is every man's case; never did any man do it who has lost his labor by not attaining what he asked. If you do not have it yet, you shall have it in the end. It is so fair a petition to ask to have your sins pardoned, that God would be friends with you, that Christ would make you love Him, and that God would be your God, that God delights in it.

This is the point then: suppose God does not answer you quickly; yet keep on knocking and seeking. That is perseverance, the thing whereby it is distinguished from temporary asking. The hypocrite will pray in a time of need and adversity, but his prayer is not constant. "Will the hypocrite always call upon God?" (Job 27:10). If they come and seek God, and He does not answer, they will do what Saul did, they will try the devil. God would not answer Saul, and he quickly went to the devil.

It is not so with God's children; they pray, and pray, and wait still; they pray with the Spirit and with perseverance: God deals not always alike with His children. Sometimes He answers right away, and sometimes He makes them wait His leisure. "I said I would confess my sin," said David, "and my transgressions, and Thou forgavest the iniquity of my sin" (Psalm 32:5). When Daniel set himself to seek God, even while he was speaking and praying, the man Gabriel appeared unto him and touched him about the time of the evening oblation. Before the word was out of his mouth, God was at his heart, and immediately sent him a dispatch. The same we see in Isaiah 65:24. Mark what a promise there is: "It shall come to pass that before they call I will answer; and while they are yet speaking I will hear." This is a great encouragement!

But God may not always do this; and what is the reason? Why, He wonderfully delights to be wrestled with, and to hear the words of His own Spirit. Nothing is more delightful to Him than when the spirit is earnest and will not give over. "I will not let thee go unless thou bless me."

It is said in the Song of Solomon that honey is under the lips of the church. Why so? It is because there is no honey sweeter to the palate than spiritual prayer to God.

And therefore God delays in answering you because He would have more of it from you. If the musicians come and play at our doors or windows, and we do not delight in their music, we throw them money right away so that they will leave. But if the music pleases us, we wait to give them money because we would keep them longer. So the Lord loves and delights in the sweet words of His children, and therefore puts them off, and does not answers them presently.

God's children, let Him deny them never so long, will never stop knocking and begging. They will pray and they will wait until they receive an answer. Many will pray to God, since prayer is a duty; but few use it as a means to obtain a blessing. Those who come to God in the use of prayer as a means to obtain what they would have will pray and not give up; they will expect an answer, and never stop petitioning till they receive it.

14

Peace with God, Part 1

"Therefore, being justified by faith, we have peace with
God, through our Lord Jesus Christ." Romans 5:1

Having declared unto you the nature of faith, and that
point which concerns the practice of it in our approach
unto God, I now come to show to you the fruits and bene-
fits Christians receive from this mother-grace. The apostle
sets down in these words the mother-grace, justification;
that whereas we were afar off, we are made near, and of
enemies made friends of God. Then there are the daughters or handmaids of this grace. For when we are justified
by faith, then:

• We have peace with God, that peace of conscience
which passes all understanding.

• We have free access by faith unto the throne of
grace, so that we need not look for any other mediators.
Christ has made the way for us to God, so that we may go
boldly to the throne of grace, and find help at any time of
need.

• There follows a joyful hope, by which a Christian has
a taste of heaven before he comes to enjoy it. "We rejoice
in hope," said the apostle. Hope is as firm a thing as faith.
Faith makes absent things to be as if they were present;
hope has patience with it, and would have us wait. We shall
be sure of it, but we must wait patiently.

• Then we not only rejoice in hope, but even those
things which spoil a natural man's joy, such as crosses,

troubles, and afflictions. These are made the matter of this man's joy, not delectable objects only. And this does not happen in time to come after afflictions, but during afflictions. So that which spoils the joy of a natural man is fuel to kindle this man's joy.

Now concerning justification by faith, though it be an ordinary point, yet there is nothing that more needs explication than to know how a man shall be justified by faith. It is easily spoken, but explicated with difficulty. Therefore, in this mother-grace, I shall show you what faith is that justifies, and what this justification is; for it is not so easy a matter either.

Concerning the nature of faith, I have spoken sufficiently already wherein it consists; but yet, notwithstanding, there is a certain thing as like this faith as may be and yet comes short of it. There are many, like the foolish virgins, who thought they were well enough, and thought they had time enough. So many think, verily they have faith, yea, and perchance go with such a persuasion to their very graves thinking that they have grace, that they labor after Christ, lay hold of Him, and are free from worldly pollutions. They feel that they have a taste and relish of the joy of the world to come, and yet are carried all this while to a fool's paradise, and think there is no fear of their safety, never knowing that they are cast away, till they come to the gates of hell and find themselves, by woeful experience, shut out of heaven. The case is woeful of those who are thus deceived.

Know then that it is not every faith that justifies a man; a man may have faith and not be justified. The faith that justifies is the faith of God's elect (Titus 1:1); there is a faith that may belong to them who are not God's elect, but that faith does not justify. That faith which justifies must be an unfeigned faith (1 Timothy 1:5; 2 Timothy 1:5). Now here is the skill of a Christian, to see what that faith is which justifies him.

This justifying faith is not every work of God's Spirit in a man's heart, for there are supernatural operations of the Spirit in a man's heart that are but temporary, that do not carry him through, and therefore are ineffectual. But the end of this faith that justifies is the salvation of our souls. We read in Scripture of apostasy and falling back. They cannot be apostates who were never in the way of truth. This being an accident, we must have a subject for it; there are certain people who have supernatural workings. Some are drawn up and down with every wind of doctrine; they have this cold and temporary faith. It is temporary because in the end it reveals itself to not be constant and permanent. We read in John 11:26 that they who are born of God never see death; they shall never perish eternally. Yet we must know that there may be conceptions that will never come to the point of birth, to a right and perfect delivery. And thus it may be in the soul of a man: there may be conceptions that will never come to a ripe birth. But let a man be born of God and come to perfection of birth, and the case is clear: he shall never see death. "He that liveth and believeth in Me shall not see death." And this is made a point of faith: "Believest thou this?"

There is another thing called conception, and that is certain dispositions to a birth that do not come to full fruition. True, a child who is born and lives is as perfectly alive as he who lives a hundred years; yet there are conceptions that do not end in birth. Now the faith that justifies is a living faith. There is such a thing as dead faith; this is a feigned faith, the other is an unfeigned faith. "The life that I now live, I live by faith of the Son of God." Do you think a dead faith can make a living soul? That goes against reason. A man cannot live by a dead thing, nor by a dead faith.

There is such a thing as dead faith. A faith that does not work is a dead faith: "Seest thou how faith wrought with his works, and by his works was faith made perfect?" (James 2:22), for "as the body without the spirit is dead," or without breath is dead, "so faith without works is dead also" (verse 26). See how the apostle compares it: "As the body without the spirit is dead, so faith without works is dead also." The apostle does not make faith the form of works, as the soul is the form of the man, but as the body without the spirit is dead, so that faith that does not work, that has no tokens of life, is dead.

But then the other word strikes home: "Faith wrought with his works." Compare this with 2 Corinthians 12:7–9, where the apostle prayed that the messenger of Satan might be removed from him. Note God's response to his prayer: "My grace is sufficient for thee, for My strength is made perfect in weakness." What! Does our weakness make God's strength more perfect, to which nothing can be added? No, it is, "My strength, and the perfection of it, is made known in the weakness of the means that I make use of for the delivery of man's soul from death."

So here the excellency and perfection of our faith is made known by works; when I see that it is not an idle faith, but a working one, then I say it is made perfect by the work. When a man has a dead faith, it does not put him to work; never believe that dead faith will make a living soul.

In Jude 20, it has another epithet attached to it, namely, "the most holy faith"—not holy only, but most holy. That faith which brings a man to God's holy of holies must be most holy. It is said that "God dwells in our hearts by faith." Now if God and faith dwell in a heart together, that heart must be pure and clean. Faith makes the heart pure. It would be a most dishonorable thing to entertain God in a pigsty, a filthy and unclean heart; but if faith dwells there, it makes a fit house for the habitation of the King of saints, and therefore it purifies the heart.

Well, then, do you think that your sins are forgiven,

that you have a strong faith, and yet are as profane and as filthy as ever? How can that be? It is a most holy faith that justifies, not a faith that will allow a man to lie on a dunghill or in the gutter with the hogs. There may be a faith that is somewhat like this, but it is but temporary, and comes short of true faith.

But there is another thing that distinguishes it, and it is the peculiar work of faith. "In Christ Jesus neither circumcision availeth anything, nor uncircumcision, but a new creature" (Galatians 6:15). And again, "Neither circumcision nor uncircumcision availeth anything, but faith which worketh by love" (Galatians 5:6). It is set down twice. Now what is a new creature? Why, it is he who has such a faith as works by love; it is not a dead faith, but a faith that works. But how does it work? It not only abstains from evil and does some good acts, which a temporary faith may do, but it is such a faith as works by love. The love of God constrains him, and he so loves God, in that he hates evil for God's sake. The other person who has a dead faith does not do it out of love for God; all the love he has is self-love. He serves his own turn by using God rather than having any true love to serve Him.

Now that we may the better distinguish between these two, I shall endeavor to show you how much further one may go than the other. I do not know a more difficult point than this, nor a case more to be cut by a thread than this, it being a point of conscience. Therefore, first, I declared unto you the nature of faith, how God first works the will and the deed, and that there is a hungering and thirsting after Christ. First, I say, there is a will and desire to be made a partaker of Christ and His righteousness; then there is the deed too. We are not only "wish-ers" and "would-ers," but we actually approach unto the throne of grace and there lay hold of Christ; we touch the golden scepter which He holds out to us.

QUESTION. But is there not an earnest and good desire in a temporary faith, an unfeigned desire?

ANSWER. Yes, there may be for a time a greater and more vehement desire in a temporary believer than in a true one, than in the elect themselves all their life.

QUESTION. Where is the difference then? I thought all was well with me when I had such a desire that I could scarcely rest till it was accomplished!

ANSWER. Beloved, it is a hard matter to tell you the difference; but you must consider:

1. From whence this desire flows, whether it comes from an accidental cause: as if by accident my heart is made more soft and I more sensible of my condition, or whether my nature is changed. To give you an example, when iron is put into the forge it is softened; and as soon as it is taken out we say it is time to strike while the iron is hot. The fire has made a change in it: it is malleable and the hammer is able to work on it. But let the fire be gone and it is as hard as before. Nay, we say that steel is harder, so that there is no change in the nature of iron; it is hard still and goes back to its former state. If it is softened, it is by an accidental cause. So it is here: as long as temporary faith is in the furnace of afflictions, when God shall let loose the cord of his conscience, and makes him see that there is no way for salvation but by Christ, then the sense of his torture will make him desire with all the veins in his heart to have Christ.

See a singular example of this temporary desire in Psalm 78:34: "When He slew them, then they sought Him, and returned and inquired early after God." So Proverbs 1:27: "When your fear cometh as desolation, and your destruction cometh as a whirlwind; when distress and anguish cometh upon you, then shall they call upon Me."

We must not desire relief with a feigned desire, but in truth and reality. "They remembered then that God was their Rock, and the high God their Redeemer." They saw a Redeemer when He was slaying them, and they believed

that God would free them, but it was only a temporary desire: "Nevertheless they flattered Him with their mouths,
and lied unto Him with their tongues; for their heart was
not right with Him, neither were they steadfast in His
covenant." Observe then this was but a temporary case, a
temporary change; there was no new creature, no new nature wrought. But in the furnace of affliction, as long as
the fire was hot, they were pliable; they were not steadfast
in His covenant.

Let this be an admonition to them who think they
never can have true faith till God slays them. I am not of
that opinion. God sometimes uses this means, but it is not
so necessary that it cannot be otherwise; and to speak
truly, I would rather have faith come another way. The
difference is this: temporary believers will have Christ while
God is slaying them, while they are in the furnace of afflictions; but the true believers seek a Redeemer when God's
hand is not on them. The true believer is sick of love, and
when he has no affliction, nor God's hand on him, with
the apostle he accounts all things dung and dross for the
excellency of the knowledge of Christ Jesus. There is an
ardent desire when affliction is not what draws him. If,
when you are out of the forge, you have your heart softened and find this work of grace and faith to drive you to
Christ, you have an unfeigned faith, and so the faith of
God's elect.

Again, there is not only this desire in him who has a
temporary faith, but, having understood the Word, he so
desires it that when he knows there is no having Christ, nor
happiness or salvation by Him, unless he denies himself
and parts with his evil ways; being persuaded of this, out of
self-love he would have Christ. And seeing that these are
the terms—that he must turn over a new leaf and lead a
new life or else go to hell—therefore he will do this too.
This is much, yet he will do this too; but how shall this be
proved? Most evidently in 2 Peter 2:20: "For if after they

have escaped the pollutions of the world through the knowledge of our Lord and Savior Jesus Christ, they are again entangled therein and overcome, the latter end with them is worse than the beginning." Here is that apostasy, and here is the subject of temporary faith. "It had been better for them not to have known the way of righteousness than, after they have known it, to turn from the holy commandment delivered unto them." This was a temporary conversion, as Ephraim, like a broken bow, turned back again in the day of battle. Observe what they did: they were like the foolish virgins; they kept their purity in respect of the pollutions of the world; they lived very civilly; they escaped the corruptions of the world, and no man could challenge them of any filthy act; they knew that Christ was the King of saints, and had the knowledge of Him; they knew that it was not fitting that the King of glory and holiness should be attended on by the wicked; that they must have sanctity that will follow Him; and, therefore, they labored to be fit to attend Him: they escaped the pollutions of the world; yet it did not last. Why so? It happened to them according to the true proverb: "The dog is returned to his vomit, and the sow that is washed to her wallowing in the mire."

By the way, take notice of the filthiness of sin; it is so filthy that the Lord compares it to the vomit of a dog! Then there follows another comparison: it is as "the sow that is washed, and returns to her wallowing in the mire." Here you see another loathsome resemblance of this temporary faith. The sow was washed, but how? Her swinish nature was not washed from her; as long as the sow is kept from the mire, in a fair meadow with the sheep, she looks as sleek and clean as they. She was washed, there is an external change, but her nature remained. Bring a sow and a sheep to a puddle. The sheep will not go in because it has no swinish nature; but the other, retaining its swinish nature, though before in outward appearance as clean as the sheep was, yet she goes again to her wallowing in the mire.

There may be the casting away of a man's sins and yet no new creature wrought in him. That I may show this to you, take this example. A man known to be as covetous a man as lives loves his money as well as his God; yet, perchance, this man has committed a misdemeanor and must be hanged for it. So this man, to save his life, will part with all he has. Has his disposition changed? No, not a whit; he is as covetous as before. He is the same man; he does it to save his life, and to this end he is content to part with his money. He has the same mind as those in Acts 27 who, in a storm, cast their wares into the sea with their own hands willingly, and yet half unwilling. To save their lives they would part with these things, yet it was with a great deal of repining and reluctance.

These men forsake their sins and hate them, yet it is but imperfectly; they part with them, but they part weeping. At this parting there may be a great deal of joy; they may taste not only the sweetness of the Word of God, but because they are in a disposition and way to salvation, they may have some kind of feeling of the joys, and taste the powers of the world to come. As the apostle says: "It is impossible for those who were once enlightened, and have tasted of the heavenly gift, and were made partakers of the Holy Ghost. . ." (Hebrews 6:4). There is a supernatural work wrought in them, and they have tasted the good Word of the Lord; they begin to have some hope, and rejoice in the glory of the world to come. What is the difference then? Here is a tasting, but, as it is John 6, it does not say that "he that eats My flesh and tastes My blood," but, "he that eats my flesh and drinks my blood shall live forever." There is a difference between tasting and drinking; there may be a tasting without drinking. Matthew 27:34 says that when they gave Christ vinegar, He tasted thereof, but would not drink. He who can take a full draught of

Christ crucified, "he shall never thirst, but shall be as a springing fountain that springeth up to everlasting life." But it shall not be so with him who only tastes.

The vintner goes round the cellar and tastes every vessel; he takes it only into his mouth and casts it out again, and yet knows by the tasting whether it is good or bad. The wine goes only to his palate, but does not reach his stomach. So a temporary believer tastes and feels what an excellent thing it is to have communion with Christ, and to be made partaker of His glory, but he merely tastes it.

Look at Hosea 5:15, where we have another instance of this temporary believer. You would think they sought God in a good sort, and in as good a manner as one could desire; but how did they seek Him? It was only in a time of affliction: "I will go and return to My place until they acknowledge their offense and seek My face; in their affliction they will seek Me early." In Hosea 5:15, the Lord complains of them notwithstanding: "They will in their affliction seek Me early." Was not this a fair returning? "Come," they say, "let us return unto the Lord, for He hath torn, and He will heal us." What comfort they seemed to gather from the ways of the Lord! But see what follows: "O Ephraim," said the Lord, "what shall I do unto thee? O Judah, what shall I do unto thee? For your goodness is as a morning cloud, and as the early dew it goeth away" (Hosea 6:4), that is, it is but a temporary thing, wrought by affliction, which will not abide.

When a wicked man on his deathbed desires that God would spare him and restore him to his health, and that he would become a new man, all this comes but from the terrors of death; for it often proves to be the case that if God restores him, he becomes as bad, if not worse than ever he was before.

2. Take this for another difference: God's children can as earnestly desire grace as mercy; the temporary believer desires mercy, but never desires grace. The believer desires

grace to have his nature healed, and to hate his former conduct. The temporary believer never had, nor ever will have this desire; should one come to the temporary believer and tell him that God will be merciful to him, yet he may go on and take his fill of sin and be sure of mercy, he would like this well, and think it the most welcome news that could be. He only fears damnation, and self-love makes him only desire freedom from that. But the child of God hates sin, though there were no hell, judge, or tormentor. He begs God as hard for grace as for mercy, and would do so were there no punishment. His nature being changed, he desires grace as well as mercy, which the temporary believer never does.

3. The last mark is taken from the words of the apostle: "Neither circumcision availeth any thing, nor uncircumcision, but faith which worketh by love." Love and the new creation puts God's children to work; their hearts are first altered and changed by being made new creatures. As the Scripture says, till a man's heart is circumcised, he is a dead man. Deadness argues impotency to do those things that a living man does. The temporary believer will not sin for fear of the consequences; but this man cannot sin like that; his heart is changed and he is dead to sin. Both abstain from sin, but the disposition is not alike. The temporary sinner perchance does not commit a sin, but he could find in his heart to. He does not say with Joseph, "How can I do this great wickedness and sin against God?" The true believer says, "I could do this evil easily enough, but I will not." "God cannot bear those who are evil," it is said in Revelation.

Now he who is born of God cannot practice sin; there is that seed, that spring in him so that for all his life he cannot sin; rather, it turns his heart from it. For all his life he could not tell you how to swear, lie, or join with others in wickedness; but this must be understood, I am speaking of the constant course of their lives. I am not speaking of

what they may do in afflictions, or when they are sur-
prised; but in the course of their lives, they commit sin as if
they did not know how to do it. The other man does it
skillfully; these do it ill-favoredly.

Your faith then must be a faith that works by love. Can
you do those good works that you do out of love? Then,
my soul for yours, you are saved. Get me any temporary
believer who loves God, and I shall say something to you.
Do you then have a faith that causes you to love God, a
working faith, a faith that will not allow you to do anything
displeasing to Him? If you have such a faith, you are justified before God.

I come now to the point of justification, the greatest of
all blessings. "Blessed is he," said David, "whose transgression is forgiven, and whose sin is covered; blessed is the
man to whom the Lord imputeth not iniquity." It is the
most blessed condition that can be; it is set down by way of
exclamation. "Oh, the blessedness of the man to whom the
Lord imputeth not iniquity!"

What is justification? The Scripture in Paul's epistles
speaks of justification by faith, and in James of justification
by works. Now it will be useful for us in this point to know
whence justification comes; it comes from "justice" (*tsedeck*,
as the original has it) and "to justify." So justification and
righteousness depend one upon the other; for what is justification but the manifestation of the righteousness that is
in a man? And therefore in Galatians 3:21 they are put for
one and the same thing: "For if there had been a law given
which could have given life, verily righteousness should
have been by the law," that is, justification would have
been by the law. Again, "If righteousness be by the law,
then Christ is dead in vain" (Galatians 2:21); that is also, if
justification had been by the law. Justification is a manifestation of righteousness, and as many ways as righteousness is taken, so many ways is justification taken,
which is a declaration of righteousness; so that if there is a

double righteousness, there must be also a double justification. Beloved, I bring you no new doctrine; do not be
afraid of that. But I show you how to reconcile places of
Scripture against the church of Rome, and those things
which the papists bring against us in this point. It stands by
reason, seeing that justification is a declaration of righteousness, that there must be as many sorts of justification
as there are of righteousness.

Now there is a double sort of righteousness: "That the
righteousness of the law may be fulfilled in us" (Romans
8:4). There is a righteousness fulfilled in us, and a righteousness fulfilled by us, which is walking in the Spirit. The
righteousness fulfilled in us is fulfilled by another and is
made ours by imputation; so we have a righteousness outside us and a righteousness inherent in us; the righteousness outside us is forgiveness of sins and pardon of them,
which is a gracious act of God, letting fall all actions
against me, and accounting me as if I had never sinned
against Him all my lifetime. Then there is a righteousness
within me, an inherent righteousness. And if a righteousness, then justification; for that is but a declaration of
righteousness. And so that which the fathers call justification is taken generally for sanctification; that which we call
justification, they call forgiveness of sins; that which we call
sanctification, they call justification. So the difference is
only in the terms.

Justification is not taken only as opposed to condemnation, which is the first kind of righteousness. "He
that is dead is freed from sin" (Romans 6:7). If you look to
the Greek in the margin, it is, "He that is dead is justified
from sin." This is not taken in the first sense, as opposed to
condemnation, but in the other sense, as it has relation to
final grace. The perfection of sanctification is wrought in
me; for where there is final grace, there is a supersedeas
from all sin. So Revelation 22:11: "Let him that is righteous
be righteous still." The Greek is, "Let him that is righteous

be justified still."

See then the difference between Paul and James. Paul speaks of that which consists in remission of sins, as in comparing the apostle with David will appear. "Blessed is the man whose sins are forgiven." James speaks of justification in the second acceptance. You need not run to that distinction of justification before God and justification before men; do not think that James was speaking only of justification before men. "Was not Abraham our father justified by works, when he offered up Isaac on the altar?" What! Justified by killing his son! This was a proper work indeed to justify him before man, to kill his son! In Psalm 106, we read how God accounted the act of Phinehas for righteousness. Thus you see how works are accounted righteousness in the second kind of righteousness. In the former righteousness we are justified by faith; for in inherent righteousness there is a goodly chain of virtues. Peter says to "add to your faith virtue," add one grace to another; "add to virtue knowledge." Faith is but one part of the crown. Now this justification in the first sense, whereby my sins are forgiven, is called the righteousness of God, because of Christ who is God, because it is wrought by Christ. In Daniel 9:24, He is called "an everlasting righteousness," which continues forever, world without end; for do not think that the saints in heaven have only the second kind of righteousness, for they have the same covering of justification by Christ in heaven that they had before. God covers their sins not here only, but there also; justification follows them forever.

QUESTION. What are the various parts of justification? We are wont to say that there are two parts: one is the imputation of righteousness, the other the forgiveness of sins.

ANSWER. For my own part, I think that justification is one simple act of God, and that it is improperly distinguished as parts. I shall show to you, both by reason and authority, that faith is but one act.

Let none say that I take away the imputation of the righteousness of Christ. No, bringing in light and expelling darkness are not two acts, but one. We are accounted righteous, that is, we have our sins forgiven. And the reason is this: if sin were a positive thing and had a being in itself, then the forgiveness of sin must be a thing distinct from the imputation of righteousness. White and black are both existent; but darkness and light are not, but only a privation one of another. Darkness is nothing of itself but the absence of light; the bringing in of light is the suppression of it. You must understand that sin has no being, no entity; it is only an absence of righteousness, the want of that light which should be in the subject. This want is either in our nature, and then it is called original sin, or it is in our person and actions, and then it is called actual transgression. Sin is an absence of that positive being which is, as I said, either in our nature or in our works.

Thus I will resolve you in another point/ If sin were a positive thing, all the world cannot avoid but that God must be the Author of it; for nothing can have a being without deriving its being from the first being, God. Now how can we avoid God's being the author of sin? Why, thus, sin is nothing.

OBJECTION. What! Sin is nothing? Will God damn a man and send him to hell for nothing?

ANSWER. It is not such a nothing as you make it; a man is not damned for nothing. It is a nothing privative, an absence of that which should be, and which a man ought to have. As when a student is whipped for not saying his lesson, is he whipped for nothing? Indeed, he has nothing; he cannot say a word of his lesson, and therefore he is whipped. It is for a thing he ought to have, and does not have. Well, if you will say there are two parts of justification, do so if you please; but this I take to be the more proper and genuine explanation.

Besides, it appears by testimony of the apostle, "As David describeth the blessedness of the man to whom the Lord imputeth righteousness without works, saying, 'Blessed are they whose iniquities are forgiven, and whose sins are covered' " (Romans 4:6–7). The apostle cites the prophet David from Psalm 32. Mark the apostle's conclusion, and how he proves it. His conclusion is, "That man is blessed unto whom the Lord imputes righteousness without works."

His argument then must be thus framed:

He whom God forgives is blessed; but he to whom God imputes righteousness without works has his sins forgiven him. Therefore he is blessed.

Now, how could this assumption hold if imputation of righteousness and remission of sins were two distinct acts? For not imputing righteousness is not to bring in light, which keeps out darkness; but observe, the apostle to the Colossians and Ephesians makes this forgiveness of sins the whole work, way, and foundation of our redemption.

But remember that I do not deny the imputation of righteousness; for that is the foundation of the other. Here is the point. How is Christ's righteousness imputed to me? It is by that positive thing which expels the other. It is not as if Christ's righteousness were in me subjectively; for it was wrought by His passion as well as His action. The apostle calls it "faith in His blood." By faith in Christ, Christ's passive obedience is imputed to me.

QUESTION. What! Do you think the meaning is that God esteems me as if I had hung on the cross, and as if I had had my sides pierced?

ANSWER. No, that would not stead me or do me any good; that which was meritorious and singular in Him reaches to us. The meaning is this, as it is in the articles of the Church of England: "That for the merits of Jesus Christ, God is well-pleased with the obedience of His Son, both active and passive, as that He takes us to be in that

state for His sake, as if we had fulfilled all His laws, and
never broken them at any time, and as if we owed Him not
a farthing." This is imputed righteousness, however the
papists may scoff at it. And this kind of justification must of
necessity be by imputation. Why? Because when a man has
committed a sin, it cannot be undone again. God, by His
absolute power, cannot make something undone once it is
done; for that implies a contradiction. The act past cannot be revoked, nor the nature thereof changed; murder
will be murder still. How then can I be justified, the sin being past, and the nature of it still remaining? I say, how can
I be justified in the first sense any other way than by imputation? It is said in 2 Corinthians 5:19 that "God was in
Christ reconciling the world unto Himself." This kind of
justification, which consists in remission of sins, cannot be
but imputative; sin cannot be changed, nor the thing done
be undone.

QUESTION. Here comes a greater question: if by justification our sins are forgiven us, what sins are forgiven, I
pray? Sins past or sins to come?

ANSWER. We are taught that, in the instant of justification, all our sins past and to come are remitted. In my
mind this is an unsound doctrine; for if we look narrowly
into it, we shall find that in propriety of speech, remission
of sins has relation to that which is past. It is said therefore,
"Whom God hath set forth to be a propitiation through
faith in His blood, to declare His righteousness for the
remission of sins that are past, through the forbearance of
God" (Romans 3:25). And remission of sins has relation to
those that are past, as appears by inevitable reason; for
what is remission of sins but sin covered? Now can a thing
be covered before it exists? "Blot out mine iniquities," said
David. Can a thing be blotted out before it is written? This
is the thing that makes the pope so ridiculous, that he will
forgive sins for the time before they are committed. But
what! Do we get nothing for the time to come? Yes, yes,

when the sin is past, by faith we have a new access unto God; and having risen by repentance, we get a new act, not of universal justification, but of a particular justification, from this and that particular sin.

QUESTION. But if there is forgiveness for sins past already, and I know that I am justified and my sins remitted, may I now pray for forgiveness of sins past? The papists say it is active infidelity, and as absurd as to pray to God to create the world anew or incarnate His Son again.

ANSWER. But there is no conversion where there is not praying; and there is need of praying for the remission of sins past and against sin for the time to come, as I shall show in the next sermon, and also consider whether there be any interruptions of the act of justification by falling into great sins. There is no man has a mind more against quirks and subtleties than I; yet for the opening of these things, and staying and settling the mind, and clearing the understanding, I shall endeavor in the next discourse to clear these things unto you.

15

Peace with God, Part 2

"Therefore, being justified by faith, we have peace with
God through our Lord Jesus Christ." Romans 5:1

In Romans 5, especially in the beginning thereof, the
apostle sets down for us those special comforts that a man
receives after God has wrought that supernatural grace of
faith in his heart; so that here is set down the mother-
grace, justification by faith, and then the blessed issues or
daughters thereof. And those are a free access to God, a
joyful hope of the glory to come, and not only a patient,
but a joyful suffering of all afflictions that shall befall us in
this life.

Concerning justification by faith, I labored to open it
unto you in the last sermon. Three things may well be considered therein: what that faith is whereby we are justified;
what that justification is we have by faith; and what relation these have to the others.

Concerning the first of these, I told you that it was not
every faith that justifies, not every kind of faith that a man
can live by. There is a dead faith, and a man cannot live by
a dead thing. And there is a living faith, and that is called
an unfeigned faith. And though it is in Scripture called the
common faith, yet it does have some restrictions; it is the
faith of God's elect.

There is also a faith which is but temporary, that being
touched with the sense of sin. Some, when they see that
there is no deliverance from the curse due to sin but by

Christ, and that there is no part to be had in Christ but by renouncing all corruptions, the consideration of the desperateness of his case without Christ makes a man long after Him; and since he cannot have Christ without leaving sin, he will resolve on that too. He will move towards Christ, and perhaps he comes to taste of the sweetness of Christ, and feels the power of the world to come; he forsakes sin, and thereby comes so near the true believer that a man must, as it were, cut a hair to divide between them. And this is a thing very necessary to be considered.

I showed you also that these are not moral matters. This is not a faith that is wrought by the power of men, but by a work of God's Spirit; for it humbles a man for sin and makes him move toward Christ and seek Him above all things. And, having laid some hold on Him, he escapes the pollutions of the world; and yet this faith is but temporary. It is a supernatural thing, yet it is without root. Now this is not different in the circumstance of time; for time does not alter the thing. A child who lives but half an hour truly lives as much as one who lives a hundred years. But it is called temporary faith, not that therein stands the difference, but therein it is shown, and that proves the man to have something wanting. Our being united to Christ, and being nigh unto Him, is as a graft put into a tree; there are two grafts put into one stock, and each of them has all the several things necessary done unto it, as cutting, binding, and so on—yet time discovers that the one thrives and the other withers, which shows that there was an unseen fault. Though he who put in the grafts never saw it, yet time discovers it. The difference is not in the time, but in the foundation of the thing itself. Now what the difference is between these, I labored to declare unto you the last day.

The use of it is briefly this: true faith is not in all these. All do not have true faith; yet some come so near and have a faith so like it that it will trouble a wise man to make the distinction. These are like the foolish virgins, who lived very civilly and kept their purity in regard of the world; none could accuse them for any evil that they had done, yet they were at length shut out.

Many think themselves in a good way and a safe condition, yea, and they go out of the world in this conceit, thinking they are entering into the gate of heaven till they suddenly are cast down to hell. Therefore, let us search and sift ourselves. If this grace were as grass that grows in every field, it would be something; but it is a precious flower which, if we do not have, Christ profits us nothing. This is the means of Christ's being applied unto you. Therefore, how it behooves every one of us to look to it, and not to gloss over the matter slightly, but to search and try and examine ourselves. And by the marks I showed you before, it is such a thing as may be likened to a conception that never comes to an actual birth. Such a thing is this temporary faith.

Among others let me add the tokens of love; it is twice set down in Galatians: "Neither circumcision nor uncircumcision availeth anything, but faith which worketh by love." And again, "Neither circumcision . . . but the new creature." They who have a temporary faith lack nothing but being a new creature. What is the new creature? It is "faith that worketh by love." If a man loves God, it is a sure token that God has loved them first; and God never gives this love to anyone without giving them unfeigned faith.

Next, he is ever careful to test himself and to prove himself. The temporary believer cannot endure to be brought to trial. He accounts every beginning of grace in himself as very great; he thinks every molehill is a mountain. Now God's children know that they may be deceived with counterfeits, and therefore they try themselves.

Mark the words of the apostle: "Examine yourselves . . . prove your own selves; know ye not your own selves how that Jesus Christ is in you, except ye be reprobates?" Let us understand the words. First, we see that it is possible to know whether we are in the faith or not. And this is flat statement against the papists; for they think a man can have only a conjectural knowledge that he has grace and faith. It may be probable, they say, but it cannot be certainly known. But does not the apostle say, "Examine yourselves, prove yourselves, know yourselves?" Perhaps no papist can know it, yet it is possible to be known. Prove and try, you shall not lose your labor. If you take pains in it, you shall attain it in this world. "Make your calling and election sure," says the Apostle Peter. On God's part it is sure enough, for the foundation of God stands sure; but make it sure unto yourselves in respect of your own knowledge. "Know ye not your own selves that Jesus Christ is in you, except ye be reprobates?" It is a thing that may well be made sure of; therefore search, try, and examine. Others are content with bare beginnings that never come to any maturity; but those who have true faith are ever bringing themselves to the trial and touchstone.

QUESTION. But someone may say, "I have tried and examined myself, and I do not find that Christ is in me! Am I a reprobate therefore?"

ANSWER. No, God forbid. I do not say the man is a reprobate who cannot discern that Christ is in him. See what may explain this. "For there must be heresies among you, that they which are approved might be made known" (1 Corinthians 11:19). There must be men who are approved, such as have endured the dint and shot of the musket, such as have put themselves to the trial, and come off well. These are the approved ones, as opposed to those who take things hand over head, do not search, and try, examine, and put themselves to the test. It is a sign that these do not have true faith. What! Is having Christ so slight or poor a thing that they will take no pains for Him, or care not for knowing whether they have Him or not? What! Neglect Christ so much as not to venture on the trial?

But he who has saving faith is ever putting himself to the trial. Again, God's child not only uses all the means in himself to try himself, but he prays for the aid of God also. He knows that his own heart is deceitful and may deceive him, but that God is greater than his heart and knows all things. And therefore he cries unto God to try him, as in Psalm 139:23–24: "Try me, O God, and know my heart; prove me, and know my thoughts; look well whether there be any way of wickedness in me, and lead me in the way everlasting." There is an everlasting righteousness, and an everlasting way that leads to it. These are not content to try themselves only, but they desire God to try them also, to make them know the uprightness of their own hearts, and not to suffer them to be deceived thereby.

Consider now what that justification is which is obtained by this true and lively faith. I showed you that justification is ordinarily taken for an acquittal from a debt. It is derived from "justice" or "righteousness." Therefore I showed that justification and righteousness are taken for one and the self-same thing: "For if there had been a law given which could have given life, verily righteousness should have been by the law" (Galatians 3:21), that is, justification would have been by the law. Now as there is a double righteousness, so there is also a double justification; not that I hold that there is any other justification, as it comprehends remission of sins, but one. What I hold is that there are as many righteousnesses as there are justifications. Now there is a double kind of righteousness, an imputed righteousness and an inherent righteousness. The one is the righteousness of Christ, an act transient from the other, which cannot be made mine but by imputation. Besides this there is an inherent righteousness in us. James speaks of the one, and John speaks of the other. One is opposed to condemnation, and the other is opposed to hypocrisy. The soundness of the heart is respected by God for righteousness in respect of the graces inherent in us.

Now I wish to give you a sense of the difference between the one and the other, and therein to declare the difference between us and Rome. Know then that the question between us and Rome is not whether justification is by faith or not, but whether there is any such thing as justification or not? The doctrine of the church of Rome is that there is no such grace as this.

But concerning the first of these, the justification which is by the imputation of Christ's righteousness, imputation in this case is as when a man comes to hold up his hand at God's bar, as it were, and it is demanded of him what he has to say for himself why he should not die; and then this justification by Christ's righteousness is opposed to condemnation. Justification by faith is such that, when I come to stand before God, though conscience says I am guilty of a thousand sins, yet I may go boldly and plead my pardon, which will acquit me as if I had never sinned at any time. "God was thus in Christ reconciling the world to Himself, not imputing their sins unto them." Now, sin is a thing past, which, being done, cannot be made undone; the sin still remains: murder is still murder and adultery is still adultery; they cannot be undone.

Now how shall a man who is guilty of murder and adultery be made just? It cannot possibly be but by not imputing his sin unto him, so that God should account it to him as if it had not been done at all by him. Rather, He puts it to Christ's account. The word "account" is also used in Philemon, where Paul says, "If he hath wronged thee, or oweth thee ought, put that on mine account." When a man's sins are thus put upon Christ's account, he is accepted of God as freely as if he had never owed Him anything or as if he had never offended Him. This is done by transferring the debt from one person to another; so we see that this imputation of sin to Christ, and of Christ's righteousness to us, is most necessary. It must be so, and even if there were no testimony for it in Scripture, yet reason shows that there can be no righteousness but by God's acceptance of us in Christ as if we had never sinned. There is the difference then. "To him that worketh not, but believeth in Him that justifieth the ungodly, his faith is accounted to him for righteousness."

QUESTION. But does God really justify the ungodly? That is a hard speech. We read in Proverbs, "He that justifieth the wicked and condemneth the just, even they both are abomination to the Lord."

ANSWER. But we must understand this as we do some other Scriptures. We read in John that "the blind see, the lame walk, and the dumb speak." It is impossible for a man to be blind and see, and to be dumb and speak, all at the same time. Paul was the chief of sinners, at least in his own account, but the act of justification altered him. God justifies the ungodly, that is, him who is even now so; but by the imputation of Christ's righteousness he is made righteous, that is, righteous in God's account.

God first justifies a man's person, and then justifies a man from this or that particular act. Scripture says, "And by Him all that believe are justified from all things, from which we could not be justified by the law of Moses" (Acts 13:39). There is justification from this or that thing. There is first justification of a man's person; he who was an enemy is now made a friend; he is now no longer a stranger at home, but is in the number of God's household. No sooner does a man receive justification but, the same hour that he receives it, the bond is cancelled, the evidence is fastened to the cross of Christ, and hangs up there. Whereas before it was an evidence against us and would have lain heavy on us at the bar, now it is fastened to the cross as a cancelled record and the bond becomes void.

But when we consider justification from this or that particular act, a man is only justified from sins past; for it is contrary to reason and Scripture that a man should be justified from sins to come. The apostle has it thus: "Whom

God hath set forth to be a propitiation through faith in His blood, to declare His righteousness for the remission of sins that are past, through the forbearance of God" (Romans 3:25). It is clear also from the nature of the thing. A thing cannot be remitted before it is committed; it cannot be covered before it has an existence, nor blotted out before it is written. Therefore justification from such or such a fault must have relation to that which is past; but for justification for the time to come, I will speak now. This is where I left off the last time.

I now have faith and I believe in Christ. I am now in relation to Him, and have remission of sins past. But why then do I pray for it? To what end is that? Bellarmine objects that it is an act of infidelity to pray for it afterwards; but we do it, and we ought to do it. See Psalm 51. David made that psalm after the prophet Nathan had told him that his sin was pardoned; yet he cried here throughout the whole psalm to have his sin pardoned and blotted out. Though there was faith and assurance, yet he still prayed for it. Bellarmine says that this cannot be; but does he dispute against our opinion? No, he disputes against the Holy Ghost, for David had received a message of forgiveness but still prayed.

OBJECTION. But it is a fallacy to join these two together; for a man to pray for a thing past is an act of infidelity, as to pray that God would create the world and incarnate His Son.

ANSWER. There is difference between an act done and an act continued. When the world was made by God, He had finished the work; and when Christ took our flesh upon Him, the act was done. But the forgiveness of sin is a continued act that holds today and tomorrow and world without end. God is pleased not to impute your sins, but cover them. Now this covering is no constant act. I may cover a thing now and uncover it later. Forgiveness of sin is an act not completed but continued, and continued world without end (and therefore we say the saints in heaven are justified by imputative righteousness, God's continuance of His act of mercy).

The point then is this: as long as we continue in the world, and by contrary acts of disobedience continue to provoke God to discontinue His former acts of mercy, and our sins being but covered, therefore so long must we pray for forgiveness. When the servant had humbled himself before his lord, it says, "The lord of that servant loosed him, and forgave him the debt." But though he forgave him, yet he did another act that caused his lord to discontinue his pardon: "Shouldest not thou also have had compassion on thy fellow-servant, as I had pity on thee?" (Matthew 18:33). He had pity on him, yet since he did another act that turned his lord's heart against him, he was cast into prison. And he was not to come out till he had paid the utmost farthing. His lord had forgiven him today and tomorrow, and would have continued his forgiveness if he had not thus provoked him; we must pray to God to continue His acts of mercy because we continually provoke Him by new acts of rebellion.

Suppose the king grants a pardon to a man; in all patents of pardon there is a clause that the man must renew his patent. If forgiveness may be renewed, then those things are to be renewed again by which the renovation of remission may be wrought. God would have me renew my acts of faith; and if of faith, why not of repentance and prayer? Ezekiel 36:29, 35–37 makes it plain that though God intends to do something, yet He appoints the means. "Thus saith the Lord God, 'I will yet for this be inquired of by the house of Israel, to do it for them.' " That is, "Though I have done it, and intend to do it, yet I will do it by the means of prayer."

God had promised Elijah that rain would come upon the face of the earth, yet he went upon the mount and saw no show of a cloud. The text does not tell us what he said,

but it does say that "he put his head between his knees."
James says, "He prayed, and he opened heaven, and
brought down rain." It was a humble, secret gesture. A
man may be more free in private than public. He prayed
and the heavens opened. God had promised it, and would
do it, but yet He would be sought. So we see that the immediate cause is prayer. So though the Lord will do this,
yet for all this He will be inquired of.

It is not with God as with men. Men who have promised would be loath to be sued to not break their promise;
they account that a dishonor to them. But it is not so with
God. God has promised, yet you shall have no benefit of it
until you sue Him for it. Therefore you must go to God
and say, "Lord, fulfill Thy promise to Thy servant, wherein
Thou hast caused me to trust." God loves to have His
bond sued out. "Lord, make good this Word; perform that
good Word which Thou hast spoken." God would have
His bond thus sued out. And as your faith, repentance,
and prayers are renewed, so your pardon is renewed.

When God will make a man possess the sins of his
youth, when a man is careless this way, it pleases God to
awaken him. "Thou writest bitter things against me, and
makest me to possess the iniquity of my youth" (Job 13:26).
When a man forgets the iniquities of his youth and does
not renew his repentance, when he does not have new acts
of faith and petition, then God makes him to possess the
iniquities of his youth. He makes his sins stand up and cry
out against him, and by this means his old evidences are
obliterated. When a man has a pardon, and it is almost
obliterated, the letters almost worn out so that they cannot be read, he would be glad to have it renewed. Every
sin puts a great blur upon your old evidence so that you
cannot read it. It may be firm in heaven, and yet perhaps
be so blurred that you cannot read it; and therefore, if
you would get them cleared again, you must go to God by
prayer and renew them again. So whether our evidences

are blurred or whether God will make us possess the iniquities of our youth, it is necessary to pray for the forgiveness of those sins which have been before forgiven.

QUESTION. But now you will say, "When I have sinned
afterward, how do I come then to be justified? A man
would think repentance only does it, and without repentance a man cannot be justified."

ANSWER. But you must understand repentance is not
an instrument at all; faith alone is the instrument. Faith
justifies me from sin hereafter as well as before. The case is
this: faith brings life. "The righteous shall live by his faith,"
as the prophet Habakkuk says.

QUESTION. What then do new sins do?

ANSWER. There are two sorts of sins. The first is of ordinary incursion, which cannot be avoided; these break no
friendship between God and us, they only weaken our
faith and make us worse at ease. But there are other sins
that waste a man's conscience. A man who has committed
murder, adultery, and lives in covetousness, which in the
apostle's estimation is idolatry, as long as a he is in this case
cannot exercise the acts of faith. We must know that faith
does not justify as a habit, but as an act applying Christ to
the comfort of the soul.

A wasting sin stops the passage of faith, and it cannot
act till it is opened by repentance. Physicians give instances
of it. Those who have apoplexies, epilepsies, and dropsy
are thought to be dead for the time, as it was with Eu-
tichus, yet, says Paul, his spirit was in him. Everyone
thought him to be dead, yet his spirit was in him. However,
in regard of the operation of his senses, it appeared that
he was dead. So if you are a careless man and do not keep
your guard, but are overtaken in some gross and grievous
sin, you are taken for dead. I am not saying that a man can
lose his life once he has it; but in the apprehension of others, and of himself too, he may appear to be so. As in epilepsies, the nerves are hindered by obstructions, so sin ob-

structs the nerves of the soul so that there cannot be that life and working till these sins are removed.

Now what is repentance? Why, it clears the passages, that as faith could not act before, now it gives him dispositions unto it. As a man in a swoon cannot do the acts of a living man till he is refreshed again, so repentance clears the spirits and makes the life of faith pass throughout. Now when repentance clears the passage, then faith acts, and then there is a new act of faith. Faith justifies me from my new sins; faith at first and at last is that whereby I am justified from my sins that I commit afterwards.

QUESTION. But what does this forgiveness of sins free us from?

ANSWER. In sin, we must consider two things: the fault and the punishment. Then consider sin as it is in itself, and as it respects the sinner, as acted by him. Respecting the fault of the sinner, it is a transgression of the law, and the punishment is death; as it respects the sinner, it is guilt. The sin is not guilt, but the guilt is the sinner's. For instance, a man who has told a lie or sworn an oath, the act is past; but a thing remains which we call guilt. As if a man commits murder or adultery, the act is past; but yet if he sleeps, walks, or wakes, the guilt follows him. If he lives a hundred years, he is a murderer still or an adulterer still; the guilt follows him. And nothing can take away the murder or adultery from the soul but the blood of Christ applied by faith.

First, God takes away the punishment. "There is now," says the apostle, "no condemnation to them that are in Christ Jesus, who walk not after the flesh, but after the Spirit." What, nothing in him worthy of condemnation? God knows we are worthy of a thousand condemnations. There are two judges and there is a double guilt. When a man is brought to the bar, first, the jury judges the facts, and then the judge who sits on the bench judges the punishment. One says guilty or not guilty; the other says guilty, then he judges him.

Now when we are justified, we are freed from both these guilts. When sin is accomplished, it brings forth death. You know the natural work of sin, it labors with death; now God will stop the acts of it so that it shall not do that which it is apt to do, which is as good as if the sin were taken away. When there were wild gourds sliced into the pot (2 Kings 4:41), it is said that the prophet "took that venomous herb away." That is, though the thing was there, it is as if it were not there; it shall do no harm. "Bring now and pour out, and there was no evil thing."

So in respect of us, though there is an evil thing in punishment, and if we had our due would bring condemnation, yet when we are sprinkled with the blood of Christ, it can do us no evil, no hurt. It is said in Scripture that the stars fell from heaven. Why, the stars are so big that they cannot fall from heaven to earth; but they are said to fall when they do not give their light, and do not do that for which they were put there. So though I have committed sin, yet when God is pleased for Christ's sake to pardon it, it is as if it were not there at all.

This is a great matter, but there is more. We are not only freed from the guilt of the punishment, but, which is higher, we are freed from the guilt of the fact. I am now no more a murderer, no more a liar; when I have received a pardon from the blood of Christ, He frees me from that charge and the world has changed for me now. "Who shall lay anything to the charge of God's elect?" If the devil lays anything to you, you may deny it. "Such a one I was, but I am justified, I am sanctified."

Suppose a man committed high treason against the king, and the king gave him a pardon. If I call him a traitor, he can have no remedy against me, for he is a traitor; the pardon does not take away the guilt. But if his prior standing is restored to him by act of parliament, then if I call him traitor, he may have remedy against me, because he is restored fully and is not liable to that disgrace. This is our case: though our sins are as red as scarlet, yet the die shall be changed; it shall not be so bloody. You have the grace of justification, and this not only clears you from the punishment, but from the fault itself. Jeremiah 50:20 is worth gold: " 'In those days, and in that time,' says the Lord, 'the iniquity of Israel shall be sought for, and there shall be none; and the sins of Judah, and they shall not be found. For I will pardon them whom I reserve." What, a sinful man and no sin! When there is search made for sin in such a man, shall it not be found?

You will say that this is meant of the grace of sanctification. No, "I will pardon them." That pardoning of sin makes the sin not to be found. What a wonderful comfort this is! When I shall come at the day of judgment, and have the benefit of my sanctification, the last absolution, such sins shall not be charged on me; my sins and iniquities shall not be remembered. "I will remember their sins no more," God says. It is a wonderful thing, and a strange mistake in many men, especially the papists. They never write comfortably of the day of judgment? They make that to be a terrible day. Alas, poor souls, they do not know that justification is that which makes sins such that they shall never be remembered. You shall hear of all your good deeds for your honor and praise, but for your sins, a search shall be made but they shall not be found. When God forgives sins, He does it fully; they shall never be cast in your teeth again. You shall hear of all your good deeds, but not of your bad ones. So lift up your heads, for your redemption draws near. Here is the blessed grace of justification: we, being justified by faith, have not only no condemnation, but no guilt; whereas all the sins of the wicked man shall be set before his face, and he shall stand quaking and trembling by reason thereof. Not one good thing that he has done shall be remembered, but he shall die in the iniquity that he has committed.

You may remember that I said that the question between us and Rome is not whether we are justified by faith or not, but whether we are justified at all. I will make good on that statement now. There are two graces: imputed righteousness, which implies forgiveness of sins, and inherent righteousness, which is the grace of sanctification begun. Romanists utterly deny that there is any righteousness but inherent righteousness. They say that forgiveness of sins is nothing but sanctification. That is a new doctrine never heard of in the Church of God till these last days, till the spawn of the Jesuits devised it. Forgiveness of sin is this: that God will never charge me with it again. They say that forgiveness of sin is an abolishing of sin in the subject where there is true remission. That is as much as to say that there is no justification distinct from sanctification, whereas the apostle distinguishes them when he says, "The Son of God is made unto us wisdom, righteousness, sanctification and redemption." He is made unto us those things by God.

Let me expound it unto you. Christ has three offices: a prophetic, regal, and sacerdotal office. He exercises His prophetic office to illuminate our understanding. He exercises His kingly office to work on our will and affection. There are two branches of it, the kingdom of grace and the kingdom of glory. How am I made partaker of Christ's prophetic office? He is made unto me wisdom. Before I was a fool, but now I am made wise. First, He enlightens me, and so He is made unto me wisdom. Well, He is also my Priest. How so? He is made an expiation for my sin. He is said in 1 John 2:2 to be "a propitiation for our sins, and not for ours only, but also for the sins of the whole world." This is such a propitiation as the party offended is well-pleased with Christ's being made a ransom. By the oblation offered unto His Father, His righteousness is imputed to us. And as a king, He rules me in the kingdom of grace and in the kingdom of glory. In the kingdom of grace He is made unto me sanctification, and in the kingdom of glory He is made unto me redemption. It is called by the apostle the redemption of our bodies. These two are thus clearly distinguished. The work of Christ's priestly office is to be a propitiation for our sins; sanctification proceeds from the scepter of His kingdom. The one is outside me, the other within me. The one receives degrees, the other does not. A man who is holy may be more holy; but imputed righteousness does not more forgive one man than another. Imputation is without augmentation or diminution. Those things that have divers contrarieties cannot be one and the same thing. Justification and sanctification have divers contrarieties. The contrary to justification is condemnation, but the contrary to sanctification is wickedness and false dealing. Thus you see the difference between these two.

I now come to the dependence one has on the other. In what respect does faith justify? Is faith an instrument to work justification, or to receive it only?

The answer is clear, it justifies in regard of the object. Romans 3:25: "Whom God hath set forth to be a propitiation through faith in His blood." Is that all? Compare this verse with chapter 5:9: "Much more then, being now justified by His blood, we shall be saved from wrath through Him." We are justified by His blood and by faith in His blood. Here are two acts that signify the same thing. It is no more than to say, I was cured by the bath, or by going to the bath. So faith is the legs of the soul that bring a man to Christ. And so my faith is an instrument not to procure my justification, but to receive it. So then, seeing that faith is an instrument to receive justification and not to procure it, then the weakest faith carries away as much forgiveness as the strongest. A strong faith rids a great deal of work because it is an active instrument. The stronger faith works the greater work; but in the point of justification, it is an instrument whereby my justification is wrought, an instrument whereby Christ is received. And the weakest hand may receive a piece of gold as well as the strongest. We must know that in the point of receiving, we live on God's alms. All our justification is His free gift, and faith is that palsy hand which receives all our comfort. It is not then any faith that justifies, but true faith; it is called by Peter a "precious faith." "Simon Peter, a servant and an apostle of Jesus Christ to them that have obtained like precious faith with us, through the righteousness of God and our Savior Jesus Christ." The meanest Christian who has a trembling hand to pitch on that and draw virtue from Him, it is like precious faith in him as much as in the great Apostle Peter, and all the rest.

16

Peace with God, Part 3

"Therefore being justified by faith, we have peace with
God through our Lord Jesus Christ." Romans 5:1

I have declared to you that in these words and the ones
that follow are set down these great graces and great blessings which you have in Christ in this kingdom of grace, before you come to the kingdom of glory. First, here is set
down the mother and radical grace of all the rest, and
that is justification by faith; then follows the blessed fruit
that issues from thence:

1. Peace with God.
2. A gracious access into His presence.
3. A joyful hope arising from the great glory that we
shall enjoy for the time to come.
4. In the worst of our troubles, and in the midst of our
afflictions, this joy is so great that it cannot be abated by
any of them. Yea, it is so far from being abated by them
that they are as fuel to kindle it. "We rejoice in affliction,"
says the apostle; that which would undo the joy of a carnal
man is made the matter of this man's joy.

Justification is the ground or foundation of all the rest;
being justified by faith is the root and ground without
which there is no fruit, no peace, no joy, no hope, much
less any kind of rejoicing in tribulation. Faith is that which
seasons all. We must first be justified by faith before we
have any other comforts; for that is the first ground, the
rudiment of a Christian in the school of Christ.

I showed you that it is not every faith that justifies. There is a dead faith, whereupon the apostle says, "The life that I now live, I live by the faith of the Son of God." A dead thing cannot make a living man; it must be a living faith.

Besides true faith, there is a temporary faith which is active too, and comes near the other. It has the operations of the Spirit, but it lacks root. It has supernatural works, but it does not make a man a new creature. This conception is but an abortive kind of birth; it does not come to maturity; it does not continue. I showed you how a man might discern one of these from the other; for herein lies the wisdom of a Christian, not to content himself or be deceived with flashes. Therefore the apostle exhorts us to prove, try, and examine ourselves. It is an easy matter to be deceived, and therefore God's people should be careful to examine themselves, to have their senses exercised herein, that however others may slight and slubber over the matter, they must and will be careful in it. Then they will not only do it themselves, but they will crave the aid of God also: "Prove me, O my God; try me."

Sometimes "justification" may be taken for righteousness in a man, and sometimes it is opposed to condemnation; so it is taken in Paul, and it signifies an acquittal. Sometimes it is opposed to hypocrisy and pollution in a man's soul; so it signifies sanctification, whereby God not only covers our sins past, but heals our natures. The first is perfect, but imputed; the second inherent, but imperfect. When the time comes that God will finish His cure, He will then make a perfect cure. When final grace comes, we shall not need to think of a popish purgatory. Death is the Lord's refining pot; then there will not be a jot of sin left in a Christian. When God has taken away our dross, then to think we shall be put in a refining fire, that an entire soul having no blot, not one spot, should be purged after final grace has made him clear and whole—this is against reason and common sense. They might have learned better of their own Thomas Aquinas; all the fire in the world will never put away sin without the infusion of grace.

The church of Rome confuses James' justification with Paul's. They confound inherent righteousness, which is begun and shall be perfected in final grace, with the other. The point between us and Rome is not whether faith justifies by works or not, but whether it justifies at all. In truth, that is the state of it. The question is whether there is another justification that is distinguished from sanctification, or whether there is another grace besides justification? Do not think that we are such blockheads as to deny faith and sanctification; yet faith is but a piece or part of that train of virtues. There justification is taken for sanctification; we acknowledge that a man is justified by faith and works; but the question between us and them is whether there is any justification besides sanctification, that is, whether there is any justification at all or not?

We say sanctification is wrought by the kingly office of Christ. He is a King who rules in our hearts, subdues our corruptions, and governs us by the scepter of His Word and Spirit. But it is the fruit of His priestly office which the church of Rome strikes at; that is, whether Christ has reserved another righteousness for us besides that which as a King He works in our hearts, whether He has wrought forgiveness of sins for us? We say that He has, and so said all the church till the new spawn of Jesuits arose. They do not distinguish remission of sins from sanctification. Bellarmine says that remission of sins is the extinguishing of sin in the soul; as water, though it is cold, yet bringing in heat extinguishes the cold. And so remission of sins is bringing in inherent righteousness, which extinguishes all sin that was before. A strange thing! And were it not that the Scripture speaks of a cup in the hand of the harlot of Rome, whereby she makes drunk the inhabitants of the earth with the wine of her fornications; unless men were drunk, it would be impossible that a learned man should thus shake out an article of their creed which has ever been believed by all the churches. When the Scripture speaks of forgiveness of sins, see how it expresses it: "Be ye kind one to another, tender-hearted, forgiving one another, even as God for Christ's sake hath forgiven you" (Ephesians 4:32).

In the Lord's prayer we pray that the Lord would "forgive us our trespasses, as we forgive those that trespass against us." Let him who has common understanding judge. Do we forgive our neighbors by extinguishing sin in the subject? I forgive you; that is, I take away the ill thing you did to me. Does he forgive thus? Alas, no! Forgiveness is outside a man. Suppose I have an action against you, perhaps an action at law. If I let my suit fall, and forgive my charges, this is forgiveness. "God justifieth, who shall condemn?" Though God has just cause to proceed against me as a rebel, yet He is content to let His action fall and to fasten it upon the cross of His Son, there to fix the handwriting against us. He will let fall that which was the ground of a suit against us, all that He could say against us.

That you may better understand that there are two kinds of righteousness, justification and sanctification, the Holy Ghost distinguishes them by various terms: "Of Him are ye in Christ Jesus, who is made unto us wisdom, righteousness, sanctification, and redemption" (1 Corinthians 1:30). You see there are two distinct graces, righteousness and sanctification; the papists make them but one, sanctification and remission of sins. "Moreover, whom He did predestinate, them He also called; and whom He called, them He also justified; and whom He justified, them He also glorified." Here justification and sanctification are nothing else but justification and glorification. Paul speaks of a thing past, not of the glory to come; that it, sanctification, which is glory begun. For what is the glory we shall have in heaven but the enlargement of those inherent graces God begins in this world? Here is the seed, there is the crop; here you have a little knowledge, but there it shall be enlarged; now you have a little joy, there you shall enter into your Master's joy; here you have some knowledge, but there you shall have a full knowledge and a full measure; here glory dwells in our land, but there we "shall with open face behold as in a glass the glory of the Lord, and be changed into the same image from glory to glory, even as by the Spirit of the Lord" (2 Corinthians 3:18). That is, we are more and more conformed to the image of Almighty God by obedience and holy qualities infused into us, so that we grow from one degree of sanctification unto another. And so you see how these are distinguished by their terms: justification and glorification, justification and sanctification.

In John it is said that, when the Spirit shall come, He shall reprove, or, as we should translate it, He shall convince the world concerning sin, righteousness, and judgment (John 16:8). Thus it should be translated, for it makes no sense to say that God shall reprove the world of righteousness. Righteousness and judgment are justification and sanctification. "When the Spirit shall come" is not speaking of Him coming upon me or you; but the Spirit here spoken of is that Spirit that should come upon the apostles on the day of Pentecost; and these should set forth like twelve champions to conquer the world and bring it under the scepter of Christ. "He shall convince the world," that is, when the Spirit shall come on you, and your tongues are tipped with that spiritual fire which shall be active, it shall convince the world concerning three particulars—of sin, righteousness, and judgment.

Of the point of humiliation for sins, Paul in Romans uses the point of justification by imputed righteousness and the glory of sanctification in judgment, which is inherent righteousness, to stop every man's mouth. First he convinces the Gentile, which was easy to be done; later he convinces the Jew that there is righteousness to be had in another, though none in ourselves. "He shall convince the world," as if to say, "To be shut up under unbelief is to be convinced (or convicted) of all sins. Now consider what the nature of unbelief is: it is to fasten all sins upon a man; and when I have faith, all my sins are taken away. They are as if they did not exist; but if we are shut up under unbelief, we are dead.

The second work of God's Spirit is the ministry of the Word. He shall convince the world that there is righteousness to be had by a communion with another; though we are guilty in ourselves, yet He will set us free. And the reason Christ gives us is, "Because I go to My Father." It is as if He should say, "Though you are convicted of your sins, that you are wholly dead in trespasses and sins, and have no means in the world to put them away, yet, notwithstanding, the second work of God's Spirit is to convince of righteousness. There is a righteousness to be had in Me because I was your Surety, arrested for your debt. I was committed to prison, where I could not come out till I had paid the utmost farthing. I made no escape, but I am now a free man. I made no escape before the debt was paid. The debt is discharged, and therefore I go to the Father to maintain My place and standing. I was given unto death for your sins, but I am risen again for your justification. And I now sit at My Father's right hand."

But there is a third thing that the work of the ministry does, which is to convince the world that there is judgment, or an inherent righteousness. It is usual in Scripture to join righteousness and judgment together. "The words of the Lord are righteousness and judgment." And the integrity of a man's heart, which is opposed to hypocrisy, is called "judgment." "As God liveth, who hath taken away my judgment" (Job 27:2). How did God take away his judgment? Had He taken away his wits? No, but "He has put His heavy hand on me," and that has put a conceit in the mind of my friends that I am a hypocrite. And therefore, "My righteousness I hold fast, and will not let it go; my heart shall not reproach me so long as I live" (verse 6). His judgment was taken away, that is, the opinion they had of his integrity; and this will expound Matthew 12:20: "A bruised reed shall He not break, and smoking flax shall He not quench, until He send forth judgment unto victory." What is that, "until He send forth judgment"? This judgment signifies nothing but those inherent graces, those infused qualities that God sends into the heart of a Christian. In a man's first conversion there are but beginnings of grace. What are faith, hope, patience, and fear? They are like a smoking flax, that is, like the smoking wick of a candle made of flax. When a candle burns in the socket, it is now up, now down, and you do not know whether it is alive or dead. So at the first conversion of a Christian, unbelief and faith, hope and despair, mount up and down. There is a conflict in the beginning of conversion, but He will not give it over until He brings forth judgment, until He gets the victory of all opposition from the flesh. And what is the reason? Because the god of this world is judged. He shall convince the world of an inherent righteousness in spite of the devil's efforts because he is condemned. He who before worked in the children of disobedience is now cast down. The strong man is cast out, and therefore, upon that ground, you have the third point. Besides the grace of justification following upon Christ's death, there is another; the devil shall be dispossessed. The devil is strong where he does wicked things, but he shall be disarmed. He shall not touch you; the wicked one shall not hurt you.

Justification is attributed to faith because faith is brought as the only instrument whereby we receive our justification, purchased by the merits of Christ's death. When we say faith is an instrument, we must understand it right well. I do not say that faith is an instrument to work our justification, Christ alone must do that; it is no act of ours, nothing is in us. Faith is said to be an instrument whereby we get our justification in respect of the object; it nears us to Christ; it is the instrument of application, the only instrument whereby we apply the medicine and the plaster of Christ's blood. Hereby we who were strangers and afar off are made near. Faith is only the hand that receives Christ. When the hand lays hold of something, it lays hold of a thing that is not part of itself; so is faith a naked hand, like a beggar's hand that receives free alms given by the donor. As the apostle says, "For if by one man's offense death reigned over all by one, much more they which receive abundance of grace, and of the gift of righteousness, shall reign in life by one, Jesus Christ" (Romans 5:17). There is an abundance of grace and a gift of righteousness; faith is the only means whereby we receive this gift, which is of great consequence. Seeing that faith does not justify as an active instrument, but only as it receives the gift of grace, it follows that the weakest faith gets as much justification as the strongest faith of any whatsoever; because faith justifies not only as a work, but as it receives a gift. Therefore our Savior said, "O ye of little faith!" Yet as little as it was, it was built upon the Rock; and though Satan desired to winnow them and sift them as wheat, yet they remained firm. Our Savior said of the faith of miracles, "If ye had faith as much as a grain of mustard seed, ye should say to this mountain, 'Be removed,' and it would obey you." So for common faith, which the apostle calls it because it is common to all the elect, if you have so much faith, you shall be able to remove mountains of corruptions. Suppose you have a trembling hand that is scarcely able to hold something, yet if you have the persuasion of the woman in the gospel, "If I may but touch him, I shall be whole," you shall be saved and healed if you can but touch Him. And mark our Savior; the people thronged about Him, and He said, "Who is it that toucheth Me?" A wonder that He, when they crowded Him, should ask such a question; but Christ knew that somebody touched Him beside the touch of the multitude. It is said in the text that the poor woman came trembling, and told Him all the truth. And He said, "Be of good comfort, though you have some paralysis and a palsied hand, yet the touch is enough." The least faith brings as much life as the greatest.

QUESTION. But what need is there for a man to strive for a great faith?

ANSWER. Though you have much comfort by a little, weak faith, yet the more faith, the more comfort; and therefore it is to very much purpose to labor after a strong faith. Abraham, it is said, "staggered not through unbelief." If you have a strong faith, you will have strong consolation. You may, by your weak faith, be healed of your disease, yet by the weakness of your faith you may lack much of the strength of your comfort; therefore you must go from faith to faith. But know this, that though a newborn child is not as strong as a man, yet he is as much alive as the strongest and tallest man. Though you are yet but a newborn babe, not so strong or lively as one who is more mature, yet you have all the lineaments of the new creature in you, though you are not as strong and lively as another may be.

QUESTION. Did you not tell me that it was not every faith that justified, but a working faith? How then does faith alone justify?

ANSWER. When we say that faith justifies, there is a subject and a predicate. Faith justifies; justification is attributed unto faith. Now look at the word "only," and ask whether it modifies the subject or the predicate. Does faith which is alone, severed from good works, justify? That proposition is false. That faith which is alone, separated from love and the fruits of good works, does not justify. But let the word "alone" be put to the predicate and it reads faith justifies alone; that is, faith is the only virtue in the soul whereby a man is justified. That proposition is true. If a man should say, "The eye alone sees," that is true. If we say that the eye severed from the members of the body sees by itself; if the eye were taken out of the head, it would neither see alone, nor at all. But the meaning is this, the living eye is the organ whereby a man discerns a visible object. So faith, though joined with other graces, yet takes no other with it to help with justification.

QUESTION. But why should God select this virtue among others that are more noble?

ANSWER. God had respect to the low estate of His handmaid, Mary. God chose the lowest and the meanest. He selected this poor beggar's hand for two reasons:

First, in respect of God, that God, by so mean a thing as a beggar's hand, should bring a man to justification. When you bring nothing but a bare hand ready to receive a pardon, this must be of grace. If God says, "You must love Me," this would be an exchange, not a free gift. I lay down something, and I take up something for it. Faith is that naked hand which fills itself with Christ; it lays fast hold of justification. If a man were ready to drown, and a cable were thrown to him to lay hold of, if he lays hold of it, he can be drawn safe to land. But when he lays hold of the cable, he must let go of all other things he was holding before. Thus must a man let go all other things and lay fast hold on Jesus Christ.

Faith has two faculties. It opens itself to let all other things fall away. Then, when it is an empty hand, it lays hold of Christ. It is of grace when a man esteems all to be dross in comparison of Christ. "Where is then rejoicing and boasting? It is excluded. By what law? Of works? Nay, but by the law of faith" (Romans 3:27). And then, chapter 4:2, "For if Abraham were justified by works, he hath whereof to glory, but not before God." Faith takes away all boasting. Let him who glories glory in the Lord. "Therefore it is of faith, that it might be by grace." This is the reason, in respect of God.

Second, in respect of ourselves: "To the end of the promise might be sure to the seed." Why do people doubt and think nothing is sure? It is because they do not come with an empty hand. We must have such a measure of faith and love, such a measure of humiliation and patience with us; but if we look on these things, we shall never be heard. If the bare acceptance of Christ with a trembling hand will not make you sure, what more can you have than the bare receiving of a gift by faith? The reason why we are not more sure is because we do not come with a naked hand.

There are many means, some before and others after faith. They are those things by which faith is wrought; though they are not so evident, yet they are most sure. When I consider that God calls me in my blood, having nothing in me, and will be friends with me, bids me take His Son, and I do not; when He bids me take His kingdom and glory with Him, and I refuse it—though this is a matter that is not so evident, yet it is more sure. Then there are other arguments that come from the fruits of faith; they are more evident, but not so sure. And thus have I declared unto you the first point of justification by faith; it is so sweet a thing that I cannot tell how to leave it.

Now let us come from the mother to the daughters. The eldest daughter is peace with God. In this peace we will consider these three particulars: What that peace is which we have; with whom we have it; and by whom, and by whose means, we have peace with God. It is procurred by Jesus Christ.

We have peace. We have this peace with God. And we have this peace with God through our Lord Jesus Christ. "Therefore, being justified by faith, we have peace with God through our Lord Jesus Christ."

The point of peace is a great matter; it is the apostolic benediction: "Grace and peace" in all the epistles. "Grace and peace from God our Father, and from the Lord Jesus

Christ" (2 Thessalonians 1:2). "Now the Lord of peace Himself give you peace always by all means" (2 Thessalonians 3:16). This is a thing by all means to be desired; you must labor to get it. The angels' song when Christ was born was, "Glory be to God on high, on earth peace, good will towards men."

This peace is a thing by all means to be sought after, and what it is you may know by the contrary. You know what a miserable thing war is. God grant that you may not know it too soon. You know what it is to have an enemy among us. This is our case till we are justified; we are at daggers drawn, at point of hostility with God. It is a foolish conceit for a man to think that by reason of God's predestination he is justified before he was; this is a foolish conceit. Until you are justified by faith, you are not justified. God's predestination does not make a change in the subject. If I intend to enrich a beggar, he is in rags still for all my intentions till my intentions are put into execution.

Paul was elected before the foundation of the world; but till he was converted he was an enemy and a persecutor, "the chief of sinners," as he speaks of himself in Romans 5:10. "If when we were enemies we were reconciled unto God by the death of His Son, much more, being reconciled, we shall be saved by His life." Before the time of peace came, we were unbelievers, enemies, in the state of enmity; whereas before God was your enemy, as soon as you have touched Christ by a lively faith, presently all the actions He has against you are gone. God is friends with you; this is a high and a deep peace, and this comprehends all kinds of blessings. Amasai, in 1 Chronicles 12:18, one of the most valiant captains that David had, speaks there of peace. One would think it not so proper; it does not belong to soldiers to talk of peace, but because peace comprehends all kinds of blessing, it is said, "Then the Spirit of the Lord came upon Amasai, who was chief of the captains, and he said, 'Thine are we, David, and on thy side, thou son of Jesse; peace, peace be unto thee, and peace be unto thy helpers, for thy God helpeth thee.' " This is a speech from a soldier to a soldier, and this is done in a military way; peace is welcome, though coming from a warrior, because it comprehends all manner of blessings. It is said that when Uriah came unto David, David demanded of him how Joab did, how the people did, and how the war prospered (2 Samuel 11:7). Look in the margin, according to the original, and it is, "He demanded of the peace of Joab, and the people, and of the peace of the war." A man would think it a contradiction that he should demand of the peace of the war; so then, this peace which we have with Almighty God after we are justified by faith, is the comprehension of all manner of good. This having peace with God is the fruit of the Spirit.

But with whom is this peace, with God? It is not with yourself. You may have a turbulent conscience, insomuch that you would give all the world to have it quiet, to be assured that there is peace between God and you—but that is not the point. The thing you get by faith is peace with God. When you are troubled with yourself and have but a weak act of faith, yet, if you believe, you are more afraid than hurt; you are quite secure, and shall be calm and quiet.

QUESTION. But why should Christians be so foolish, so troubled? Why do the children of God so disquiet themselves?

ANSWER. Because they are fools. God is liberal and free, but there is some hope of worthiness in us, and we do things we should not do. We are always poring on ourselves, and do not bring a naked hand; this is the reason we are so full of distractions.

Also, many peevish people among us simply will not be comforted. When news was brought to Jacob that Joseph was slain and lost, it says, "All his sons and daughters rose up to comfort him, but he refused to be comforted; and he said, 'For I will go down into the grave unto my son, mourning' " (Genesis 37:35). They have a kind of pettishness, peevishness, and willfulness; they will not be comforted. It may be that there is some kind of pride in it too; they would perhaps be thought to be the only mourners of Israel, of the kingdom. "As Rachel mourned for her children, and would not be comforted," they shut their eyes against all comforts. God commands them to be comforted, and they will not; it is no marvel then that they eat the fruit of their own hands. It is a part of the minister's office to bring comfort; we have an injunction to it in Isaiah 40:1: "Comfort ye, comfort ye, My people." We bring the tidings of peace, and our feet should be beautiful (Romans 10:15). We bring good news that all is well, as Noah's dove did coming with an olive branch in her mouth. We are to comfort you, but if you stop your ears, who can help it? The Lord is gracious, and charges us to comfort you. And can there be any better news than to hear, "All is peace; all your sins are done away. God has blotted out as a thick cloud your transgressions"? This is the tidings of such good things that all within you is too little to praise the Lord; and therefore it is not a thing to be slighted. "Blessed is the man whose sins are forgiven" (Psalm 32:1). The word "blessed" is not of a singular number; it signifies blessedness, as it were, a heap of blessings. They commonly call them the eight beatitudes, but were there eighty-eight they are all simply one: to have your sins forgiven you is the sum of all happiness.

Additionally, when a man sets his eyes too much upon his sins, more upon his sins than upon the mercies of God freely offered in Christ, this is a strong hindrance to peace. You look at the wrong object, looking too much on your sins when you should be looking at Christ, that brazen Serpent offered to you. Then it is no wonder that you do not see Christ, though He is near you. Mary Magdalene complained and wept to the gardener that they had taken away her Lord, and she did not know where they had laid Him, whereas He was standing at her elbow. Her eyes were so full of tears that she could not behold her Savior. Therefore do not stand in your own light, but look upon Christ as well as upon your sins.

And though there may be peace and calm, yet all turmoils will not immediately cease after humiliation. When there is a great storm at sea which lasts perhaps twenty-four hours and then ceases, are the waves quiet as soon as the storm is over? No, there will be tossing and rolling many hours afterwards because there must be a time of settling. So though there is peace between God and you, and the storm is over, yet there must be a time of settling.

I wish to show you the difference between the peace that wicked men have and this peace with God. Theirs is not peace, for "there is no peace to the wicked." It is a truce only, and we must make a great difference between a truce and a peace. When a truce expires, commonly the result is more war. With them there is a cessation of trouble; their consciences do not accuse them. But when the time is over and conscience again breaks loose, it will be more unquiet and unsettled than ever before. It will be open war again for them.

17

Peace with God, Part 4

"Therefore being justified by faith, we have peace with God, through our Lord Jesus Christ; by whom also we have access by faith into this grace wherein we stand, and rejoice in hope of the glory of God." Romans 5:1–2

Having out of these words declared to you the mother-grace, justification by faith, I proceeded to the consideration of her daughters, those fruits or graces which spring from a true justifying faith. So here we have the great charter and privilege that a justified man is endowed with. First, he has peace with God; second, he has free access to Him; third, he has unspeakable joy, and that joy not only in respect of that delectable object, the hope of the glory of God in heaven hereafter, but here also, that which spoils the joy of a natural man. Afflictions and the like are made the matter of this man's joy.

Now concerning peace with God through our Lord Jesus Christ, I declared to you that it was an inconceivable thing: "The peace of God that passeth all understanding." It is a thing into which our shallow understandings cannot reach; we cannot comprehend the excellency of this grace. Consider its excellency by the contrary; there is no misery in the world like that when a man stands at enmity with God. Do we provoke the Lord? Are we stronger than He? "If a man sin against a man," said Eli, "the judge shall judge him; another man may take up the quarrel, but if a man sin against God, if the controversy be between God and us, who shall intercede for us?" Were it not for our peacemaker, Christ Jesus, we would be in a woeful condition.

It is a great matter to come to the fruit of peace; the fruit of peace is to them who make peace. We have this fruit of peace. We do not sow fruit, but seed—the fruit comes afterwards. It is not so with a Christian; he is as sure as if the thing were in hand. He sows not only the seed, but the fruit of peace; as soon as he is justified, at that instant he has the fruit of peace.

So we have peace, but with whom? It is between God and us. God and a justified man are at peace through Jesus Christ. At the very same instant that a man is justified, he is at peace with God. This peace is a gift of a high nature, which belongs not to every man, but to the justified man only; he only who is justified by faith has peace. In Ephesians there is a general proclamation of peace: "Peace be unto them that are near, and unto them that are afar off." The word the apostle uses in Ephesians alludes to Isaiah 57:19: "I create the fruit of the lips. 'Peace, peace to them that are afar off, and to them that are nigh,' saith the Lord, 'and I will heal them.' But the wicked are like a troubled sea that cannot rest. 'There is no peace,' saith my God, 'to the wicked.' " Though the proclamation is ever so general to Jews and Gentiles, yet it belongs only to those who have peaceable minds towards God, those who will not stand on terms of rebellion against Him.

What madness it is to think that, if I stand in point of rebellion against God, I should have peace with Him! I must cast down my treasons, and I must come with a subject's mind. Then and only then will there be peace. When Jehu came to revenge the quarrel of God, Joram asked him, "Is it peace, Jehu?" He answered, "What peace, so long as the whoredoms of thy mother Jezebel and her witchcrafts are so many?" (2 Kings 9:22). As long as you continue in a course of rebellion, what are you doing talking of peace? Why are you thinking about peace when you are the chief rebel? As long as wickedness continues in your heart, you do not have the peace of God by Jesus Christ.

There may be a kind of quietness in the conscience of a wicked man; but we must make a great distinction between a peace and a truce. A truce is but a cessation of war for such a time; and many times, when the truce is over, it ends in greater war because they have more time to gather strength and increase their forces. So there may be a peace or a truce between God and wicked men; but it is the worst judgment that can be put upon a wicked man to be thus let alone. It is not so with a godly man: God breaks their peace and hedges up their way with thorns, and many times torments their conscience and breaks their peace. But when God allows a sinner to thrive in sin, when He allows him to go on so long that His own honor is almost touched, when God holds His peace, then the sinner thinks that God does not heed his actions. "I held my peace," said God, "then thou thoughtest Me to be altogether such a one as thyself."

However the preacher may amplify these things, the wicked man thinks that God is not as terrible as they make Him out to be. But though God holds His peace long, yet at last He will speak. Oh, consider this, you who forget God, "lest He tear you in pieces and there be none to deliver you." When the time of the truce is over, then the conscience will be like a fierce mastiff: the longer he is tied up, the more fierce he is when he is let loose. So conscience, when it has been long quiet and tied up, when God lets loose the cords thereof, it will be more fierce than ever before; it will then fly like a mastiff in your face and, as it were, tear your throat—and then there will be in you the very flashings of hell.

There is also a great difference between the peace of

God's children and this little cessation of war in the consciences of wicked men: "When the strong man armed keeps the house, the goods that he possesseth are in peace." When Satan is the master and you do his will, when he has you at his command, he does not trouble you. When he keeps the house, the goods are in peace. "But when a stronger than he comes, and puts him out of possession, then comes the strife and debate." Look therefore to your peace; is it such a peace as you never have any conflict, any stirring or striving between the strong man and the weak? Suspect that peace; that is not the peace of a justified man, but of such a one who is held by the prince of darkness.

Again, how can this peace come to wicked men? They neither consider the wrath of God or the danger of sin; they do not consider that "Tophet is prepared of old." If they considered this, it would spoil their sport and break their peace.

But a justified man knows what sin is and what hell is; and at that very time when he is thinking of his sins and of damnation, when he knows that this is the reward of God's enemies, he has peace even then. The others shut their eyes so that they may not see their danger; and because they do not discern it, therefore they are at peace. A man on a dark night going over a dangerous bridge, if he misses just a step, he is drowned; yet he passes over securely and is unafraid because he lacks the light to discover the danger. But bring him back the next day and show him what a danger he escaped, and the thoughts of it will make him quake and tremble, though the danger is past. So these men, being in darkness, do not see their danger, and therefore do not fear. But God's child, having his eyes in his head, discerns the danger, and sees also how he is delivered by Jesus Christ. He is at peace, not because he does not see the danger of the way, but because he knows that God has made the way broad by Jesus Christ, and so he is freed from sin and death.

Now to them who have this true and sound peace, your peace is with God. This peace is not always in their own conscience, but it is no less legitimate on God's part, which is the safest part. There are many reasons why God does not show it to them. Still, though all is quiet between God and them, they have no apprehension of it in their consciences.

Many times this is their own fault, because they will not be comforted; all their thoughts are bent upon their sins and their provocations of God, and they have no eye open to look upon the mercies of Christ. They put it off and will not be comforted; and if they put it off from themselves, no wonder that they have no peace in their consciences.

This may come by reason of the great conflict before in the conscience. God raises a great storm and, when He intends to bring a man to do some great work or to enjoy a great deal of joy, He first humbles him. The Prince of our salvation was consecrated by afflictions, and we must be conformable unto Christ our Head. When the storms are past, the sea will continue raging for a while; and when you have turned the wheel round, if you take away your hand, it will go round itself for a time. So when you are justified by faith, the storm is over, yet the roaring of the waves will continue. It will be so with the children of God: though there is a calm, yet there will be some remainders of a storm.

Again, they are in travail, and that is a painful thing. "My little children with whom I travail." They have the pangs of the new birth, and it is a good while before they can find that quietness their heart longs for.

Again, though He is friends with them, God purposely takes away from them the sense of peace because He takes delight in their finding that strength of faith. Faith is manifest to be most strong when there is the least sense of it. "My God, My God, why hast Thou forsaken Me?" The less sense, the faster the hold; and God loves this confidence, that when He spurns and frowns the man will not let go nor be put off. "Let Him kill me, He shall kill me with Christ in my arms. I will not let go my hold. God cannot fail, He has given me His Word, and therefore I will not let go."

Such a strong faith had Abraham, contrary to reason: "God's Word is true. He gives me His Word, and I will trust Him." So a child of God will not be put off; though God writes bitter things against him, he will not forgo Him. We have an excellent example in the woman of Canaan. Jesus said of her, "O woman, great is thy faith." But how did the greatness of it appear? "Lord, have mercy upon me; my daughter is grievously afflicted." Why did she not rather say, "Lord, have mercy on my daughter"? The reason is because she was afflicted in her daughter's affliction.

By the way, we may hereby understand the meaning of the statement, "I will visit the iniquities of the fathers upon the children, unto the third and fourth generation of them that hate Me." But why to the third and fourth generation? Because I may see the third and fourth generation, and may see the judgment of God on them, and may remember my sin for which they are plagued. The case is mine, and not theirs only. "Lord, have mercy upon me, for my daughter is diseased. I see my own sin is punished by the judgment on her in my sight." Poor woman, the disciples were weary of her clamorous cries, and said, "Send her away, for she troubleth us." What did Christ say? "Is it fit to take the children's bread and cast it unto dogs?" This was enough to dash her hopes; before she was discouraged by silence, but to be called a dog would be quite enough to discourage her. But see the fruit of faith: she sought comfort out of that which would have undone another person. "Well, if I am a dog under the table, then it is there I shall get a crumb; other children who are better, let them have the loaves. I account myself happy if I may but get a crumb." Then to her Jesus said, "O woman, great is thy faith." This is great faith when it goes contrary to all sense; that when God calls me a dog, when He spurns me and frowns on me, I will not be put off. Faith is of the nature of the vine: if it has but the least hold on the wall, it makes use of it, and climbs higher and higher. Out of the least thing that drops from her Savior's mouth, this woman raised her faith higher. So, though we have this peace with God, yet oftentimes He withholds the notification of it to us.

The last thing is to note the difference between the peace of a carnal and a spiritual man. Carnal peace is mixed with a great deal of presumption and pride; but the more spiritual peace you have, the more you are dejected in yourself, the more cast down. See it in Ezekiel 16:60–63: "I will establish with thee an everlasting covenant; then shalt thou remember thy ways, and be ashamed when thou shalt receive thy sisters, thy elder and thy younger; and I will give them unto thee for daughters, but not by thy covenant; and I will establish my covenant with thee, and thou shalt know that I am the Lord, that thou mayest remember and be confounded, and never open thy mouth any more because of thy shame, when I am pacified towards thee, for all that thou hast done." Even when God is pacified, yet they hold their heads down and are ashamed; when a man knows that God has pardoned his sins, he is ashamed that he has carried himself so wickedly against God, of whose mercy he has now such experience. When God is pacified, a man remembers his former sins and is confounded, as it is in Ezekiel 36:31: "Then shall you remember your own evil ways, and your doings that were not good, and shall loathe yourselves in our own sight for your iniquities, and for your abominations" in that time when I am pacified toward you.

That which would work security and pride in a carnal man (for he never thinks himself better than when there is

peace within) will work in the child of God the spirit of
humiliation. In the last chapter of Job, God had manifested Himself wonderfully to Job and, however, before he
had very sharp afflictions, his sufferings in soul were next
to the sufferings of Christ. I believe never any man suffered so much as Job did, insomuch that the arrows of the
Almighty stuck in him: "Thou hast eaten up my flesh." This
was the case with Job, and he stood upon terms of justification; he wished that God would dispute with him, that
God would either be the opponent or the answerer. If
God would answer, he would oppose; or if God would oppose, he would answer. God comes as he would have Him,
and Job is not at that point that he was before. When God
drew nigh to him, Job said, "I have heard of Thee by the
hearing of the ear, but now my eye seeth Thee" (Job 42:5).
Well, this may make a man a proud man and elevate him.
"No," Job said, "now I abhor myself in dust and ashes."
The nearer God draws unto us, and the more merciful He
is unto us, by that light we the more discern our own
abominations. That which would make another man
proud brought Job to the knowledge of this vileness:
"Therefore I abhor myself, and repent in dust and ashes."

Now, another thing is who this Peacemaker is. This I
shall but touch: "We have peace with God." But how?
"Through our Lord Jesus Christ." He is our Peacemaker,
and interposes between His Father's wrath and us. "For
He is our peace, who hath made both one, and hath broken down that partition wall between us" (Ephesians 2:14).
We not only have peace with God through Christ, but
Christ is the very peace. He is not only the Peacemaker,
but He is the peace. There was a middle wall of partition
between the Jews and the Gentiles, and between God and
us. Christ broke it down; sin shall no longer be a wall of
partition. "Having abolished in His flesh the enmity, even
the law of commandments contained in ordinances, for to
make Himself of twain one new man, so making peace,

and that He might reconcile both unto God in one body by the cross." There was hatred between God and us. Christ has crucified that hatred with the nails wherewith He was fastened to the cross. He has killed it by His crucifixion, and now, enmity being slain, peace must be alive; there is peace and reconciliation made. "You are come," says the writer to the Hebrews, "to the blood of sprinkling." Whereas the blood of Abel cried for vengeance against Cain the murderer, this blood cries for peace; it outcries all our sins.

Sin has a voice; it is said in Scripture: "The cry of Sodom and Gomorrah went up into the ears of the Lord." Every sin you commit has a voice to cry; but the blood of Christ has a shriller voice, and outcries the cry of your sins. It is so preeminent that it speaks for peace and outcries the voice of our sins.

The high priest was a type of Christ. He must have on his frontlet, "Holiness to the Lord" (Exodus 28), as one who bears the holy one of the Lord, standing in the person of Christ. Moses said (when wrath had gone out from the Lord) unto Aaron, "Take a censer and put fire therein from off the altar, and put on incense, and go quickly unto the congregation, and make an atonement for them, for there is wrath gone out, the plague is begun" (verse 46). So when the wrath has gone out, this High Priest comes and offers Himself up as a sweet incense acceptable unto God. "And Aaron took as Moses commanded, and came into the midst of the congregation, and behold the plague was begun among the people, and he put on incense and made an atonement for the people." When wrath has come out from the Almighty, and His army is sent out to destroy the rebels, then our High Priest stands between the living and the dead and offers Himself as an oblation to Almighty God to make peace.

Look at the case of Balaam. When the people had committed fornication, Phinehas executed judgment;

wherefore the Lord said, "Phinehas hath turned away My wrath from the people" (Numbers 25:11). And if that one act of Phinehas, his zeal for the Lord in killing the fornicators before the congregation, appeased God's wrath for the whole congregation, how much more does that act of our Phinehas, who has fulfilled all righteousness, whom the zeal of God's house had eaten up? He is nothing but zeal itself, and all that He does unto His Father is for our good. How much more shall Christ pacify God's wrath, who has received the gash of God's sword upon His own body, and would not have Himself spared that He might do it? "As Jonah was three days and three nights in the whale's belly, so shall the Son of Man be in the heart of the earth." There was a mighty storm, Jonah was cast out into the sea, and immediately the storm ceased. Since Christ has suffered for us, there is peace, and the storm is over.

The next part of the text: "By whom we have access by faith into this grace wherein we stand and rejoice in the hope of the glory of God." The first privilege that a justified man has is a gracious access unto God. Suppose he sins (and who does not)? "If any man sin, we have an Advocate with the Father, Jesus Christ the righteous. These things have I written that ye sin not; but if any man sin, we have an advocate with the Father."

This is the state of a justified man: though by his relapses he provokes God, yet he is still one of God's subjects. He may be a disobedient subject, yet he is still a subject, not a foreigner as before. But now "ye that were not a people are become the people of God." A child of God in the midst of rebellion, as soon as he is in a state of grace, is under God's protection; he is no stranger. Though he has his blood about his ears and is in his rags, yet he may come to God. By Jesus Christ he may come boldly to the throne of grace that he may find help in time of need. In Ephesians 2:18, Paul sets down twice the great privileges Christians have: "for through Him we both have access by one Spirit unto the Father." It is Christ who makes the way. To have a friend at the court is a great matter, especially when a man has need of him. Christ has gone before us, and He lives forever to make intercession for us." Hence we need no other Mediator. Thus He speaks to His Father: "Father, this is one of Mine whom I shed My blood for, one of those whom Thou gave Me. I beseech Thee, have pity upon him, and, I beseech Thee, give him audience."

"By Him," that is, through Christ, "we have access by one Spirit unto the Father, in whom we have boldness by the faith of Him, and access with confidence" (Ephesians 3:12). I do not now go doubting to God. I offer my suit with boldness. Mark the Apostle James: "If any man lack wisdom [or any other thing], let him ask it of God, that giveth to all men liberally, and upbraideth not."

It is otherwise with men. When one does a great man wrong and later desires a favor at his hands, that man will say, "O sir, do you not remember how you used me at such a time, or in such a place?" The offender is upbraided, his offense cast in his face. But it is not so with God. He gives liberally and upbraids no man.

So there is a free and a bold access with faith and confidence: "By whom we have boldness and access." That is a notable place; here is bold access by faith unto God, and by that we may be assured of whatever we ask. If it is forgiveness of sins, we may be sure they are forgiven; if we ask in faith, we may be assured.

By the way, take notice here of the folly of the papists, who think that a man can have no confidence or assurance that his sins are forgiven. "This is our confidence, that if we ask anything according to His will, He heareth us." Now is it not according to His will to ask forgiveness of our sins? Does not He enjoin us to do it? Therefore what infidelity it is not to be assured of it! And what impudence it is in them to go about cutting off that which is the whole comfort of a Christian, the assurance of his salvation. Thus it is indeed with those who have no feeling or confidence as those who are in hell think there is no heaven; and they who teach such uncomfortable doctrines can receive no comfort further than the priest gives it them. It is true there is no true assurance but in the true church, but there it may be found.

And as I began with sowing in tears, so I would end with reaping in joy. That is the next thing in the text. I began with humiliation, but end with joy; and not only that joy which we shall have in the kingdom of heaven, but on earth while we have these things but in hope and expectation. A man who would reckon up his estate does not only value what he has for the present, but he reckons his reversions also: what he shall have after such a time and what will come to him or his heirs. God's children have a brave reversion—glory, honor, and a kingdom. "It is your Father's good pleasure to give you the kingdom." And "we are the children of God, but it does not appear what we shall be . . . when He appears, we shall be like Him, and appear as He is." He shall change our vile bodies and make them like His glorious body; we are here sons, but yet in a strange country. Let not the people of God be discouraged by the taunts, jeers, and reproaches of wicked men; they do not know what you are, and therefore make light of you as they did Christ Himself.

Besides what we have in reversion, the very hope we have of it works wonderful joy in the heart of a Christian. David did not live to see the glory of Solomon's temple, but he made provision for it, cast the model of it, and took much delight in the contemplation of what it would be. The consideration of these hopes "makes my flesh rest in hope, and my heart rejoice" (Psalm 16:9). The consideration of the resurrection made David's heart rejoice. The consideration of that which is to come should bring an abundance of joy to a Christian. These are strange things, not like the joy of a natural man; for his heart is sad in the midst of laughter. But these "rejoice with a joy unspeakable, and full of glory." Here are some sparks, some beginnings of the glory of heaven, and of that great joy which we shall have hereafter. But I cannot speak much of these things in just an hour.

But as the devil transforms himself into an angel of light, there is no work of God's Spirit in the hearts of His children but Satan, like an ape, labors to imitate in the hearts of wicked men to make them secure. There are joys in some who are not regenerate. They who received the Word on the rock received it with joy. If the Word is apprehended and has but the least footing, it brings joy with it.

But now, how comfortable a thing it is to have such a comfort on earth as to know that I have this true joy, and to be able to distinguish this joy from those fleeting joys of the wicked, which are but as the crackling of thorns under a pot. Theirs is but as a blaze that suddenly goes out. Now if you would know your joy aright, and whether it differ from that counterfeit joy which flesh and blood and the devil suggest, look to the things that go before, and which produce this joy.

1. The first thing that goes before true joy and produces it is an opening unto Christ when He knocks at the door of your heart. Note that famous passage in Revelation 3:20: "Behold, I stand at the door and knock; if any man hear My voice and open the door, I will come in to him and sup with him, and he with Me." There is, if you will open the door, a sweet and familiar communication between Christ and you. He communicates Himself at dinner and supper. A man does not come melancholy to meals. Christ will come and make merry with you. He will sup with you familiarly.

But how is it with you? Has Christ knocked, and you

have given Him an improper answer, and do you have joy? Then it is a false joy. When Christ knocks at the door of your heart, there must be an opening the door on your part when He knocks by His Word and Spirit. Do you give such an answer as the spouse did in Song of Solomon 5:1: "I am come into my garden, my sister, my spouse. I have gathered my myrrh with my spice, I have eaten my honeycomb with my honey"? Christ comes to supper, knocks at the door, and would bring in a great deal of joy. "I sleep," said the spouse, "but my heart waketh; it is the voice of my well-beloved that knocketh, saying, 'Open to me, my sister, my love, my dove, my undefiled.' "

When God comes and woos us, desires to communicate Himself unto us, and desires us to put off our clothes, do you look for comfort if you do not open to Him? "At last I opened to my beloved; but he had withdrawn himself, and was gone, my soul failed when he spake; I sought him, but I could not find him, I called him, but he gave me no answer" (Song of Solomon 5:6). If you do not give Christ entertainment when He comes, you may seek and not meet with Him. It is observed that the keepers of the wall are the greatest strikers. Those whom God has set to be watchmen, instead of comforting, they smite: "The watchmen that went about the city, they found me, they smote me, they wounded me, they took away my veil from me" (verse 7). She gets rapped by them who should protect her because she did not entertain the beloved. If you find any comfort after Christ has knocked and you have opened unto Him, then it is true joy, and you may make much of it.

2. If it is true joy, faith goes before it. "For being justified by faith we have peace with God through our Lord Jesus Christ." So that exercising the acts of faith is a spiritual means to raise comforts in our souls. I need to speak of John 6:56, for there is lack of the exercises of faith; is it enough, do you think, to have faith exercised just once?

"He that eateth My flesh and drinketh My blood dwelleth in Me and I in him." It is not enough to eat once a year. A man will not be in good health who eats but once a year; a man must eat once a day at least. A Christian should feed on Christ every day, make Him his ordinary food, renewing every day the acts of his faith, receiving Christ crucified by faith every day.

If a Christian would consider that God offers Christ unto him every day, and you renew your faith and clasp Him anew every day, it would be a special way whereby joy would be raised in the soul. The apostle says in Romans 5:2, "We rejoice in the hope of the glory of God." And Romans 15:13: "Now the God of hope fill you with all joy and peace in believing, that ye may abound in hope through the power of the Holy Ghost." Thus, when you have exercised the acts of faith in believing, and then upon that rejoice, then it is seasonable and true joy, and not the counterfeit joy of the wicked. When it arises and springs from believing, when that procures it, it likewise distinguishes it from all false joys. The apostle tells us, "Having this confidence, I know that I shall abide and continue with you all, for your furtherance and joy of faith" (Philippians 1:25). It is called "the joy of faith" because it springs from that principle of rejoicing, from the mother grace, so that your rejoicing may be the more abundant.

The preaching of the Word, whereby faith is wrought, brings an abundance of joy. 1 Peter 1:8 is remarkable: "Whom having not seen, ye love; in whom though now ye see Him not, yet believing, ye rejoice with joy unspeakable and full of glory." Yet believing, that is, yet exercising the acts of faith, which we too much neglect. If we exercised these acts every day, we would have our charter of joy renewed every day. "Yet believing, ye rejoice."

3. "Pray and be thankful." Praise and thanksgiving are those fruits which fulfill all our joy. When you pray, you converse with God; you speak with Him face to face, as

Moses did. He who can pray spiritually and pray hard unto God will be as Moses. Moses' face shone when he talked with God, and so your soul will thrive. Praying hard and being thankful; there are no greater means than these to get this joy: "Rejoice in the Lord, O ye righteous, for praise is comely for the upright" (Psalm 33:1). Upon this hangs all our comfort; praise always brings rejoicing, the one begets the other. In Isaiah, the comfort there that God's children receive is the changing of raiment. Christ preaches "the acceptable year of the Lord to appoint unto them that mourn in Zion, to give to them beauty for ashes, the oil of joy for mourning, the garment of praise for the spirit of heaviness." The ground of praise is joy; one follows the other. Observe, God will give us the oil of joy. Christ was anointed with this oil above His fellows (Psalm 45:7). Christ has fullness of joy; this oil does not come on His priesthood alone, but it trickles down unto the lowermost hem of His garment.

In the last place, consider the great things that are given to us by God, and what an estate we get by Christ. We have forgiveness of sins, and "blessed is the man whose sins are forgiven." Christ's blood is wine, and our names are written in the book of life. "Do not rejoice," said our Savior, "because the devils are subject unto you; but because your names are written in the book of life." When we consider that we are not on the black roll, and it is our faith that strengthens us, which makes us reckon Christ as our chief wealth, this makes us rejoice in our inheritance, and in hope of the glory of God. When we consider the great reward in the world to come, this is a great cause of rejoicing; and therefore God's children long for the coming of Christ. It is made a mark of those who shall be saved that they "long for the appearance of Jesus Christ, looking for, and hastening unto the blessed hope, and the glorious appearing of the great God, and our Savior Jesus Christ" (Titus 2:13). And 2 Peter 3:12: "Looking for, and hastening

unto the coming of the day of God." A longing expectation; not only they, but we also that have the first fruits of
the Spirit, groaning and longing for its coming. And therefore the last breath of the Scripture is breathed in this:
"He that testifieth these things saith, 'Surely I come
quickly.' Amen, even so be it; come, Lord Jesus" (Revelation 22:20). Song of Solomon 8:14 sweetly allegorizes this:
"Make haste, my beloved, and be like the hind, and like
the roe."

Come, Lord Jesus; come quickly, and come as the hind,
and as the roe, and as the deer upon the mountain of
spices. Make haste and come quickly; be swift and do not
tarry. And I could not end in a better place.

18

The Seal of Salvation, Part 1

(God's Spirit witnessing with our spirits that
we are the children of God)

"For ye have not received the spirit of bondage again to
fear; but ye have received the Spirit of adoption, whereby
we cry, 'Abba, Father.' The Spirit also beareth witness with
our spirit, that we are the children of God." Romans 8:15–
16

The apostle sets down in this epistle a platform of
Christian doctrine, whereupon all persons and churches
might safely build themselves. He shows therein a sure way
how those might come to the Lord Jesus Christ who are to
obtain salvation by Him, which he delivers in three head-
ings:

First, he shows how God will convict the world of sin.

Second, he reveals to them what that righteousness is
which is outside themselves and is imputed to them.

Third, he sets forth that inherent righteousness, created in us by sanctification of the Spirit, with the effects
thereof, and motives and helps thereunto.

This answers that threefold work of the Spirit in John
16–18, where Christ promises that when the Comforter
should come, He will reprove the world of sin, of righteousness, and of judgment.

He shows the Comforter shall work a conviction of sin,
showing a man that he is as vile, empty, and naked as may

be. This is not a bare confession of sin only—which a man may have and yet go to hell—but such a conviction as stops a man's mouth so that he does not have a word to speak, but sees a sink of sin and abomination in himself, such as the apostle had: "For I know that in me (that is, in my flesh) dwelleth no good thing" (Romans 7:18). To attain to this sight and measure of humiliation, there must be a work of the Spirit. Therefore the apostle begins, in the Romans 1, with the Gentiles who, failing grossly in the duties of the first table of the law, God had given over also to err in the breach of all the duties of the second table.

The next chapter, and most of the third, he spends on the Jews. They bragged of many excellent privileges they had above the Gentiles, such as to have the law, circumcision, to be leaders of others, and to have God among them; and therefore they despised the Gentiles. The apostle reproves them, showing that in condemning the Gentiles they condemned themselves, since they had a greater light of knowledge than the Gentiles, which should have led them to the true and sincere practice of what they were instructed in. Then he goes on and shows all naturally to be out of the way (verse 19), and so concludes them to be under sin, "so that every mouth may be stopped, and all the world become guilty before God." This is the end of the first part.

This being done, in the latter end of the chapter he proceeds to speak of the second work of the Comforter, which is to convict the world of righteousness. But on what grounds? "Because I go to my Father, and ye see me no more." That is, He shall assure the conscience that now there is a righteousness of better things purchased for us. Christ was wounded, arraigned, and condemned for us. He was imprisoned, but now He is free, who was our Surety; yea, and He is not free as one who has escaped, who has broken prison and run away (for then He could not have stayed in heaven any more than Adam could stay in paradise after his fall), but now Christ remains in heaven, perfectly and forever reconciled with the Father. This is a sure sign to us that the debt is paid, and everlasting peace and righteousness have been brought in for our salvation. This the apostle enlarges, and shows this to be the righteousness that Adam had, and which we must trust in. And this he does unto the sixth chapter.

From here the apostle goes on to the third point, convicting the world of judgment and of righteousness, unto the ninth chapter, which are two words signifying one and the same thing; but because he had named righteousness before, which was the righteousness of justification (outside a man) in Christ Jesus, he calls the third use "judgment," which is that integrity which is inherent, bred, and created in us; to wit, sanctification, as we may see in Isaiah 42:3, where it is said of Christ: "A bruised reed shall He not break, and the smoking flax not quench, till He bring forth judgment unto victory." Here he shows judgment to be a beginning of righteousness in sanctification, even such a one as can never be extinguished. So Job 27:2–6: "As the Lord liveth who hath taken away my judgment . . . all the while my breath is in me, and the Spirit of God is in my nostrils, my lips shall not speak wickedness, nor my tongue deceit. God forbid that I should justify you; till I die I will not remove my integrity from me; my righteousness I will hold fast, and will not let it go." Here you see that by "judgment" is meant integrity, that righteousness which is created and inherent in us. So the substance of that place in Isaiah is that God will never give over so to advance and make effectual that weak righteousness and sanctification begun in us until it shall prevail against and master all our sins and corruptions, making it in the end a victorious sanctification. And the ground hereof is, "For the prince of this world is judged"; he is like one manacled, whose strength and power is limited. So now, though he is strong, yet he is cast out by a stronger one than he, and he cannot, nor shall he ever, rule again as in times past.

The apostle follows this strain of doctrine in this epistle, showing that, as the righteousness of justification by the blood of Christ is a thing outside us, so the righteousness of sanctification is a created and inherent thing in us, and the ground of the witness of our spirits. So the blood of Christ does two things unto us: in justification it covers our sins and in sanctification it heals our sins and sores; if there is any proud or dead flesh, it eats it out and then heals the wound. Therefore the apostle says, "Ye are not under the law, but under grace." He who sees that the law is satisfied by another, and all to be of free grace, will not much stand on anything in himself for his justification, but, as a poor beggar, he will be content that all should be of mere grace. Therefore he concludes, "Sin shall not have dominion over you; for ye are not under the law, but under grace."

After this the apostle goes on to other particulars, showing divers things, especially the 12th verse of this chapter, where he drives into the point of sanctification, as though he should say, "You are freed from the law indeed, as it is a judge of life and death; but yet the law must be your counselors. You are debtors of thankfulness (seeing whence you are escaped) so that you may not live after the flesh."

Then he proceeds to show them how they should walk, seeing they had received the Spirit. They should "walk after the Spirit." Now that they had received that which should subdue and mortify the flesh and the lusts thereof, they should be no more as dead men, but quick and lively in operation by living after the Spirit; otherwise, they could not be the sons of God (verse 16). And then he comes to the words that I have just now read: "For ye have not received the spirit of bondage again to fear, but ye have received the Spirit of adoption, whereby we cry

'Abba, Father.' For the Spirit itself beareth witness with our spirits that we are the children of God."

Here the apostle shows the ground of our union and communion with Christ, because, having His Spirit, we are of necessity His. This John says in 1 John 3:24: "Hereby we know that He abideth in us by the Spirit which He hath given us." What ties together and makes one of things far asunder, but the same spirit and life in both? So that Spirit which is in Christ is a full running-over fountain descending down; and being infused into us, it unites us unto Him; yea, that Spirit communicated unto me in some measure (which is in Him such fullness), ties me as fast to Christ as any joint ties member to member, and so makes Christ to dwell in my heart. The apostle speaks to this in Ephesians 2:21. By one Spirit we are built up and made the temple of God, and come to be the habitation of God through the Spirit; so that by this means we are inseparably knit and united unto Him. What is it that makes one member to be a member to another? Not that nearness of joining or lying one to or upon another, but the same quickening spirit and life which is in both, and which causes a like motion; for otherwise, if the same life were not in that member, it would be dead and of no use to the other. So it is the same spirit and life in the things conjoined which unites them together.

To explain this more, imagine a man were as tall as heaven (the same spirit and life being diffused into all his parts). What is it now that can cause his toe to stir, there being such a huge distance between the head and it? It is that self-same life which is in the head being in the toe. No sooner does the head will the toe to stir than it moves, and so is it with us. That very Spirit which is in Christ is in us, and thereby we are united unto Him, grow in Him, live in Him and He in us, rejoice in Him, and so are kept and preserved to be glorified with Him. He is the second Adam, from whom we receive the influence of all good things, showering down and distilling the graces of His Spirit upon the least of all His members.

It was said of Aaron (who was a type of the second Adam), and of that holy oil (representing the graces of God's Spirit) which not only ran down his head and beard, but the skirts of his garments also, and all his rich attire about (Psalm 133:2). So when I see the oil of Christ's graces and Spirit not only rest upon the head, but also descend and run down upon the lowest of His members, making me now as one of them, and in some sort another man than I was or my natural state could make me—by the same Spirit I know I am united unto Christ.

This purpose is what Christ so stands on in John 6 to the Jews, where, speaking of eating His flesh and that bread of life that came down from heaven (lest they should be mistaken), He adds, "It is the Spirit that quickeneth; the flesh profiteth nothing. The words that I speak unto you, they are spirit and they are life." So we see that it is the Spirit that gives being to a thing. And therefore the apostle proceeds to show that "as many as are led by the Spirit of God, they are the sons of God" (Romans 8:14).

As Christ is the true Son of God, so we are truly, by conveyance of the same Spirit into us, His sons by adoption, and so heirs with God, yea, and joint heirs with Christ. This He begins to show in verse 15. So that, being in this excellent state, they were not only servants and friends (a most high prerogative), but they were now the sons of God, having the Spirit of adoption whereby they might boldly call God "Father." In this verse the apostle opposes the spirit of bondage, which makes a man fear again unto the Spirit of adoption, which frees a man from fear.

Now two things may be observed here:

First, the order the Spirit of God keeps ere it comforts; it shakes and makes us fear. This the apostle speaks to in Hebrews 2:14–15, where he shows that the end of Christ's coming was that "because the children were partakers of flesh and blood, He also Himself took part of the same; that through death He might destroy him that had the power of death; that is, the devil, and deliver them who, through fear of death, were all their lifetime subject unto bondage." The first work then of the Comforter is to put a man in fear.

Second, here he shows that until the Spirit works this fear, the heart will not stoop. The obstinacy is great; yea, so great that if hell's gates were open, ready to swallow up a man, he would not yield until the Spirit sets in to convince the heart. Therefore John 16:8 tells us that "when the Spirit is come, He will reprove the world of sin," that is, He will convince and show a man that he is but a bond-man—and so from this sight He makes us to fear. No man must think it strange that God deals with men at first after this harsh manner, to kill them, as it were, before He makes them alive. Nor should any be discouraged, as if God had now cast them off as none of His; for this bondage and spirit of fear is a work of God's Spirit, and a preparative to the rest, yet it is but a common work of the Spirit, and such a one that, unless more followed, it can afford us no comfort.

QUESTION. But why then does God allow His children to be first terrified with this fear?

ANSWER. In two aspects this is the best and most wise course to deal with us, or else many would put off the matter and never attain a sense of mercy.

1. It is best and most wise in respect of God's glory; and that first because, as in the work of creation, so in the work of redemption, God will have the praise of all His attributes. As in the work of creation there appeared the infinite wisdom, goodness, power, justice, mercy of God, and the like, so will He, in the work of our redemption, have all these appear in their strength and brightness. And when we see and acknowledge these things to be in God in the highest perfection, hereby we honor Him. On the

contrary, when we will not see and acknowledge the excellency of God's infinite attributes, we dishonor Him. And the work of redemption was a greater work than the work of creation; for therein appeared all the treasures of wisdom and knowledge in the conveying of it unto the Church. Herein appeared, first, infinite wisdom in ordering the matter so as to find out such a way for the redemption of mankind as no created understanding could possibly imagine or think of. Second, as for the mercy of God, there could be none comparable to not sparing His own Son, the Son of His love, so that He might spare us who had so grievously provoked Him. Third, there could not be so much justice seen in anything as in sparing us and in not sparing His Son. God laid His Son's head, as it were, upon the block and chopped it off. Indeed, the death unto which He gave His Son was not only more vile than the loss of His head, but far more painful and terrible to nature, the death on the cross, in rending and tearing that blessed body of His. As the veil of the temple was rent (which was a type of Him), so was He rent, torn, and broken for us, when He made His soul an offering for sin. This was the perfection of justice. And thus was He just, as the apostle speaks, and the Justifier of him who believes in Jesus. God would have justice and mercy meet and kiss each other, and that for two reasons, to magnify His justice and to magnify His mercy.

He would magnify His justice. The Spirit must first become a spirit of bondage and fear to magnify God's justice. Thus the prophet David, having sinned, was driven to this confession: "Against Thee and Thee only have I sinned, and done this evil in Thy sight, that Thou mightest be justified when Thou speakest, and be clear when Thou judgest" (Psalm 51:4). Thus he, a holy man, was brought to confess his sin in order to give God the glory of His justice.

And so to this end, that a man might pass through or by, as it were, the gates of hell unto heaven, the Lord will have His justice extended to the full; for which cause lessening or altogether, for a time, abstracting all sight of mercy, He turns the law loose to have its course. And thus, as in the work of redemption, He would have the height of justice appear, so would He have it appear in the application of our redemption that justice should not be swallowed up by mercy. But even as that woman who had nothing to pay was threatened by her creditors with taking her two sons to prison (2 Kings 4:1), so, though we have nothing to pay, the law is let loose upon us to threaten imprisonment and damnation in order to frighten and terrify us—and all to magnify God's justice. Know that we do not satisfy God's justice by what we suffer, yet it is fitting that we should acknowledge and learn thereby more highly to value the suffering of our Savior.

God has set forth many terrible threatenings in His Word against sinners, and shall all these be to no purpose? Because the wicked are insensible of them, must they therefore be in vain? Some people there must be in whom they shall work. "Shall a lion roar and we not be afraid?" (Amos 3:8). Since then those who should will not, there are some who must tremble, and those even of God's own dear children. This the prophet excellently sets forth in Isaiah 66:2, where the Lord shows whom He will regard: "But to this man will I look, even to him that is of a contrite spirit, and trembleth at My Word." Even some of God's own must tremble and be thus humbled of necessity; and it is not without a just cause that God deals with His children after this manner, though it is sharp in the experience. We must fear, tremble, and be humbled, and then we shall receive a spirit not to fear again. That vain courage which some brag they have so as not to fear death is not that which is meant here; for, alas, such braggers, out of ignorance of the thing, and a desire to be out of misery in this life, may embrace death willingly, hoping it may put an end to their sorrows. But this spirit not to fear again is such a spirit that assures me of the forgiveness of all my sins, showing me my freedom by Christ Jesus from hell and eternal damnation, making me live a holy life, and from hence not to fear, and so sealing me up unto the day of redemption.

2. It is requisite that the Comforter should first work in men a fear for the glory of God's mercy, which would never be so sweet, relished so well, nor be so highly esteemed by us if the awful terror of justice had not formerly made us sting. We may see this in that parable whereunto our Savior likens the kingdom of heaven to the man who owed ten thousand talents unto the king. His master showed him mercy and forgave him all his debt; but what did he do first? First he required the whole debt of him, and because he had nothing to pay, he commands him, his wife, his children, and all that he had to be sold so that payment might be made. He would have him pinched thoroughly so that he might know how much he was indebted, and how great that favor was which he received in having all that he owed forgiven him. Thus a king, many times, casts men into prison, allows the sentence of condemnation to pass on them, and perhaps orders them to be brought to the place of execution before he pardons them; and then mercy is mercy indeed—and so God deals with us.

Many times God makes His children fear. He shows them how much they owe Him, how unable they are to pay, casts them into prison, and threatens condemnation in hell forever, after which, when mercy comes to the soul, then it appears to be wonderful mercy indeed, even the riches of exceeding mercy. Why do so many find no favor in the gospel? Is it because there is no sweetness or matter of delight in it? No, it is because such have had no taste of the law and of the spirit of bondage; they have not smarted, nor found a sense of the bitterness of sin, nor of that just punishment which is due unto the same.

The king will sometimes suffer the law to pass on some grievous malefactor for high treason, bring him to the place of execution, and lay his head on the block before a pardon be produced. We have had experience in this country of a man who, otherwise, would not cry nor shed a tear for anything; despising death, he was not afraid to meet a host of men. Such a one, having now at an instant a pardon brought from the king, how wonderfully it worked upon him, causing softness of heart and tears to flow from his eyes when nothing else could. While the wonder of this mercy, which now appears so sweet and seasonable, is beheld and admired, he was so struck that he knew not what to say.

For this cause, therefore, God shows us first a spirit of bondage to prepare us to relish mercy, and then He gives the Spirit of adoption not to fear again. And thus, by this order, the one is magnified and highly esteemed by the foregoing sense of the other.

If, therefore, this terror and fear is hard and troublesome unto us, yet, if it is for God's glory, let us endure. If He will give me over to a wounded, terrified conscience, to fears, tremblings, and astonishments, yea, or to draw me into the fire itself, or any other punishment, so He dealt with His church of old. He brought her through the fire and water before she came into a wealthy place (Psalm 66:12). Since it is for His glory, I must be content.

But He gets nothing from us of all that we do; all is for ourselves. Our acknowledgments of Him make Him no stronger, wiser, juster, or better than He is; but in glorifying Him we glorify ourselves, and so pass from glory to glory until we come to be fully transformed into His image. And herein consists our happiness, in acknowledging His wonderful attributes, that by the reflex and knowledge of them, we grow up in them as much as may be. God was as glorious, powerful, wise, just, happy, and good before the world was made as He is now; and if the case is put concerning glorifying Him, the three persons of the Trinity were only fit and worthy of so great honor, not we, as we may read in Proverbs 8:30. There Wisdom shows how He was with the Father before all time, and that they mutually solaced themselves in the contemplations of one another's glory: "Then was I by Him as one brought up with Him, and I was daily His delight, rejoicing always before Him." And in John 17:5 we read the same thing in effect, where Christ prays, "And now, O Father, glorify Thou Me with Thine ownself; with the glory which I had with Thee before the world was." So that the admiring, beholding, and magnifying God's glory (as much as may be), laboring to be like Him, is our glory.

This course is not only for God's glory, but for our good; and this appears two ways: In our justification and in our sanctification.

As for justification, we are such strangers to God that we will never come unto Him till we see there is no other remedy, being at the pit's brink, ready to starve, hopeless of all other helps, being frozen in the dregs of sin, and delighting in our ways. We see this in the parable of the prodigal son, who would never think of any return to his father till all other helps failed him; money, friends, acquaintance, and all sorts of food. Nay, if he might but have fed upon husks with the swine, he would not have thought of returning any more unto his father; but this being denied him, the text says that he then came to himself, which shows us that while men run on in sinful courses they are mad, even as we see those in bedlam are kept under, and comforts denied them, till they come to themselves. And then what does he say? "I will arise and go to my father." He confessed that he had sinned: "and I will say, 'Father, I have sinned' " (Luke 15). So is it with us until the Lord humbles and brings us low in our own eyes, showing us our misery and sinful poverty, and that in us there is no good thing; that we are stripped of all help in and without ourselves, and must perish forever. Unless we beg His mercy, we will not come unto Him.

We see it was so with the woman whom Christ healed of her bloody issue in Luke 8:43. How long it was before she came to Christ! She had been sick twelve years, had spent all her substance upon physicians, and nobody could help her—and this extremity brought her to Christ. So this is the means to bring us unto Christ, to drive us to our knees, hopeless, as low as may be, to show us where help only is to be found, and run us to it. Thus, therefore, when men have no mind to come to Christ, He sends, as it were, fiery serpents to sting them so that they might look up unto the brazen serpent, or rather unto Jesus Christ, of which it was a type, for help. Unto others, being strangers to Him, He sends a variety of great and sore afflictions to make them come to Him so that He may be acquainted with them, as Absalom set Joab's corn on fire because he would not come to him, being twice sent for.

So God deals with us before our conversion, many times, as with iron whips lashing us home, turning loose the avenger of blood after us, and then, for our life, we run and make haste to the city of refuge. Thus God shoots off, as it were, His great ordnance against us to make us run unto Him. Thus John the Baptist came preaching repentance, being in attire, speech, and diet strong and harsh, clothed with camel's hair, and with a girdle of skin about his loins. His meat was locusts and wild honey; his place was the wilderness; his speech was harsh and uncomfortable. He thundered with his voice, calling the people a generation of vipers, and telling them that "now also was the axe laid to the root of the tree, that every tree that brought not forth good fruit, was hewn down and cast into the fire."

We know in this manner the Lord came to Elijah. First, a great "strong wind rent the mountains, and brake in pieces the rocks before the Lord, but the Lord was not in the wind; and after that went an earthquake, but the Lord was not in the earthquake; and after the earthquake a fire, but the Lord was not in the fire" (1 Kings 19:11–12). These were as a peal of great ordinance shot off to prepare the way, showing the king was coming. And after the fire came a still small voice, and there the Lord was. So the Lord rends, tears, and shakes our consciences and rocky hearts many times to prepare the way for Him; and then He comes to us in the still and soft voice of consolation.

For our sanctification, it is good for us that the Comforter first works fear in us; for we are naturally so frozen in our dregs that no fire, in a manner, will warm and thaw us. We wallow in our blood, and stick so fast in the mire of sin that we cannot stir; so this fear is but to pull us from our corruptions and make us more holy. If a man has gangrene beginning in his hand or foot that may spread farther, and be his death if it continues so, he is easily persuaded to cut it off lest it should go farther. So God deals with us with this fear of bondage that we might be clothed anew with His image in holiness and righteousness.

Now, to effect this, the sharpest things are best, such as the law, the threatenings of condemnation, the opening of hell, the racking of the conscience, and a sense of wrath present and to come. So hard-hearted are we by nature, being as children of the bondwoman unto whom violence must be used. If we see a man riding a wild and young horse to tame him, he will run him against a wall so that this may make the horse afraid. If this will not do, he takes him up into the top of some high rock, and, bringing him to the brink thereof, he threatens to throw him headlong, making him shake and quake, whereby at last he is tamed. So deals the Lord by us: He gives us a sight of sin, and the punishment due thereunto; a sense of wrath sets the conscience on fire, fills the heart with fears, horrors, and disquietness, opens hell to the soul, brings a man, as it were, to the gates thereof, and threatens to throw him in, and all this to make a man more holy and to hate sin the more.

So there must be a strong mortifying and subduing of us by a powerful hand to bring us unto Christ for our sanctification; nothing but a fiery furnace can melt away that dross and tin which cleaves unto such corrupt metal as we are. See this method excellently set forth in Ezekiel 22:19–20: "Because ye are all become dross, behold I will gather you into the midst of Jerusalem, as they gather brass, and iron, and lead, and tin, into the midst of the furnace to blow the fire upon it to melt it; so will I gather you in Mine anger and in My fury, and I will leave you there and melt you."

Before I proceed further, give me leave to answer an objection of a troubled soul that may arise hence.

OBJECTION. Oh, what comfort then may I have of the first work of the Spirit in me? For as yet I have found none of these things. I have not been thus humbled nor terrified, nor had such experience as you speak of in that state under the spirit of bondage.

ANSWER. Though this is a work of the Spirit, yet it is not the principal justifying and saving work of the Spirit; yea, the children of the devil may come to have a greater measure of this than God's own dear children whom, for the most part, He will not frighten and afflict in that terrible manner as He does some of them. But the consequence of this is more to be accounted of than the measure, to see whether that measure I have (whatever it is) leads me. For if the measure were ever so absolutely necessary to salvation, then all God's children would have enough of it. But I make a distinction still between humiliation and humility, which is a grace of itself, and leads me along with comfort and life. Thus, therefore, I think of humiliation if I have so much of it as will bring me to see my danger, and cause me to run to the medicine and city of refuge for help. To hate sin for the time to come, and to set myself constantly in the ways and practice of holiness, is enough. And so I say in the case of repentance, if a man has a sight of sin past, and a heart firmly set against all sin for the time to come, the greater and firmer this were, the lesser measure of sorrow might suffice for sins past. A wise father would never beat his child for faults that are past, but for the prevention of that which is to come; for we see in time of correction the child cries out, "Oh! I will never do so anymore." So God deals with us because our resolutions and promises are faint and failing; and without much mourning, humiliation, and stripes we do not attain this hatred of sins past nor strength against them for time to come. Therefore it is that our humiliation and sorrow must be proportionate to that work which is to be done; otherwise any measure of it would be sufficient which fits us for the time to come.

But I will add, there are indeed divers measures of it, according unto which the conscience is wounded or eased. When there is a tough, melancholy humor so that the powers of the soul are distracted, good duties omitted, and the heart so much the more hardened; when upon this the Lord lets loose the band of the conscience, oppressing the same with exceeding fears and terrors—this the Lord uses as a wedge to cleave asunder a hard piece of wood. God then shows us, because we would not plow ourselves, we shall be plowed. If we would judge ourselves, says the apostle, we would not be judged; and therefore the Church confesses and complains that "the ploughers ploughed upon her back, and made deep furrows" (Psalm 129:3). Why did this happen? Because she did not plow up her own fallow ground, therefore the Lord sent her other strangers and harsh plowers who plowed her soundly indeed. Why does God thus deal with His children? Because He is the great and wisest Husbandman, who will not sow among thorns. Therefore, when He is about to sow the seed of eternal life in the soul, which must take deep root and grow forever, He will have the ground thoroughly plowed.

The way, then, to avoid these things that are so harsh and displeasing to flesh and blood is to take the rod quickly and beat ourselves; for when we are slow and secure and omit this, God does the work Himself. But yet God makes a difference of good education in those who have kept themselves from the common pollutions and gross sins of the times; it pleases God that faith should come into them. They know neither how, nor the time; grace drops in little by little; now a little and then a little; by degrees sin is more and more hated and the heart inflamed with a desire of good things in a conscionable life. But, in a measure, I say, such must have had, have, or shall have fears and terrors so much as may keep them from sin and quicken them to go on constantly in the ways of holiness. Or else, when they fly out of the way, they shall smart of it, and be whipped home again. Yet they may find themselves, as it were, in heaven they know not how. But if a man has stuck deep and long in sin, he must look for a greater measure of humiliation and fear, and a more certain time of his calling; there must be hauling and pulling such a man out of the fire with violence; and he must not look to obtain peace and comfort with ease. God will send thunder and lightning in such a man's conscience on Mount Sinai before He speaks peace to him in Mount Sion.

A second time there is also of a great measure of humiliation, which is (though a man may be free from great, gross sins and worldly pollutions) when the Lord intends to show the feeling of His mercy and the sense thereof to any in an extraordinary measure, or to fit them for some high services. Then they shall be much humbled before, as we see Paul was in Acts 9:9. God thundered upon him, and beat him down in the highway to the ground, being stricken with blindness for three days after.

Thus much shall suffice to have been spoken of the

15th verse, touching the spirit of bondage and the Spirit of adoption. The apostle tells them that they may thank God the spirit of fear thus came, so that hereafter they might partake of the Spirit of adoption to fear no more. He stirs them up, as it were, to be thankful, because now they had obtained a better estate. What estate? A very high one. "The Spirit itself beareth witness with our spirit that we are the children of God" (verse 16).

19

The Seal of Salvation, Part 2

"The Spirit itself beareth witness with our spirit, that we
are the children of God." Romans 8:16

Having spoken concerning the spirit of bondage and
the Spirit of adoption in the former verse, the apostle, in
these words that I have now read, stirs up those unto
thankfulness to whom he writes because they had now at-
tained to a better state; the Spirit itself bears witness with
their spirits that they are the children of God.

The thing then is to know ourselves to be the children
of God; there must be sound evidences. Here then are two
set down whose testimony we cannot deny. I will touch
them as briefly as I can, and so will make an end. The first
is the witness of our spirit. The second is the witness of
God's Spirit with our spirits.

These are two evidences, not single but compounded,
wherein you see there may be some work of our spirit.

QUESTION. But our spirit can be deceitful. How then
can our own spirit work in this manner to testify?

ANSWER. In this place our spirit is, as it were, an evidence of God from heaven, as a loud token given, as-
suring me upon good grounds that I have not misapplied
the promises; but though God writes bitter things against
me, yet I love Him still and cleave to Him. For all this I
know that I still hunger and thirst after righteousness; that
I will not be beaten off, nor receive an ill report of my
Lord and Savior; that I rest, wait, fear, and trust in Him

still. When thus our valor and faith is tried, then comes the
same Spirit and seals with our spirit that we are the children of God. When our seal is first put, then God seals
with our spirit the same thing by His Spirit. To this effect is
1 John 5:8, where we read that three witnesses are set
down—the Spirit, the water, and the blood—and these
three agree in one. These three witness that we have everlasting life, and that our names are written in heaven. How
do these three agree with these two witnesses? Very well.
John ranks them according to the order of their clearest
evidence; first the Spirit, then the water, then the blood.
The apostle here ranks them according to their natural
being. First our spirit in justification and sanctification,
and then God's Spirit. As to the Spirit, of all others this is
the clearest evidence; and when this is bright and manifest,
there needs be no more; the thing is sealed.

So the testimony of water is a clear evidence (whereby
is meant sanctification). This is put next to the Spirit; for
when the Spirit is silent, yet this may speak. Though I have
many wants and imperfections in me, yet if my spirit can
testify to me that I have a desire to please God in all things;
that I resolve upon and set up His service as the pitch of all
my utmost endeavors; that with allowance I willingly cher-
ish no corruption, but set myself against all sin—this water
will comfort and hold up a man from sinking, as we see in
all the sore trials of Job, chapter 27:5. Still he stood upon
the integrity of his own spirit and would not let that go,
though he was sorely beaten by the Almighty, and slan-
dered for a wicked person.

QUESTION. But the water may be muddy, and the
struggling of the flesh and spirit so strong, that we may not
be able to judge which is master. What then?

ANSWER. Then faith lays hold of the blood in justification, which, though it is the darkest testimony, yet is as
sure as any of the others.

Now, in comparing these witnesses together in John

and in my text, I rank the water and the blood with the testimony of our spirit. And the Spirit mentioned in John and in my text are all one; not as though we wrought them, but we believe them to be so. If a man asks how I know that I am sanctified, the answer must be, I believe and know it to be so. The work of producing these things in me comes from God; but for the work of discerning how our affections stand in this case, it comes from us.

The testimony of our spirit I conceive to be when a man has taken a survey of those excellent things belonging to justification and sanctification; when, according to the substantial truths that I know in the Word, I observe and follow as fast as I can what is there commanded. When I take the candle of the Word, and with that bright burning lamp search into the Word for what is there to be done, and so bring it home to myself, thereby mortifying my corruptions—this is the groundwork of the witness of our spirit. First, as in the blood, with my spirit I must see what is needful to be done in order unto justification, what free promises of invitation belong thereunto. I must see how God justifies a sinner, and what conditions on our part are required in justification. I must see what footings and grounds for life, and what way or hope there is for a graceless man to be saved, yea, even for the worst person that may be.

In this case a man must not look for anything in himself as a cause. Christ cannot be had by exchange, but received as a free gift, as the apostle says, "Therefore it is of faith that it may be by grace, to the end the promise might be sure to all the seed" (Romans 4:16). I must bring a bare hand to receive Christ; it must be of grace. God for this cause will make us let fall everything before we shall take hold of Him. Though qualified with humiliation, I must let all fall, not trusting it to make me the worthier to receive Christ, as some think. When I first received Christ for my justification, I had to let everything I have fall to lay hold of Him so that then He may find me naked, as it were, in my blood; and in this manner God will take us so that all may be of mere grace.

The apostle adds another thing, and that is that the promise may be sure. If anything in us might be a cause or help to our justification, a man would never be sure; therefore it is all of grace that the promise might be sure. It is as though God should say, "I care for nothing else; bring Me My Son and show Him to Me, and then all is well." And in this case you see that He does not name hope, love, or any other grace but faith; for the nature of faith is to let fall all things in laying hold of Christ. In justification faith is a sufferer only; but in sanctification it works and purges the whole man, and so witnesses the certainty and truth of our sanctification, and so the assurance of salvation.

Hence, from the nature hereof in this work, the apostle, in 2 Peter 1:1, writes to them who had obtained like precious faith. In this case it is alike to all in virtue of this work, whatsoever the measure is. And I may liken it thus. Paul writes: "With these hands I get my living." Now, though strong hands may work more than weak hands, and so earn a great deal more, yet a beggar who holds out his hand may receive more than he or any other could earn. So faith justifies only receiving, not working, as we may see in John 1:12: "But as many as received Him, to them gave He power to become the sons of God, even to them that believe on His name." To "receive Him" means "to believe in Him." How? Come and take Him. How? As it is in Revelation 22:17: "And let him that is athirst come; and whosoever will, let him come, and take of the water of life freely."

When I see that God keeps open house, come who will, without denying entertainment to any; and when God's Spirit has wrought the will in me, what hinders me now from receiving Christ? When the Spirit has wrought this will in me, and I come and take God at His Word, and believe in Christ, laying hold by degrees on the other promises of life, winding and wrapping myself in them as I am able, that is faith. But that mere persuasion that many have that they shall go to heaven is not faith, but rather a consequence thereof. The promise is made to those who believe in Christ. "For in Him," says the apostle, "all the promises are yea, and amen." If a man weeps much, and begs hard for the remission of sins, he may weep and be without comfort unto the end of his life, unless he has received Christ and applied His virtues to his trembling soul. A man must first receive Christ, and then he has a warrant to interest himself in all the promises.

So if this is done, if such a man were asked, "Have you a warrant to receive Christ?" He could reply, "Yes, I have a warrant, for He keeps open house unto all who come, welcoming all; and I have a will to come. This is a good and sufficient warrant for me to come, if I have a will wrought in me." And then if he comes, this is the first thing to be observed in the witness of the Spirit.

Now, if a man staggers while the King keeps open house, so as he will not or does not come, then, in the second place, comes the invitation. Because we are slow to believe, therefore God invites us, as in Matthew 11:28: "Come unto Me, all ye that labor and are heavy laden, and I will give you rest."

OBJECTION. Oh, but I am not worthy to come!

ANSWER. But, you see, here is invitation to encourage you to come. Yea, the sorer and heavier your load is, you should come so much the rather.

So if the Lord should ask a man, "Friend, what brought you here? What warrant did you have to be so bold?" Then he shows forth his ticket, as if he should say, "Lord, Thou gavest me a word of comfort, a warrant of Thy invitation. In obedience to Thy Word, and by faith in Thy promise, I have come here."

Now this invitation is directed to those who, as yet, have no goodness in them. When then my spirit warrants this much in me, that upon this word of promise and invitation I have come in for relief and ease of my miseries unto Christ Jesus, the great Physician, relying on Him for cure, and lying, as it were, at His feet for mercy—this is the testimony of my spirit that I believe, and sufficient ground for me to rest on that now I am in the way of life and justified by His grace.

Sometimes Christ meets with a dull and slow heart, a lazy and careless heart. What becomes of it for not knowing or weighing the dangerous state it is in, or for making excuses? Here Christ may justly leave (for is it not much that the King should invite us for our good?) as He did those in the gospel who, for refusing to come to His supper, were excluded from ever tasting thereof, strangers being fetched in their places. God might so deal with us. But you see in 2 Corinthians 5:20 that God sends an ambassador to entreat us. He erects, as it were, a new office for our sakes. Paul says, "Now then we are ambassadors for Christ, as though God did beseech you by us; we pray you in Christ's stead, be ye reconciled unto God."

This may seem to be needless, we being weaker than he. Ambassadors seeking peace for the most part are sent unto those who are stronger. The apostle reasons thus: "Are we stronger than He? Do we provoke the Lord to anger?" But here we see and may admire His infinitely rich goodness, that He comes and sues to us to be reconciled. It is a kind of indignity for a great monarch to sue for peace to them who are far below him. This dishonor God is willing to put up with at our hands, and sues unto us first, when it rather became us upon our knees to beg and sue first unto Him. The effect of the embassy is that we would be friends with Him, and receive that which is so highly for our advancement.

When, therefore, I see that this quickens in my heart so

that (as James speaks of the engrafted Word that is able to save our souls) I can bring it home, having some sweet relish and high estimation of it in my heart, that it begins to be the square and rule of my life, then I am safe. If this, or any of these, fasten upon my soul, and thereupon I yield and come in, it is enough to show that I am a justified person. And from hence our spirit may witness, and that truly; this is a hard thing in the witness of our spirit.

If none of all these will do, then comes a further degree, a command from the Highest: "You shall do it." See 1 John 3:23: "And this is His commandment, that we should believe on His Son Jesus Christ, and love one another as He gave us commandment." In the parliament of grace there is a law of faith that binds us as strictly to believe as to keep any of the commandments. So the apostle asks, "Where is boasting then? It is excluded. By what law? Of works? Nay, but by the law of faith" (Romans 3:27). So that if I will not believe on the Lord Jesus, who eases me of the rigor of the law, and so is my righteousness, I must perish forever.

OBJECTION. What! Must I believe?

ANSWER. Yes, you are as strictly bound to believe as not to murder, as not to be an idolater, as not to steal, and as not to commit adultery. Nay, I will add that your infidelity and contempt of that gracious offer, your disobedience to the law of faith, is greater than your breach and disobedience to the law of works, when you fling God's grace in His face again and trample under foot the blood of the covenant. For this see John 16:9. What is that great sin which Christ came to reprove? Even this infidelity. He says, "because they believe not in Me." This is a great sin in two respects: first, because it is a sin against God's mercy; and, second, because it is a chain which links and binds all sins together. Thus our faith is sure when it relies on the Word; otherwise, all other thoughts are but presumption, and will fail a man in the time of need. For what is faith but my assent to believe every word of God He has commanded me to believe, and so endeavor to practice it?

If none of these prevail, then comes threatening; then God swears that such as refuse shall never enter into rest. If a prince should ask for the hand of a beggar's daughter in marriage, and she should refuse and condemn him, do you think he would be well-pleased? So it is with us. When the King of heaven's Son asks us, "Will you be married to Me?" if we refuse, the Son takes it horribly ill. Therefore He says, "Kiss the Son, lest He be angry and ye perish in the way, when His wrath is kindled but a little. Blessed are all those that put their trust in Him" (Psalm 2:12). In Hebrews, God swore that, because of infidelity, those unbelieving Jews should never enter into His rest. All the rest of the threatenings of the law were not backed with an oath; there was some secret reservation of mercy unto them upon the satisfaction of divine justice. But here there is no reservation. God has sworn such shall never come into heaven. Do not look for a third thing in God now as a mitigation of His oath; it cannot be; He has sworn that an unbeliever shall never enter into His rest.

These five things are the grounds of faith, even unto the worst and unworthiest persons that may be; and by all or some of them He creates faith in us which, once wrought in the heart by the Spirit of God secretly, and we discerning the same, is the witness of our spirit.

Now our spirit having viewed all these things, and the promises upon which they are grounded, thus it witnesses. It is as if one should demand of a man, "Are these things presented to your view true?"

"Yes," he will say, "as true as the gospel."

"Is all good and profitable?"

"Oh, yes," he says, "all is very good and desirable."

Then the upshot question is, "But is this good for you particularly?"

If your soul answers now, "Yes, very good for me," if

then you accept this, and wrap and fold yourself in the promises, you cannot find yourself out of the comfort and assurance of being in Christ Jesus; for what, pray, makes up a match but the consent of two agreeing? So the consent of two parties agreeing (upon this message) makes up the match between us and Christ, uniting and knitting us unto Him.

There are also other means to make us grow up in Him, by which time discovers what manner of engrafting we have had into Him; for we see four or five scions are engrafted into a stock, yet some of them may not be incorporated with the stock, but wither. So, by the Word and sacraments, many are admitted as retainers and believers of the promises who shrink back and do not hold out because they were never thoroughly incorporated into Christ, but were imperfectly joined unto Him. But, however, all who come to life must pass this way if they look for sound comfort.

But the testimony of our spirit goes further, wherein I might show how in sanctification our spirit says, "Lord, prove me; see if there be any evil in me, and lead me in the way everlasting." The true believer loves the brethren and desires to fear God, as Nehemiah pleads, "Be attentive to the prayer of Thy servant, and of Thy servants, who desire to fear Thy name" (Nehemiah 1:11). So the true convert says, "This is the warrant that I am partaker of, that inward, true washing, and not of that outward only of the hog which, being kept clean and in good company, will be clean till there is an occasion offered of wallowing in the mire again." But when he finds that though there were neither heaven to reward him nor hell to punish him, if opportunity were offered, yet his heart rises against sin because of Him who has forbidden it—this is a sure evidence, and testifies that he is a child of God. This is the first thing in bringing a man in, to survey the promises belonging to justification and sanctification, wherein our spirit sees itself to have an interest, and truly and on sound judgment witnesses assurance of salvation.

Second, when I find Christ drawing me and changing my nature, that upon the former reasonings, view, and laying hold of Christ, making me now have supernatural thoughts and delights (for this a man may have), then certainly my spirit may conclude that I am blessed; for, says the Scripture, "Blessed is the man whom Thou choosest, and causeth to come unto Thee." But some, like dreamers, only dream of this. But do I do this waking with my whole soul? Does my spirit testify it upon good grounds? Why, then I may rest upon it; it is as sure as may be. This much is the testimony of our spirit. Now it is clear that faith is wrought briefly in two ways, which the Lord uses to bring a man to the survey of those grounds upon which our spirit witnesses. First, He works upon the understanding; second, on the will and affections.

It is a strange thing to consider how this work is begun and finished; so that we may say hereof as the Lord poses to Job, "Who hath put wisdom in the inward parts? Or who hath given understanding to the heart?" (Job 38:36). And in another place He asks, "Where is the way where light dwelleth, and as for darkness, where is the place thereof?"

First, God enlightens the understanding with the thunderings of the law when He shows a man such a sight as he could not have believed, and convinces him in general that his estate is not good, that without mercy hell attends him. This is a flash of lightning from Mount Sinai. Then comes a thunder clap, laying down all, laying flat the will and affections, dejecting a man; so that this first secret work of faith is a captivating of the understanding, will, and affections. Now the act of both the understanding and the will is set forth in this case: "These all died in faith, not having received the promises, but having seen them afar off, were persuaded of them, and embraced them"

(Hebrews 11:13). In this Scripture is set down the two hands and arms of faith: believing Christ who is out of sight, and laying hold of and embracing the promises.

Those in the Old Testament did not receive Christ in the flesh, and so are said to look afar off, as the apostle says, "Whom having not seen ye love, in whom, though now ye see Him not, yet believing, ye rejoice" (1 Peter 1:8). But the apostle adds, they were persuaded of the promises and embraced them. This was the work of the Spirit on the understanding, convicting the soul of sin, showing there is a remedy, telling the soul that all is marvelously true that God has revealed in His Word, and then drawing the soul to this conclusion: "Christ came to save sinners, whereof I am chief; therefore He came to save me."

Yet all this while the will may be stubborn and rebellious, and the affections disordered; therefore here comes the second arm of faith, not only being persuaded of the Word as the Word of truth, but as a good promise of good things to me. So that here is another degree of the working of the Spirit to compel the will and affections, so sweetly grace having removed that perverseness and disorder which governed them before. Now, this gentle enforcing and often beating upon the will again and again, what the understanding had rightly conceived at last works upon the will and moves it; for we see the most wicked man in the world laying hold on the worst things as being good and profitable unto Him. So when the best thing is presented to the will as the best thing, and the necessity thereof urged by dangers ensuing inevitably if I will not choose it, then it apprehends that, and says of it as Peter at the transfiguration, "It is good for us to be here, and let us build tabernacles."

Hence you see what faith is in this working. It is an act of the understanding forcing, in that way of conviction that we mentioned, the will and the affections. And thus, when the understanding is captivated and the will brought to be willing, then the first act of faith is past.

From here we proceed to the second, which is running to the city of refuge, the application and believing of the promises, and so to apprehending Christ, surveying the promises belonging to justification and sanctification, and bringing them home to the soul, from whence comes the witness of our spirit.

Before we come to speak of God's Spirit witnessing with our spirit, (because between this work there may be many times, and is, an interposing trial ere the Spirit of God witnesses with our spirit), we will first remark that when our spirit has thus witnessed in justification and sanctification, God may now write bitter things against me, seem to cast me off, wound me with the wounds of an enemy, and remove the sense of the light of His countenance from me. What then is to be done? Why, I will trust Him though He kills me. I am sure, "I have loved and esteemed the words of His mouth more than my appointed food," as Job says. "I have laid hold of Christ Jesus by the promises, and I believe them. I have desired, and do desire, to fear Him and yield obedience to all His commandments. If I must die, I will yet wait on Him and die at His feet." Here is the strength of faith. Christ had faith without feeling when He cried out, "My God, My God, why hast Thou forsaken Me?" When sense is marvelously low, then faith is at the strongest. Here we must walk and live by faith; we shall have sense and sight enough in another world. The apostle tells us, "Now we walk by faith, and not by sight, and by faith we stand," as we may see a pattern of the woman of Canaan in Matthew 15:22. First she was repulsed as a stranger, yet she went on. She was then called a dog; she might now have been discouraged so as to have given up on her request. But this is the nature of faith, to pick comfort out of discouragements; to see out of a very small hole those things that raise and bring consolation. She caught at this quickly, "Am I a dog? Why yet it is well, for the dogs eat the crumbs that fall from their master's table." Thus faith grew stronger in her, and when this trial was past, Christ said unto her, "O woman," not, "O dog," now, "great is thy faith; be it unto thee even as thou wilt."

Then from our believing God in general, believing and applying the promises, and valorous trustings in God and resting on Him, and taking Him at His Word, comes the testimony of God's Spirit witnessing with our spirit that we are the children of God. This being done, and God having let us see what His strength in us is, He will not let us stand long in this uncomfortable state, but will come again and speak peace to us so that we may live in His sight. It is as if He should say, "What! Have you believed Me so on My bare Word? Have you honored Me so as to lay the blame and fault of all My trials on yourself for your sins, clearing My justice in all things? Have you honored Me so as to magnify mercy, to wait and hope on it for all this? Have you trusted Me so as to remain faithful in all your miseries?" It is then that the Lord puts to the witness of our spirit the seal of His Spirit, as we may read in Ephesians 1:13: "In whom also ye trusted after that ye heard the word of truth, the gospel of your salvation; in whom also, after that ye believed, ye were sealed with the Holy Spirit of promise, which is the earnest of our inheritance."

Here is the difference between faith and sense: faith takes hold of general promises, draws them down to particulars, applies them, and makes them her own. Faith lives and walks by the promises, squaring the whole life by them in all things. But sense is another thing, even that which is mentioned in Psalm 35:3. When there is a full report made to the soul of its assured happiness, "Say unto my soul, 'I am thy salvation.' " When a man has thus been gathered home by glorifying Him and believing His truth, then comes a special evidence to the soul with an unwonted joy, and says, "I am thy salvation." In effect, this is what Christ said in John 14:21: "He that loveth Me shall be loved of My

Father, and I will love him, and will manifest Myself unto
him." And as in Song of Solomon 1:2, then He will kiss with
the kisses of His mouth, so we shall be able to say, "My Beloved is mine, and I am His." When God has heard us cry
awhile till we are thoroughly humbled, then He takes us
up into His arms and cuddles us.

So that a meditation of the Word being past, a man
having viewed His charter and His promises, surveying
heaven, the privileges of believers, and the glory that is to
come, then comes the Spirit and makes up a third evidence, with which comes joy unspeakable and glorious in
such a measure that, for the present, we can neither wish
nor desire anything else, the soul resting wonderfully rav-
ished and contented. This cannot, and shall not, always
continue, but at sometimes we shall have it; yet it remains
always so, as it can never finally be taken away. Our Savior's promise is, "And ye now, therefore, have sorrow, but
I will see you again, and your heart shall rejoice, and your
joy shall no man take from you" (John 16:22). The root of
all consolation is that God will not forsake forever, but will
at last come again and have compassion on us, according
to the multitude of His mercies.

OBJECTION. What! Does the Spirit never seal but
upon some such hard trials after the witness of our spirit?

ANSWER. The sealing of God's Spirit with our spirit is
not always tied to hard foregoing trials immediately; for a
man may be surveying heaven and the glory to come, or
praying earnestly with a tender and melting heart, applying the promises and wrestling with God, and at the same
time God's seal may be and is put many times upon the
same. For as the wind blows where it wills, and no man discerns the coming thereof, so may the Spirit seal at divers
times and upon divers occasions. Yea, and why may it not
seal in time of some great suffering for the truth, as we
read of the apostles in Acts 5:41, who went away from the
council "rejoicing that they were counted worthy to suffer

shame for His name."

Last, for trial, we must now see how to distinguish this testimony of the true Spirit from the counterfeit illumination of some who will have strange, sudden joys, the devil, no question, then transforming himself into an angel of light to them. This trial, therefore, is made by three things going before and three things following after.

For the things that go before:

1. See that the groundwork is true. If a man is in the faith and believes the Word; if upon believing and meditation there can be an opening to the knock of Christ at the first, and not delaying Him like the lazy spouse in the Song of Solomon; if in this case the Spirit comes and fills the heart with joy—then is all sure and well, for then Christ promised to enter. But if a man has a dull, dead, delaying ear, and therewith great, fantastic joys, he may assure himself the right Spirit has not wrought them. They are but idle speculations; but if this joy comes upon surveying our charter and evidences, it is sure we may build upon it.

2. A man must consider if he has as yet overcome strong passions and temptations, and passed through much hazard and peril for Christ, having been buffeted with divers temptations of which he had obtained mastery. For the seal of God's Spirit with our spirit comes as a reward of service done, as you may see in Revelation 2:17: "To him that overcometh will I give to eat of the hidden manna, and I will give him a white stone, and in the stone a new name written, which no man knoweth saving he that receiveth it." He means that He will give a secret love token to the soul, whereby it rests assured of the unspeakable love of God, and freedom from condemnation. Now, what was this white stone? The Athenians had a custom, when malefactors were accused and arraigned, to have black and white stones by them; and so, according to the sentence given, those condemned had a black stone and

the acquitted had a white stone given to them. This is what the Holy Ghost here alludes to, that this stone, this seal, shall assure them of absolute acquittal from condemnation, and so free them from the cause of fear. Again, He tells them that Christ will give a man a new name, that is, write his absolution in fair letters in the white stone with a clear evidence. It is as if He should say when Christ has seen a man overcoming, and how he has conflicted with temptations, and yet holds out, pressing for the crown unto the end of the race, Christ will then come in and stroke him on the head, easing him of all his pains and sores with such a sweet refreshing as is unspeakable. When a man has won it, he shows he then shall wear it.

3. If the Spirit seals after meditation on the Word, it is right; the apostle says, "In whom after that ye believed, ye were sealed." Examine the root of this joy. The Spirit gives no comfort but by the Word. If a man meditates on the promises, and thereupon has a flame of love kindled, this is sure, and a man may say that the Word stirred it up. If it is God's comfort, God will have His Word to make way unto it.

There are some who find no sweetness in the Word. What is the cause of that? Because they do not chew on the Word to imprint it in their memories and in their heart. If comfort comes while a man, meditating on the promises, wedges it home upon his heart, it is of God; otherwise it is counterfeit and false. These are the forerunners to this seal.

In the next place, there are three things that follow after this sealing, which the Spirit leaves behind it:

1. Humility. As is true in knowledge, so in sense. It makes a man more humble. There is naturally in all a certain pride which must be overcome. The apostle says, "What hast thou that thou hast not received?" But on the contrary, the nearer a man comes to the glory of God, the more rottenness he finds in his bones. We see this in Job: "I

have heard of Thee," he says to God, "by the hearing of
the ear; but now mine eye seeth Thee." The result is,
"therefore I abhor myself, and repent in dust and ashes"
(Job 42:5–6).

2. Another thing the Spirit leaves behind it (if it seals
rightly) is a prevention of security for time to come. In this
case, we must look for a new encounter; a false persuasion
makes a man to fall into security. Because Satan is then
most malicious and busy, a man must stand faster than
ever. The devil hates them most who are most endued with
God's image. Because he cannot reach God, he perse-
cutes Him in His members. And, therefore, in this case, it
must be with us as it was with Elijah in 1 Kings 19:8. After
such an enlightening, a man must now think that he has a
great journey to go, and so walk on in the strength of that
a long time. The devil, we see, watches a man, and when
he is at the best, then endeavors to overcome him. We may
see this in Adam and Eve: no sooner were they placed in
that state of innocence but he tempted them. How much
more may a man, having a sweeter taste of the Spirit, and
less strength now, look to be set upon. And, therefore, in
these feasting days, he needs to be more on his watch and
pray more; for we have more given us than Adam had. We
have a new name given us, a secret love token.

Further, we see Christ says, "Behold, I stand at the door
and knock; if any man will open unto Me, I will come in
and sup with him and he with Me" (Revelation 3:20). Now,
in this case, if we are such persons who let our hearts fly
open to let Him in, we are safe. It is as if He should say, "If
you would be sure of reconciliation to be at peace with
Me, sup with Me, and I will sup with you." For we know if
men who were enemies are once brought to keep company together, and to eat and drink one with another, we
use to say that all is done and wrapped up in the table-
cloth; all old reckonings are taken away. Now they have
certainly become friends. But if, like the spouse in the

Song of Solomon, we let Him stand knocking and will not let Him in, we also may have great and sound knocks and blows ourselves before we find Him again. As we read it befell the Church there whom the watchmen found, beat, and took away her veil as she was seeking Christ. If we would have comfort, therefore, let us mark the knocking of the Spirit, and not grieve Him by withstanding holy motions. And then we shall find Him sealing up our salvation, witnessing with our spirits that we are the children of God. Men, you see, wait for the wind, and not the wind for them; otherwise, they may wait long enough before they reach home. So must we watch the knockings of Christ, and let Him in, so that His Spirit may seal us up to the day of redemption.

3. Another thing the true witness of the Spirit leaves behind is love. It makes a man more inflamed with love to God. If a man does not love God more after such an enlightening, it is false and counterfeit. "I will love Thee dearly, O Lord, my God, because Thou hast heard my voice" Psalm 116. And, says the apostle, "The love of Christ constraineth us" (2 Corinthians 5:14). And, therefore, if we are obedient sons, we will show it in loving and honoring our Father more and more. The prophet Malachi says, "A son honoreth his father, and a servant his master; if then I be a Father, where is Mine honor?" (Malachi 1:6). These are the trials before and after a true illumination to distinguish it from the counterfeit, so that we may always find and observe it in ourselves.